Exploring Through Writing

A Process Approach to ESL Composition

5234516

maysaa

Exploring Through Writing

A Process Approach to ESL Composition

ANN RAIMES
Hunter College

St. Martin's Press
New York

To
JAMES RAIMES
with love and gratitude

Library of Congress Catalog No.: 86-60641
Copyright © 1987 by St. Martin's Press, Inc.
All rights reserved.
Manufactured in the United States of America.
10987
fedcba

For information, write:
St. Martin's Press, Inc.
175 Fifth Avenue
New York, NY 10010

cover design: Darby Downey
cover art: *Untitled*, 1985, by Esther Frederiksen
text design: Leon Bolognese

ISBN: 0-312-27769-5
Instructor's Edition ISBN: 0-312-00222-X

Acknowledgments

Text Credits

p. 187: Excerpt from *Diary of a Young Girl*, pp. 14–17. Anne Frank. Selection from "Thursday, 9 July, 1942." Pocket Books © 1952. Reprinted by permission of Vallentine Mitchell & Co. Ltd. and Ms. Anne Frank Fonds.

p. 192: Excerpt from "Returning to a Beloved Island." Ruth Gordon. Reprinted by permission of The New York Times, July 22, 1984. Sect. X, 14:1.

p. 193: "Mr. Doherty Builds His Dream Life," pp. 77 + . Jim Doherty. Reprinted from May 1984 issue of *Money* magazine by special permission; © 1984, Time Inc. All rights reserved.

p. 198: Excerpt from *Growing Up*, pp. 42–43. Russell Baker. Reprinted by permission of Don Congdon Associates Inc., Copyright © 1982, by Russell Baker.

p. 199: Excerpt from "Homey Ski Spa in the Italian Alps." © 1985, by Barbara Lazear Ascher. Originally published in The New York Times, February 24, 1985. Sect. XX, 19 + . Reprinted with permission of the Rhoda Weyr Agency.

p. 209: "The Chrysler and the Comb." From *Mrs. Bridge*, pp. 113–114. © 1959 by Evan S. Connell. Reprinted by permission of Harold Matson Co., Inc.

p. 210: Excerpts from "Introduction to Interview with Ernest Hemingway," pp. 183–185, by George Plimpton. From *Writers At Work: The Paris Review Interviews*, Second Series, edited by G. Plimpton. Copyright © 1963 by The Paris Review, Inc. Reprinted by permission of Viking Penguin, Inc., and Martin Secker and Warburg Ltd.

p. 212: "Treasures," p. 108. Joan Costello. Copyright © 1984. From *Parents* Magazine Enterprises. Reprinted from *Parents* with permission.

p. 214: "Lure of Possessions: Do You Cling to Objects or Throw Away Your Past?" Barbara Lang Stern. Courtesy *Vogue*, p. 173. Copyright © 1983 by The Condé Nast Publications, Inc.

p. 217: "Object Lessons." From *The Meaning of Things: Symbols in The Development of The Self*, pp. 78–85. Mihalyi Csikszentmihalyi and Eugene Rochberg-Halton. Permission granted by Cambridge University Press © 1981.

p. 224: Excerpts from *Minor Characters*, pp. 13–14. Joyce Johnson. Copyright © 1983 by Joyce Johnson. Reprinted by permission of Houghton Mifflin Co. and Pan Books Ltd.

p. 234: Excerpts from "Nancy Rogers." From *Working: People Talk About What They Do All Day and How They Feel About What They Do*, pp. 344–346. Studs Terkel. Copyright © 1972 by Studs Terkel. Reprinted by permission of Pantheon Books, a Division of Random House, Inc. and The International Creative Management.

Acknowledgments and copyrights continue on pp. 310–311, which constitute an extension of the copyright page.

Preface: To the Instructor

Writing well, whether in a first or a second language, is a process that can be learned and practiced. Unfortunately, good writing doesn't just happen. Most writers, whether they are writing in their native language or not, have to write draft after draft, first to generate and organize their ideas and then to convey those ideas clearly to readers. Ernest Hemingway, for example, wrote the ending to *A Farewell to Arms* thirty-nine times.

Taking time over writing; doing a lot of reading, thinking, talking, and writing about a subject; trying out options; and rewriting—none of these are punishments for poor and unskilled writers. Rather, these activities are an absolutely essential part of the writing process. For second-language students, these activities are especially valuable, as they provide many opportunities for communication in the new language. *Exploring Through Writing: A Process Approach to ESL Composition* will ask your students to read, think, talk, and write in English. It will lead them through the process of writing, providing three things that all writers—including professional writers, businesspeople, and student writers—need to improve their writing: time, familiarity with the options available to them, and a lot of advice and support from readers, including skilled advice from a teacher.

In addition to giving students the opportunity to explore topics by writing about them, the book emphasizes the specific rhetorical and linguistic needs of second-language writers; that is, it addresses the commonly accepted forms of written English and its syntactic and grammatical conventions. These needs are addressed as individual parts of the writing process. Writing is such a complex process that if we teachers try to concentrate on everything at once, we will surely run into trouble. Student writers, particularly those who are writing in a new language, can benefit from approaching the task of writing in a systematic way.

What the Book Does

This book provides the systematic approach to writing that ESL/EFL students at the intermediate-advanced level need, whether they are in an academic program or an intensive English-language institute. With their wide variety of educational and cultural backgrounds, and their variety of exposure to the written word in their native languages, second-language students can benefit from methodically working through the processes that most skilled writers of English use, accumulating language experience (and thus acquiring more language) as they do so. This book leads students from the blank sheet of paper, through the various stages in the whole process of writing, to a polished final product ready for the critical eyes of a reader.

The book should be used in the following way:

1. Students work through Part I, "Processes," more than once during a term. At the same time, they refer to Part II, "Grammar: Twenty-One Troublespots," and Part III, "Materials." As they go through the chapters in Part I, they explore one particular subject through reading, talking, and writing about it. They write a lot, and all the writing contributes to the production of one essay—one that is polished, carefully worked, re-worked, and edited. In working through the sixteen chapters in Part I, the students pay attention to techniques of invention, to rhetorical development, and then to correct grammar and syntax.

2. When students come to the end of Part I and hand in the final draft of the essay, they go back to the beginning of the process for their next essay—back, that is, to Chapter 1 for more reading, discussing, and writing, through which they explore a new topic. Now, in an abbreviated way, selecting from or skipping some chapters, they once more work through the processes of discovery, drafting, revising, and careful editing. After exploring their new subject by writing about it, they produce another essay.

   Chapters contain individual assignments (reading or writing tasks that can be done at home or in class), or classroom activities (individual, group, or whole-class activities during class time), or both. Journal assignments, intended to give students more opportunities for communicative and ungraded writing, are included in the first eight chapters. Thereafter, students work intensively on the drafts of their essay, returning to the journal again as they start to explore another topic for writing.

3. Students use Part II, "Grammar: Twenty-One Troublespots," along with Part I. Part II is a kind of handbook. It provides review and editing advice for the grammatical areas that frequently trouble ESL writers. Although students are directed to use it to check specific points as they work on editing and proofreading, instructors and students can refer to it for help at any time.

4. Part III, "Materials: Pictures and Readings," provides pictures and readings in five subject areas. Students are first referred to these resources in Chapter 2 ("Look and Read"); they use the pictures and readings and the activities grouped around them to build the vocabulary and sentence structure the subject demands, and to stimulate thinking. They can thus use the materials to refer to, emulate, quote from, agree with, or refute. In addition, rhetorical and grammatical concepts explained in the book are often illustrated with examples from the readings in Part III.

What the Students Do

Students do not begin by imitating a model or making up a canned essay to fit an all-purpose outline for a "comparison-contrast" essay—although they might later decide that such a format could be a useful way to explain their ideas. Nor do they begin by worrying about sentence style, grammar, and spelling, although they will address all of those things at the appropriate time. Instead, they start by working on the processes of writing, exploring through the act of writing what they want to write about and how they want to write it.

In the "Getting Started" chapters, students begin by gathering ideas from their own experience and knowledge, and then turn to other sources as they search for their own topic to write about or search for ideas on a topic suggested by their instructor. Five broad subject areas are suggested for exploration. Within these, the students, in consultation with their instructor, develop their own specific topic. A file of resources, the thematically grouped sets of pictures and readings in Part III, provides information and springboards to thinking about a subject.

Next, in "Finding Ways In," to help them develop their own ideas on a topic within these five broad subject areas, students are given the opportunity to explore a variety of systematic methods of discovery while they read, write, talk to each other, and respond to each other's ideas—all in English, their target language. After this preparation and fitting new knowledge in with old, the students have on paper a lot of material to use in writing. For ESL/EFL students, this means that they already have experience with some of the vocabulary, idioms, sentences, and rhetorical possibilities that they can use.

In "Writing and Rewriting," which encompasses Chapters 9 through 12, students can now make decisions about the purpose, audience, and organization of their piece of writing; they can write a first draft, read it critically, get advice from others, and use the readers' reactions to revise the draft.

Finally, in "Editing" (Chapters 13 through 16), students are given careful and systematic instruction on how to edit their piece of writing for grammatical and mechanical errors. Whenever in the process their attention has been drawn to a troublesome grammatical point, they can turn to a chapter in Part II that gives an explanation, provides an exercise or two, and then asks a series of questions that the students can apply to their own drafts.

The sixteen chapters devoted to writing processes do not, therefore, ask students to do sixteen separate and discrete on-the-spot writing assignments, turning their attention from one topic to another before they have had a chance to delve into the complexities of each. Instead, students may produce only three, four, or five essays in a term, but each of these will be a finished, carefully worked, and polished essay. And in the course of preparing their essays, students will be using one of the most useful tools for developing writing skills and learning about a subject and a new language: writing itself. So, as they work through the sixteen chapters a few times, they will produce a great deal of writing of various kinds: memories, stories, lists, notes, freewriting, journal entries, descriptions, summaries of readings, plans, outlines, drafts, *and* completed essays.

What the Instructor Does

What many student writers need is a chance to explore the options available to writers and language learners. Thus, the teacher must serve as guide, reader, editor, and expert in the forms of the language—a more creative and responsive role than that of mere error-finder. The Instructor's Manual that accompanies this book assists you by providing specific guidelines for the activities in each chapter as well as an overview of the following:

1. How to organize your coursework and how to use Part I again after the first essay has been completed.
2. How to adapt these activities to the demands of your school, your curriculum, and the demands of your students' other writing assignments.
3. How to select and organize groups for collaborative learning.
4. What to do when groups are working together.
5. What to do if groups don't work well.
6. How to respond to students' writing—at different times and for different purposes.
7. The rationale for the approach: the research and theoretical underpinnings.

Acknowledgments

A lot of people were a great help to me as I wrote this book. I want to thank my colleagues at Hunter College who used some of the materials in their classes: Martha Cummings, Steven Haber, Susan Price, and Susan Stempleski. Randy Russell also tested out materials with his ESL class at Jersey City State College. A constant source of information and inspiration for me was the writing that the students produced and their enthusiastic reactions to the tasks; in particular, Alvaro Bermejo, Mihail Katsaros, Siao Tao Kuo, Tzvi Kushnir, Vanila Patel, Pari Songhorian, and Aura Tello have all contributed pieces of writing to this book. I am indebted, too, to the many colleagues whose work on the process of writing has influenced my own: particularly to Ann Berthoff, who introduced me to the idea of the double-entry notebook, to Peter Elbow's use of freewriting, to Stan Jones, who alerted me to the technique of writing a story with a given ending, and to Vivian Zamel, with whom I have had many wonderful discussions.

The following people read my developing manuscript with great care, and offered valuable advice and suggestions: Frances Boyd, Columbia University; Charlotte Gilman, University of Texas at Austin; Donna Jurich, San Francisco State University; Robert Kantor, Ohio State University; Alexandra Krapels, University of South Carolina; and Vivian Zamel, University of Massachusetts/Boston. My thanks to all of them.

The staff at St. Martin's Press made writing this book not only smooth but also pleasurable. Special thanks go to Jane Smith and Vivian McLaughlin for their assistance with pictures and readings; to Christine Pearson, production supervisor; to Patricia Mansfield, senior project editor, for her keen editorial eye and gracious way of pointing out errors and infelicities; and particularly to Susan Anker, acquiring editor, for guiding this book from start to finish, always offering expert advice and warm encouragement.

Acknowledgments often end with references to a writer's family. Anyone who has written a lot knows exactly why: writing a book always ends up being a collaborative enterprise. So, heartfelt thanks go to my daughters, Emily and Lucy Raimes, for not grumbling too much when I spent evenings and weekends writing—and wouldn't let them get near my (originally *our*) Apple and Word Juggler. And, as always, my biggest debt is to my husband, James Raimes. He helps more than he could ever know.

Ann Raimes

Contents

PART III MATERIALS: PICTURES AND READINGS 177

1 Places 179

2 Possessions 201

3 Work 227

Exploring Through Writing

A Process Approach to ESL Composition

Introduction

In this book, you will be asked to write a lot, to read each other's writing, and to discuss it. So, we will begin that way with some in-class activities.

1. With the other students in your class, compile a list of topics that you think you would enjoy writing about. These topics can be put on the chalkboard.

2. Choose your two favorite topics, and write a short response (no more than one page) to one of these topics. (You will write about the other one later.) Write in class for about 7 to 10 minutes *in your own language.* Write to tell any classmates who speak your language (or friends outside class) what you know about the topic, and try to make them interested in your ideas.

3. Form a small group with three or four classmates, and tell each other what you wrote about and what difficulties you had. If the students in your group speak the same language as you do, read your composition aloud. Otherwise, try to tell the others in English what you wrote about in your first language, and show them what your own language looks like on the page.

4. Now, take the same amount of time (approximately 7 to 10 minutes) to write in English on the other topic that you selected. Write as if you were writing the first draft of an article to be published in a class magazine. Again, keep your response short.

5. Look at your two pieces of writing, and assess each of them separately on the scale at the top of page 2 by putting a checkmark in the appropriate column.

6. Read aloud to the students in your group what you wrote in English. Tell them what was the most difficult part of writing that assignment. Exchange papers with one person in the group, and assess his or her piece of writing by using the scale on page 2. Obviously, this kind of assessment is quite personal, so there will be no "right" answers. Compare your ratings to see how much you agreed or disagreed with each other.

7. As a class, list on the chalkboard what conclusions you can now draw from this exercise about writing in your first language and in English; for example, what are the similarities and differences? What did you do first

	Writing no. 1			Writing no. 2		
	Needs Work	Average	Well Done	Needs Work	Average	Well Done
Information about topic						
Interest to a reader						
Clarity of organization						
Sentence effectiveness						
Accuracy of grammar and spelling						
Assessment of the whole piece						

      in each case? What did you worry about most in each case? What helped you most in each case?

8. Discuss with your classmates the experiences you had with writing before you started this course. First, write down your answers to the Language and Writing Questionnaire (see top of page 3) on a sheet of paper. Then, either as a class or in a small group, compare your answers.

9. Give your instructor the answers you wrote to the questionnaire. Also, give your instructor the piece you have just written in English. Your instructor will assess it so that you can see which areas you need to work on. Your instructor might refer you to one or more chapters in Part II, "Grammar: Twenty-One Troublespots," so that you can review the grammar areas that cause you trouble.

What You Need

So far, you have been engaged in activities that run through this book: writing, reading what others write, discussing ideas with other students, and listening to comments on your own writing. As you work through the chapters in this book, you will do different types of writing, all intended to help you explore techniques for writing on your own choice of subject as well as on a specific, assigned subject.

The basic tools you will need to work with are:

• Your notebook, a three-ring looseleaf binder, 8½ by 11 inches, with section dividers. You will do your own writing on the right-hand page of the

LANGUAGE AND WRITING QUESTIONNAIRE

1. How much instruction have you received in writing in your first language? in English?
2. What are the two most important things you have learned about writing in your first language? in English?
3. Outside a school setting, when and why do you ever write, in your first language or in English? (For example, do you write notes, letters, stories, diary entries, or essays?)
4. On these occasions, do you know who your reader will be, and can you anticipate how that reader will respond?
5. How have teachers—in first-language and second-language classrooms—responded to your writing? (For example, have they commented on content, made suggestions for revision, corrected errors?)
6. How confident do you feel about writing in your first language and in English?
7. What language do you dream in?
8. When you write in English, do you mainly plan and think in English or your first language?
9. Which language do you prefer to write in? Why?

open book, and leave the facing left-hand page free for comments, questions, and responses from yourself, your classmates, or your instructor. With a looseleaf binder, you can take out your pieces of writing and give them to your classmates and your instructor to comment on. The binder should open flat so that you can write on both sides of the paper. Divide the notebook into four sections:

Section 1: for *class writing*, including many "double-entry" activities and assignments.

Section 2: for the *drafts* you write.

Section 3: for your *journal* entries: frequent, ungraded writing that you do out of class and show to your classmates and instructor for a few minutes at the beginning or end of a class.

Section 4: for exercises from Part II ("Grammar: Twenty-One Troublespots") and for your own notes about *spelling and grammar*.

- A package of white, 8½-by-11-inch looseleaf paper, lined, with margins, and with punched holes that fit the binder. (If you type your drafts, then some of your paper should be unlined, without ruled margins.) To begin, put about twelve blank sheets of paper into each section; add new sheets as you go along. (When your instructor returns the pieces of writing you have just handed in, add them to section 3, the journal section.)
- Pens and pencils.

- Eraser.
- Tape and scissors (so that you can "cut and paste" while revising).
- A pack of 4-by-6-inch index cards.
- A dictionary. Recommended are *Oxford Student's Dictionary of American English* (Oxford University Press, 1983) and *Oxford Advanced Learner's Dictionary of Current English* (Oxford University Press, 1974), both specially written by A. S. Hornby for students of English as a second language. The latter book is a dictionary of current British English. Also recommended is *The American Heritage Dictionary of the English Language: New College Edition* (Houghton Mifflin, 1982), which is used by many American students.
- A lot of time to devote to reading and writing.

Throughout this book, you will be asked to read and write, to let others read your writing and comment on it, and to rewrite. In return, you will read what other students in your class have written, and you will comment on it. Samples of the writing of students learning English as a new language appear throughout this book. Unless otherwise noted, these samples have been corrected so that you will not be confused by incorrect grammar and spelling; however, the content, vocabulary, and organization of the student writing remain unchanged.

As you use this book, if you do any writing that you are particularly happy with, please send me a copy of it: Ann Raimes, College Department, St. Martin's Press, 175 Fifth Avenue, New York, NY 10010, U.S.A. I would love to read it.

PART I ✳

PROCESSES ✳

Getting Started

In the first three chapters, you will do a lot of writing, but you will not be writing polished essays. Here you will be concentrating on exploring a subject—by examining your own experience, by talking to others, by reading, and by writing. To help you get started, materials to look at and read are included in Part III. In addition, you should also gather ideas from other sources, such as what you know already, what others say, and what you read elsewhere. The activities in Chapters 1 to 3 will help you discover and organize these ideas so that you can begin to develop a topic that is interesting to both you and a reader. As you get things down on paper, you will like some parts of what you write more than others, so there will be pieces you want to keep and pieces you want to throw out. The decision will be yours.

Your instructor will not necessarily correct the writing you do in these chapters. The purpose of this writing is not to test whether you can spell and use the grammar of English; instead, the aim is to let words suggest more words and to let ideas suggest more ideas. In this way, you can find and explore a topic that interests you. Then, when you begin work on an essay, you will not be faced by a blank sheet of paper. You will, of course, have an opportunity to work on correcting errors and fixing up your spelling later. But first you need to find a subject to explore.

Search Your Memory

Chapter 1 asks you questions that lead you to think carefully about your own experience and your own knowledge. We usually draw heavily on both of these as we write.

Individual Assignments

1. Take a few minutes to think about one of the following questions. (Your instructor will assign one or will let you choose your own.)

Question 1. What vivid memory do you have of a place in your past? For instance, think about a specific room, a house, a building, a town, or a natural setting. Think about it as if you were filming it with a movie camera, trying to capture all the details, so that someone else can see it as you saw it.

Question 2. What details can you remember about a treasured possession you had when you were younger or a treasured possession you own now? You might think, for example, of a toy, a doll, a bicycle, or a souvenir. Think about what it looks (or looked) like and why it is (or was) important to you. What special features would you include if you tried to draw this possession? Where did you get it? Why do (or did) you like it?

Question 3. What do you remember about the events of one specific day of work—either one of your own or one that you have heard or read about? You might think about a good day, a particularly hard day, your first job, or work around the house. Or, you might recall a time when you watched a family member work or heard a relative tell a story about a working day.

Question 4. What can you remember about a family event in the past that was important to you? Think about the family members who were there. What did they look like then? What were they wearing? What did they do? How did they relate to each other? What was your role in that event?

Question 5. What can you remember about an occasion when someone was described as acting "just like a man" or "just like a woman"? What was the situation, who was involved, and what happened? What did the person do that was seen as "typical" male or "typical" female behavior?

Whichever question you choose, try to picture the whole scene in your mind as if you were watching a movie. Try to get all the details clear.

2. Now, use section 1 of your notebook, the section reserved for class writing. Think for a few minutes of the important words that you will need to tell someone else about your memory. Then, list the words in your notebook on the second right-hand page (page 3); it will face an empty left-hand page (page 2). If you can't think of a word in English, write it in your first language. Later, you can ask a friend or use a dictionary to determine the English translation.

3. Read the list written by Mihail, a student from Greece:

> construction
> difficult
> dangerous
> frightened
> traveling
> dirty clothes
> sick
> accident
> ράμματα [stitches]
> money

Decide which question you think Mihail was answering, and try to imagine what he was describing. (You will read his story on pages 9–12.)

Classroom Activities

1. Join up with a partner, and take a few minutes to tell your partner about the memory you recalled. Use the list of words you made to help you. Then, listen carefully to your partner's description of his or her memory, and ask questions if you want to have any more explanation or any more details. Tell your partner what you think is the most interesting part of the story. If at any time you cannot think of a word or a phrase in English, ask your partner or your instructor to help you.

2. Write about the memory your partner described. Begin writing on a new right-hand page in section 1 of your notebook. When you have finished writing, exchange notebooks with your partner for a response.

3. Read what Aura wrote about her partner's story, and note how Tao responded on the left-hand page. (See pages 10–11.)

Now read what your partner wrote about your story, and comment on it on the left-hand page of your partner's notebook (that is, on the page facing the story your partner wrote). Concentrate on the details of the story. Does it describe exactly what you had in mind when you told the story to your partner? You might want to add details, change them, rearrange events, or correct a part of the story your partner got wrong.

4. With your partner or the whole class, decide how you would answer the following questions about "Tao's First Moving Picture Machine" (page 11):

   a. What question in this chapter was Tao responding to?
   b. How clearly can you picture the scene described?
   c. Where did Tao, the storyteller, want some more details in Aura's version of the story?
   d. Where would you like more details?
   e. When did the story take place, and what verb tense did Aura use most often?

5. When you get your own notebook back from your partner, carefully read your partner's comments. Discuss the following questions with your partner.

   a. Which comments added information that the listener had heard but had forgotten to include?
   b. Which comments added information that the storyteller had not included but then wanted to add?
   c. Which comments corrected information?
   d. Which comments corrected spelling or grammar?

Journal Assignment

Before you begin to write in your journal, read what Mihail, the student from Greece, wrote:

September 1983. I never want to forget that month because I arrived in the Big Apple [New York]. I will always remember that month and my first difficult days. At that time, I had many problems because I had no money. A lot of people dream of making money and do it in a bad way. My way was good. I decided to find a job, and so I bought the newspaper every day and, with the help of my friends, I finally found a job.

and he thought that was the most important
No! He was tired of his children going to neighbors' houses.
No! 26-inch
And he paid the full amount. That was important to him.
In the evening after dinner

Name: Margaret. She also took the best seat in the livingroom.

He picked it up and even moved it to the window and threatened to throw it out.

Tao's First Moving Picture Machine

This story took place in Taiwan, Republic of China, around 1973. Tao's family didn't have a television set so they had to go to a neighbor's house to watch TV. They kept asking their father for a TV, but he was opposed to the idea because he said that a new TV would affect their school grades.

Finally, the day came. Tao's father was getting a little tired of going to other houses to watch TV. He decided to buy a TV set, but not an ordinary 14-inch TV set. He wanted a 25-inch Phillips TV, brand new. Also he wanted to buy it with cash, so he paid in advance.

When the TV arrived, the whole family assembled, and a new member of the family joined them: the TV set. The family's first reaction was that they wouldn't change their position for a million dollars. But gradually the excitement became more like a routine. The oldest sister had the authority to handle the TV. She wanted to watch her favorite actor, Robert Wagner, all the time, and nobody dared to argue with her. But then a higher authority took over—Tao's father—and almost threw the TV set out of the window because the children spent so much time in front of it.

My job in a construction company was hard and dangerous work for eight hours a day, but the pay was good. The company built houses, office buildings, and parks, and also fixed government buildings like post offices or army buildings.

Every day at 6 A.M., I would meet the other guys in the warehouse, and then we would drive sometimes 100 miles from New York. When I started work in the fall, the weather was very bad, but nothing stopped me from working because I needed money to pay my rent and school tuition fees, and to buy food and clothes. As I was working outside, I had to wear a lot of clothes, and it was difficult to move around comfortably.

A lot of times I got sick because I was very tired and I ate very little. Also, I felt lonely; I missed my family, my mother's hot, delicious food, my friends, and my life back home. All those things affected me, but nothing stopped me.

Many times I went back to my room and, with an empty stomach, slept in my dirty clothes until the next day. Then next day, with only a cigarette in my hand, I went to work again and worked patiently all day in snow or rain. But when I got my paycheck, I could forget my problems and start work all over again.

In the last week of work before I started school, I had a little accident. A big piece of wood flew from the roof of the post office building where we were working and hit me on the head. Fortunately, nothing serious happened. I just had to get five ράμματα [stitches] in my head and spend a week in bed. I needed that week. It was a nice end to my career in construction. After that, I started school and found a new part-time job. Have you ever had this kind of job? I hope not. It's not a real pleasure.

Did Mihail use all the words in his list (see p. 8)? Did he use them in the same order as in the original list, or did he change the order?

Now, in the journal section (section 3) of your notebook, on right-hand pages only, write your own version of your memory. After you have finished, read carefully through your journal entry, count how many of the words on your original list you have used (Individual Assignment 2, p. 8), and note the order in which they appear. Give your journal pages and the facing left-hand pages to your instructor for response.

Note: When you are given a specific topic to write on (by a teacher or an employer), it is a good idea to first search your memory in your journal to uncover what you know about the topic. This will help you get started and will help you decide what new information you need. So, your journal can guide your research.

CHAPTER 2

Look and Read

Chapter 2 will provide you with some background material on the subject you chose in Chapter 1. You will be asked to examine this material closely and to report on it in detail. Such detailed observation will provide more subject matter for discussion and writing.

Individual Assignments

1. Look at the list below. According to the question you chose in Individual Assignment 1 in Chapter 1, turn to the corresponding pages in Part III, "Materials: Pictures and Readings."

Question	Section in Part III
1	Places, pp. 179–200
2	Possessions, pp. 201–225
3	Work, pp. 227–249
4	Family, pp. 251–270
5	Men and Women, pp. 271–296

Now, in section 1 of your notebook, on a right-hand page, write your answers to the Preview Questions. Then, look closely at each picture in the section, and think about the questions that follow it. Finally, choose *one* picture, and write down short answers to the accompanying questions to prepare for discussion in class.

2. Imagine that you are trying to get a blind person to "see" the picture you have chosen. On a new right-hand page in section 1 of your notebook, describe exactly what you see in the picture. Include as many details as you can.

3. Read carefully all the selected passages—or those your instructor assigns, along with the questions that accompany the passage. Some of the difficult words and phrases are explained in the margin, but you may still come across other words or sentences that you do not understand. For now, do not let that hold you

I wonder why she doesn't quit.

Why is he a supervisor if he is so bad?
what does status mean?

Do tellers ever steal money? Why does she
only have a small amount?

A twenty-eight-year-old woman has been working as a bank teller for six years. She doesn't like it much. She dislikes the time clock, her boss, and the fact that she doesn't know a lot of the people who work at the bank. The problem with her boss is that he yells at her, doesn't answer her questions, and hasn't won anyone's respect. The thing she likes about the job is talking to her customers, but she doesn't like those who talk about money and try to impress her. To her, the money is just pieces of paper. Some people talk about stealing money from the bank, but she wonders what the point would be for the small amount of money in her drawer.

up. There is no need to turn to a dictionary yet. You do not have to know exactly what every word means. Just read through the passages, and try to understand as much as you can with what you already know.

Now, choose the reading that interests you the most. On a new right-hand page in section 1 of your notebook, write down your answers to the questions following the passage.

4. Read what one student, Aura, wrote about the excerpt on p. 234 from Studs Terkel's book *Working*. Note her own comments and questions on the facing page. (See pages 14–15.)

Now, in your own words, on a new right-hand page in section 1 of your notebook, summarize the main points of the reading you chose. Again, if you can't think of a word or an expression in English, write it in your own language. On the facing left-hand pages of your notebook, enter any comments or questions you have about the passage you chose, including questions about any words, phrases, or sentences you don't understand. If you open your notebook six months from now, you should be able to read your summary and from it recall the subject matter, the main points, and any pertinent details of the selection. Write with that aim in mind.

Classroom Activities

1. In class, work with students who chose the same section of materials as you did. Tell each other the answers you wrote to the Preview Questions. If you want to change or add anything to your answers, write the new information on the facing left-hand page of your notebook.

2. Read what Vanila, a student from India, wrote about the picture on page 181:

An old man is working in his gas station on a nice quiet evening. There is no traffic and everything seems to be silent. There is nobody on the road at all. The place is deserted except for the old man. It is nighttime, and we see lights on in the little cabin of the gas station on the right of the picture. The sign, which says "Mobilgas," is lit up, too, and so are the three gas pumps. The man is doing something at these pumps. I think it is summertime because he isn't wearing a coat. There are a lot of dark trees around the gas station and along the road. It looks like a lonely place to work.

Which details has Vanila included that help you to "see" the picture clearly? Underline them. Has Vanila left out any important details that you think should be included? If so, what are they?

3. In a small group, each student reads aloud a description of the picture he or she chose. After each student reads, the other members of the group give their answers to the following questions.

   a. If you were blind and listened to this description of the picture, would you be able to "see" it clearly in your mind, with all the details?
   b. Did the writer leave out any details that you would need to be able to draw the picture on paper or to "see" it in your imagination?
   c. What did the writer mention first? and last? Why do you think the writer chose to do it that way?
   d. Would you suggest a different order of presentation? If so, why?

If you want to make any changes in your description as the group discusses your writing, note the changes on the facing left-hand page of your notebook.

4. Exchange notebooks with a partner. Read your partner's answers to the questions accompanying the reading passage (Individual Assignment 3) and the summary that your partner (Individual Assignment 4) wrote. Then, see if you can help each other answer the questions each of you raised. Use a dictionary if you find it helpful.

5. Hand in to your instructor your description of the picture and your summary of the reading passage. If you would like some response to your comments and questions, then hand those in, too. In addition to answering your questions and commenting on your content, your instructor might also refer you to particular chapters in Part II, "Grammar: Twenty-One Troublespots," so that you can review them, do the exercises in your notebook, and discover ways to avoid errors in the future.

Journal Assignment

Over the next few days, as you read, watch television, or just go about your daily life, look for images and scenes that make you think of the pictures you have just looked at and the passages you have just read. Whenever you see something that you associate with these materials, write a description of it in section 3, the journal section, of your notebook. Then, let your classmates and your instructor read what you have written.

CHAPTER 3

Focus

In Chapter 3, you will look at all the ideas and information you have collected so far and use them to focus in on a topic that you can explore.

Individual Assignments

1. Read through (a) all the notes in section 1 of your notebook and (b) your journal entries. Then look once more at the pictures you chose in Part III, and skim two or three of the reading selections as quickly as you can.

2. On a right-hand page in section 1 of your notebook, write the heading, "Topics I Could Write About." Now, still keeping to the same broad subject area (e.g., Places), think about narrower aspects of the subject that would be interesting to read and write about (e.g., beaches, vacation spots, city versus country). Make a list of the focused topics of interest that you have some material for and could possibly write about. Try to list ten to twelve possible topics. Remember, though, that you are only exploring here; you will not necessarily have to write about any of these topics.

3. Following is a list of four purposes that most nonprofessional writers have in mind when they write:

    a. to explore and express feelings and ideas (in journals, diaries, and note-books)
    b. to entertain a reader (in stories, poetry, songs, and letters)
    c. to inform a reader (in memos and in essays and articles containing facts, instructions, opinions, analysis, problem-solving, comparisons, and definitions)
    d. to persuade a reader (in editorials, essays, and letters)*

Which of these purposes might a writer have for each of the topics listed in

Note: If you want to improve your writing mainly for academic reasons—to do well in college—it will be helpful for you to choose topics that concentrate on the last two purposes: to inform and to persuade.

Topics for subject of "Places"	Purpose
How to choose the best place for a vacation	*c ,*
A crowded beach is worse than a crowded bus	*c*
My dream house	*a b*
The houses of Le Corbusier	*c*
Architecture influences our lives more than we think.	*c, d*
Which does the choice of a home reflect more: personality or money?	*c d*
The house I grew up in and the apartment I live in now	*a, b*
The day the movers came—and what they did to my cat and me	*b*
Eastern and Western landscape painting	*c ,*

the accompanying box? Often, you will find that more than one purpose seems to fit the topic. In the right-hand column, enter the letter or letters of whichever purposes fit each topic.

4. Which of the four purposes seems to be most appropriate for each of the topics *you* have chosen? Write the purposes on the left-hand page of your notebook, opposite each topic you chose.

5. If you have not found topics that you can match up with all four purposes listed in Individual Assignment 3, read through your notes again and try to find topics that will fit.

Classroom Activities

1. In class, find a partner who has been working on the same set of materials as you, and compare the topics that you have discovered. Together, decide on four topics that you like best and that you both think you could write about.

2. In a class discussion, students now tell their choices of topics. As each topic is proposed and written on the board, discuss the purpose that a piece of writing on the topic might have. Discuss, too, what a reader might expect to find when reading about that topic.

3. Give your pages with your list of topics and purposes to your instructor, who will make recommendations as to which ones are the most suitable for you and your classmates to explore.

Journal Assignment

Choose a topic you identified as having the purpose of persuading a reader. In the journal section of your notebook, write a letter to a classmate, trying to persuade him or her to accept your point of view. Provide as much evidence as possible to show why you are right. In your next class session, give the letter to the student you chose. He or she will tell you whether you have been convincing in your arguments.

Finding Ways In

Writers use many different ways to find out what to write about, what to include, and how to organize the ideas they want to express. The next five chapters will introduce you to a variety of approaches; you can use them in any sequence with any type of subject, whether it is assigned or not. However, there is no need to use all or even any of these "ways in" to your subject every time you write. Most writers find one or two that suit them, and they use these most often. The first time you work through this book, try all the techniques. Then, as you work on future essays, decide which techniques you feel most comfortable with and find most helpful. These will be the techniques that you will probably use again and again to help you find ways to discover ideas for your own writing.

In Chapter 3, you listed some possible topics for writing, and you have already done some thinking and writing about them. In the following chapters, you can explore these topics further as well as investigate other possibilities by using techniques such as making lists and brainstorming, freewriting, asking questions, using a system to explore new viewpoints, and telling a story.

Another useful "way in" to any piece of writing is to write in your journal about any ideas that interest you. If you set aside a short amount of time every day to write in your journal, you can use the journal to explore and develop ideas.

CHAPTER 4

List and Brainstorm

Brainstorming is an activity that lets one idea lead to another through free association and quick follow-up of related words, thoughts, and opinions. Essentially a group activity, brainstorming allows us to share ideas, learn from others, and produce new ideas of our own. This chapter introduces you to some techniques that help you generate these new ideas—or at least recall ideas from your memory—either alone or with others, through writing or through discussion. Brainstorming is one of these techniques, and making lists is another. Many of us use lists frequently in our everyday life. Lists remind us what to do next, and often in the writing of a list, one item suggests another.

Classroom Activities

1. Work with students who are working on the same broad subject area that you selected in Chapters 1 and 2. Together, using the headings given in the following pages, compile lists of ideas about your subject. For example, under the heading, "What makes a place memorable," you might list:

> view
> climate
> happy times spent there
> frightening event occurred there
> new friendship formed there
> painful memory associated with the place

Include five to ten ideas under each heading. In addition, add two headings and lists of your own, and relate them to the focus you chose in Chapter 3. Write the lists you compose in section 1 of your notebook on a right-hand page.

> Subject 1: Places
>   1. What makes a place memorable
>   2. The best type of place to spend a vacation
>   3. What makes a place beautiful
>   4. The advantages of the city

5. The advantages of the country
6. The ideal house or apartment
7. (Provide your own heading.)
8. (Provide your own heading.)

Subject 2: Possessions
1. Valued possessions in your country
2. Valued possessions in the United States
3. Possessions that are advertised on television and in magazines
4. What a 20-year-old student needs for college
5. Possessions you would want after being married
6. Things we should be able to throw away easily
7. (Provide your own heading.)
8. (Provide your own heading.)

Subject 3: Work
1. The features of a good job
2. Choosing a career
3. The best jobs to train for in the future
4. What makes a job tedious
5. A good boss
6. Being self-employed
7. (Provide your own heading.)
8. (Provide your own heading.)

Subject 4: Family
1. Living close to the different generations of one's family
2. The generation gap
3. The issues families disagree about
4. Big or small families
5. The only child
6. Rules parents make
7. (Provide your own heading.)
8. (Provide your own heading.)

Subject 5: Men and Women
1. Household jobs usually done by women in your country
2. Household jobs usually done by men in your country
3. The roles of the sexes 50 years ago
4. Mothers and fathers as role models
5. Bringing up sons and daughters
6. Changing roles of men and women in the United States and other countries
7. (Provide your own heading.)
8. (Provide your own heading.)

2. Which were the most unusual and interesting ideas that emerged as you made your lists? Write those ideas in your notebook on the left-hand page opposite the lists you made. Put an asterisk (*) next to any ideas that you might be interested in writing about in the future.

3. With the students in your group, select three narrower topics to explore—for example, under "Work," such topics as "Office work," "Nursing," and "Good jobs for college students."

4. Gather ideas on these three topics by brainstorming with your group. First, let the topic create its own free associations in your mind. And then, as fast as you can and without stopping to think about grammar, organization of ideas, or correctness, tell each other all the words, phrases, and ideas that come into your head when you think about these topics. Recall the pictures you have looked at, the passages you have read, and your own experience. Of course, you can also do brainstorming on your own (in your head or on paper), although you usually pick up more ideas when you work with others.

5. On a new right-hand page of your notebook, write down the ideas that the students in your group produced.
     Here are some of the ideas that one group produced for the topic "Office work":

> Typing
> Boring
> Lunch hour is the best.
> Lots of jobs are boring.
> Freedom to make decisions is important.
> Pressure
> Bosses
> It's important to have a good boss.
> 9 to 5
> Routine is one of the worst things about an office job.
> Money
> The only reason to work is for the money.
> Nursing is better than office work.
> Is office work a job or a career? What's the difference?
> How many men are secretaries? Do you know any male secretaries?
> Some secretaries have to be like maids: they get coffee, buy presents for the
>   boss's spouse, and all that.
> Do you want to wear a suit to work?
> Some jobs make you feel tired but not satisfied.
> I might look for an office job after college.

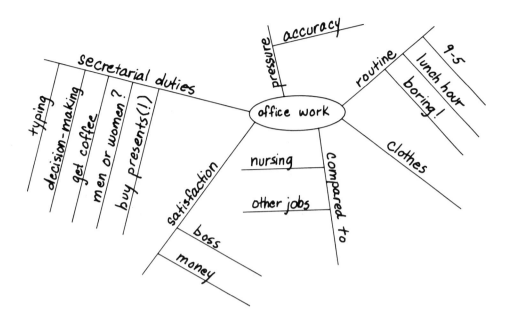

Another way to organize the results of a brainstorming session, either by yourself or with others, is shown in the accompanying diagram. The chosen topic is in the center of the diagram, with associated ideas arranged around it and with ideas growing out of ideas.

Individual Assignment

Individually, look at your brainstorming notes, and try to sort the ideas into groups. Which ones belong together? For example, from the list in Classroom Activity 5, one student saw the ideas as fitting under these headings:

Bosses
The routine of office work
Bad things about office work
A comparison of office work and nursing
Is office work a career—or just a job?

On the left-hand page facing the list of ideas you wrote in Classroom Activity 5, write the headings for the groups of ideas you can form from that list. Under each heading, put the ideas that belong to it. Put an asterisk (*) next to the two most interesting groups. In your next class meeting, compare with the other students how you sorted your brainstorming ideas.

Journal Assignment

In the journal section of your notebook, write about how you discover ideas on a topic when you write in your first language. What were you taught in school? What would you do if you were going to write in your first language about one of the topics you have just chosen? Let your instructor read what you have to say on this subject.

CHAPTER 5

Freewrite

Freewriting is a technique used by professional and student writers to let ideas emerge freely and to let one idea suggest another on the page. They write as quickly as they can without stopping to think about organization, the effect on the reader, or accuracy. Often, they find that new and important ideas emerge as they write, especially if they write quickly, without concern for spelling or grammar. They find that, when the purpose is simply to get as much down on paper as possible, they can discover new ideas through writing. So, when you freewrite, write as much as you can, in connected sentences (not lists), and write as quickly as you can, without stopping to think about organization or grammar. If you cannot keep on writing—if your ideas dry up for a moment—then just write something like "I'm stuck and I can't think what to write next," or "I wish I could think of something more interesting to say." Often, as you are writing this, more ideas will come to you and you will be able to continue.

Individual Assignments

1. Look back over all the material you have on your subject in your notebook. Then, freewrite for about 5 to 10 minutes (your instructor will tell you how long), starting on a new right-hand page in section 1 of your notebook. Write about anything that comes into your mind as a result of what you have just read. Do not be concerned about how your writing will appear to a reader.

Here are some suggestions:

You might write about one of the topics you chose in Chapter 3.

You could write about a topic that came up as you made lists in Chapter 4.

You might write about why you chose the event you first wrote about.

You might want to write about the pictures you have looked at and the passages you have read, pointing out their similarities and differences or relating them to other information you know about.

You could even start all over again and explore another memory, particularly if something you read in this book, discussed in class, or wrote in your notebook made you think of something you hadn't thought of before.

See how much you can write in the time your instructor gives you. If you cannot think of a word, an expression, or even a whole sentence in English, then write it down in your first language. The purpose is to capture as many ideas as you can and to keep on writing, even if you feel you are not being organized or correct, or feel you are not sticking to the topic. None of this is important for freewriting. What is important is to fill the page with all the ideas you can produce.

2. Read an example of what Alvaro, a student from Colombia, wrote. So that you can see what freewriting looks like, his piece appears uncorrected, as he originally wrote it, with the errors he made.

I have been living in the U.S.A. for about four years. When I came here, I brought with me a few books, my favorite T-shirts, and a little hand-made pillow from my mother.

Among some of the books I brought with me is one called *The Little Prince*, is a very interesting book. Every time I read it, I find new and different ideas that I can practice in my life. Some of my favorites T-shirts are souvenirs from places which I had visited in Colombia where I come from and they remind me of the good times I had. The little handmade pillow from my mother is a small cotton square, with five lines around it and my Christian name on it. Sometimes when I have difficulties in my courses I look at it, asking for help like my mother used to give me when I was living at home.

And what I left behind was a happy family life, my good friends and a pretty city in the north of Colombia near the Atlantic Ocean, where is always sunny and windy. It is pleasant to live there. I hope I can go back pretty soon.

What do you think is the most important point that this student makes? What idea sticks in your mind? What is the most important idea the writer is trying to convey? Below, write one sentence that captures that main idea:

---

3. Now read the uncorrected freewriting of Tzvi, a student from Israel.

Atsuko Toyama, author of "A Theory on the Modern Freshman" [see p. 239] says, "the younger workers do what they are told and not one iota more." I think that sentence has to worry teachers and the people who related to education. Because the skills that child get in the school he use when he is grown up. And if the child has developed carefulness and creation he will continue the same as an adult. I myself usually do much more than I am told. Except the job that I don't like. In that case I do only what I was told to do. But anyway I try not to get job like that.

Now write in one sentence the most important idea that Tzvi is trying to convey.

---

4. Read through your own piece of freewriting. Imagine that a reader only has time to read *one* sentence and not your whole piece. What could you say in a sentence that would tell your reader the most about your ideas? Now, on the left-hand page opposite the freewriting, write one sentence that tells a reader the most important idea that your piece of writing is expressing.

5. On a new right-hand page of section 1, freewrite for another 5 to 10 minutes. Begin with the sentence that you have just written to express your most important point. Include as many ideas as you want from your first piece of freewriting. When you have finished, write on the facing left-hand page the one sentence that captures the central idea of this new piece of writing.

Classroom Activities

1. In class, read through your two pieces of freewriting, and translate anything you wrote in your own language into English. Also, note whether writing quickly made you leave out any words or make any careless errors. Make any corrections you want.

2. Exchange your two pieces of freewriting with a partner. After reading each other's writing, tell your partner what you regard as the most important ideas of his or her pieces.

3. Give your second piece of freewriting (but not your second summary sentence) to your instructor, who will write a sentence that states the main idea of the piece. Compare it with the sentence you wrote in Individual Assignment 5.

Journal Assignment

At home, over the next four or five days, do some freewriting for 5 to 10 minutes each day. If you need help with finding topics, look at the suggestions in Individual Assignment 1, or ask your classmates or instructor for advice. Later, submit the piece you like best to your instructor.

CHAPTER 6

Ask Questions

Asking questions about your initial notes and ideas helps you get closer to a plan for a longer and more complex piece of writing. Of course, everything you write when you explore a subject can serve as material for inclusion in a completed essay. But asking questions about the material helps you focus your thinking. Remember that, even after you decide on a focus, you are not necessarily committed to it. Plans can always be changed.

Classroom Activities

1. Form a group of three or four students. It does not matter whether the students are all working on the same subject area. Take a few minutes to choose either one of the topics you selected in Chapter 3 or a new topic that arose from your brainstorming and listing. The topic should be one that you need some help with in generating ideas. Then, tell the members of the group, "I think I'll write about _____," and complete the sentence.

2. After you have announced what you think you will write about, the group will decide which of the following four categories your topic fits into best. (It may fit into more than one category, but the group should decide which *one* category is your main focus.)

   a. Something you can see, hear, or touch (a place, person, or object).
   b. Something that happened.
   c. Something you can't see, hear, or touch (an idea, or an abstraction, such as *happiness, marriage*, and so on).
   d. Something the writer wants you to believe (an idea or opinion with points for and against it).

3. Your group will now ask you questions about the topic you proposed. The questions should begin with these words: *What, Who, How, When, Where, Why.* Listen carefully to the questions, and then give your answers.

   The answers you give to these questions will lead you to consider ways of developing and presenting your ideas to a reader. Some sample questions follow, with a space for your chosen topic. For example,

What does _____ look like, exactly?

will become

What does *your great-aunt's room* look like, exactly?

Note that not every question will fit every topic.

Some of them

For something you can see, hear, or touch
What does _____ look like, exactly?
Where is _____ located?
How was _____ produced or made?
When did _____ first make its appearance, and in what setting?
What are the most striking characteristics of _____?
Who likes _____?
Why do people like or dislike _____?
What does _____ do?
Who uses _____?
When is _____ most active, most used, or most useful?
How might _____ change?
How many parts can _____ be divided into?
What (or whom) is _____ similar to or different from?

For something that happened
What happened, exactly?
When did _____ happen?
Where did _____ happen?
Why did _____ happen?
In what order did the events occur?
What caused _____ to happen?
What happened as a result of _____?
Who was there?
Which people did _____ affect?
When did the effects stop?
How was what happened similar to or different from other events?
How many separate divisions (of time, place, and so on) can be seen in _____?
How could _____ have been different?
How was _____ connected to other events?
Where else could _____ have happened?
Why was _____ important enough to you to choose to write about it?

For something you can't see, hear, or touch
What does _____ mean?

What special meaning does _____ have for you?
What else is _____ closely related to?
Who knows a lot about _____?
Who is affected a lot by _____?
How can _____ be changed to improve it?
How do others view _____?
How has _____ affected people's lives?
When does _____ have its most powerful effects?
Where can we see the causes and effects of _____ most clearly?
Why is _____ important to you?
Why is _____ important to others?

For something the writer wants you to believe
What do you know about _____?
What do others need to know about _____?
Who believes _____ now?
Who is affected by _____?
How is everyday life affected by _____?
How will things change if people change their minds about _____?
How can people's opinions about _____ be changed?
When did people first begin to think the way they do about _____?
When do views about _____ change?
Who feels strongly about _____?
Where is support for _____ found?
Where is opposition to _____ found?
Why is it important to convince people about _____?

Read it   These questions will lead you to explore your subject matter more fully, but they should also turn your attention to the formal possibilities of developing a piece of writing. Forms commonly used by people writing in English include using examples, illustrations, or facts; describing what happened or describing the exact appearance of something or someone; defining a term; comparing and contrasting; analyzing; classifying; examining change, causes, or effects; and examining what others have said and done. In the next chapter and in Chapter 11, "Explore Alternatives," you will work some more on the options available to you when you develop your ideas in writing.

Individual Assignment

On the right-hand page of your notebook, write down the most interesting questions your group asked you. Now write detailed answers to these questions on the facing left-hand page.

Journal Assignment

In the journal section of your notebook, write about a question that interests you and that you like to discuss with other people. An example might be: Why do some governments spend more on defense than on education? Write about why you think your question is interesting or important, and consider the different answers that could be given. As you write, remember to ask yourself a series of questions beginning with *What, Who, How, When, Where,* and *Why* to help you generate ideas. Let your classmates read your journal entry.

Explore New Viewpoints

The purpose of the writing you will do in Chapter 7 is to expand the ways in which you think about and explore a topic. These patterns of thinking will also help you develop patterns of organization for your writing. Thus, when you begin to write your first draft, you will have more options to choose from, as you consider what your reader will need to know in order to understand the point you want to make.

Individual Assignments

1. Summarize what you have done so far under these headings:

General subject: _____

My topic: _____

Here is what one student wrote:

General subject: Family
My topic: Single-parent families

And here is what a teacher wrote:

General subject: Places
My topic: My great-aunt's room

You are in control of what you write about. So, if the activities of listing, brainstorming, freewriting, and asking questions have given you new ideas for topics, you can make any changes necessary to the list you produced in Chapter 3, Individual Assignment 2.

2. Now look at your chosen topic from different viewpoints. You might find some of them useful in determining what to include in your writing. They might also suggest ways to structure and organize your essay. That is, they might provide you

with more ideas of what information to include to inform your reader. From the lists of exploratory viewpoints that follow, select only the ones that seem to apply most directly to your chosen topic. Write them on a new right-hand page in section 1 of your notebook, and then write your responses on the opposite left-hand page.

a. *Define your topic.*
   Look up the definition in the dictionary.
   Write down your own definition.
   Note any other definitions possible.
   List any synonyms or similar terms.

b. *Describe your topic.*
   Use your senses to describe how it looks (color, shape, size), sounds, feels, smells, or tastes.
   Describe it from a new perspective: for example, from above, from below, from a great height.
   Give facts and figures about its measurements and location.
   Divide it into parts if possible.
   State what group of things it seems to belong to.

c. *Compare your topic.*
   List what it is similar to.
   List what it is different from.
   State how it is similar to or different from the things you have just mentioned.
   State what could be seen as its opposite.

d. *Tell a story about your topic.*
   Tell about something that happened that involved your topic.
   Ask someone else to tell you a story about this topic.
   Make up a story about your topic.

e. *Associate your topic with other things.*
   State what causes or produces your topic.
   List what effects your topic has on people or events.
   List other things that your topic is related to.
   List things that your topic reminds you of.

f. *Find out what others say about your topic.*
   Ask friends what they have to say about it.
   Interview someone, and ask for a story about your topic.
   Go to the library, and read about your topic in journals or books.
   Write down what you remember having read or heard about your topic.

g. *Examine points of view about your topic.*
   List the points of view that people hold about your topic.
   State the strongest opinion that *you* have about your topic.
   List the way (or ways) in which your topic could be controversial.

Ask yourself what opinion you hold about your topic that you would like
  to convince others of.
Make a list of reasons why you feel the way you do about your topic.

3. Which of these different ways of looking at a topic was most productive for
you? As you worked through this chapter, which were the best ideas that came to
you? Put an asterisk (*) next to these ideas in your notebook. Give your instructor
the pages with the exploratory viewpoints you used and your responses so that he
or she can comment on your ideas and recommend other viewpoints to explore.
Your instructor might also indicate which grammatical troublespots (in Part II)
you need to review to help improve the accuracy of your writing.

Journal Assignment

In section 3 of your notebook, write a journal entry telling your instructor
and your classmates what has been the most interesting and helpful activity in this
book so far. Explain why.

CHAPTER 8

Tell a Story

The ability to tell a story is important for writers. It is useful not only for expressive or creative writing (that is, for novels and short stories), but also for nonfiction and for academic writing. When readers read an expository essay, which presents an argument or gives information, they expect to read examples that support the writer's opinion. These examples are often stories from the writer's own experience and reading. Even when the topic is abstract (for example, a definition of a "successful career"), readers expect to find concrete examples to support the writer's generalizations. They will, therefore, not be surprised to read, somewhere in a piece defining a successful career, a story about a real person's successful career. Chapter 8 concentrates on the use of narrative to tell a story for its own sake or to provide a concrete example in an informative piece of expository writing.

Classroom Activities

1. Choose the same subject area (i.e., Places, Possessions, Work, Family, or Men and Women) as you did in previous chapters. Imagine that the sentence given below for your subject is the last sentence of a short story.

Subject 1: Places
So, even though that place seemed to Sam to be one of the most beautiful spots in the world to pitch a tent, he decided that what the wild animals had just done made it too terrifying to visit again.

Subject 2: Possessions
Harold watched in horror as Mandy, showing her long-hidden scorn for his hobby of collecting, picked up his treasures one by one, ripping them, breaking them, and throwing them across the room, until only one was left—his elephant's tusk.

Subject 3: Work
That was how Susan's boss, tearing up the two pieces of paper that had caused so much trouble, changed the nature of the company—and of her whole life.

Subject 4: Family

And so another family picnic ended, with the usual wet clothes, squashed cake, and a crying child; this time, though, there was also a broken heart.

Subject 5: Men and Women

It was Uncle Richard's courageous act that saved the day; without him, Sarah would never have discovered how her fiancé would react in a life-threatening crisis.

Work with a group of three or four students, and try to decide on a story that might lead up to such an ending.

2. When you have decided on a story line, write out the story, with all its details, on a new right-hand page in section 1 of your notebook. Write 1 to 2 pages if you can. Remember to try to include all the elements that appear in the ending.

3. Read the following two stories written by students as they worked together in groups:

---

a. The expected day finally came. My three sisters, Mary, Veronica, and Gloria, and I were getting ready for the picnic. We didn't know what to wear: jeans, shorts, or just a swimsuit and a skirt. My mother was putting the food in the car, and my father was gathering up his fishing equipment. My father decided to invite my older brother, Lucy, his wife, and their child. My brother and his wife were very different. Lucy was a very *vinagreta* [sour, bad-tempered] person, who never dared to expose herself to the sun's rays, so she wore a big, exaggerated hat with a feather. Also she felt she was better than we were, and she had to be better-dressed—no jeans for her! Instead, she was wearing a *traje sastre* [tailored suit] and high heels. We had all learned to understand her, but my brother Alfonso was always teasing her.

We got to the picnic place and enjoyed ourselves. My father went fishing, and we went swimming. My mother took a strawberry cake out of the basket. Everything seemed very quiet. I noticed that Alfonso wanted to persuade Lucy to go swimming, but she said that she hated the river water and the fish and rocks and everything, so he took her hat and stepped on it. While she was trying to get it back, she pushed him, and he fell right in front of my mother, squashing the strawberry cake flat. Then he felt embarrassed, so he went to Lucy and threw her in the water, along with her high heels and big hat. Lucy climbed out of the water, picked up the baby, who was crying because she was scared, and burst into tears herself. She ran up to Alfonso and yelled

at him, "How could you do that? That's not a joke. How could you be
so mean? I'm leaving you—forever!" and ran off. And so another family picnic ended, with the usual wet clothes, squashed cake, and a
crying child; this time, though, there was also a broken heart.

---

     b. Sam went camping on Hunter Mountain last summer. He
wanted to explore and to go fishing, hunting, and climbing. At night, he
heard strange sounds from wild animals and birds, and he couldn't
sleep because he was scared, but he really liked it there. So, even
though that place seemed to Sam to be one of the most beautiful spots
in the world to pitch a tent, he decided that what the wild animals had
just done made it too terrifying to visit again.

    With your class or group, decide which story is the most effective, and why.
Consider these questions:

    How many story elements are there in each of the last sentences these
        writers chose? (In other words, how many separate people and events
        does the writer have to introduce and explain?)
    Have both writers developed and accounted for all the elements in the last
        sentence?
    Are the two stories equally interesting?
    Which story has more details, allowing you to almost experience the event?
    What do your answers to these questions tell you about your own story?

4. Working with a partner, make a list of the story elements that appear in the
concluding sentence your partner chose. Then, exchange notebooks with your
partner, and read each other's stories. As you read, ask yourself whether the writer
has included in the story all the elements that appear in the conclusion. If any
elements are not covered, write them on the left-hand page facing the story. In
addition, tell the writer what you think is effective about the story.

5. Give your own story to your instructor for a response.

Journal Assignment

    For the next few days, carry your looseleaf notebook and a pen with you. If
you experience anything that would tie in with the topic you chose in Chapter 6,
record it in the journal section of your notebook. Whenever you see an interesting
incident or hear about or read an interesting story, write it down for your class-

mates and your instructor to read. Tell where and when the story happened, and describe the main characters. Imagine you have a movie camera instead of a pen, and get in all the details. Pass your stories around at the beginning of a class session, so that your classmates and instructor can ask you questions about them. Then give the stories to your instructor for comment.

Writing and Rewriting

In the previous chapters, you explored a topic in several different ways. You thought about it, talked about it, looked at pictures about it, read about it, and wrote about it in your journal. Perhaps you also did some brainstorming, listing, and freewriting; asked questions; explored the topic from different viewpoints; wrote notes; read your classmates' notes and lists; and told stories. So far, you have a lot of words and ideas on paper, and a lot of short pieces of writing that explore a variety of perspectives on the subject area you chose.

In the next four chapters, you are going to work on putting all your ideas together by sorting and organizing them into a clear piece of writing. Remember, few writers—even professional ones—"get it right" in their first draft, so do not expect to produce a polished essay immediately. Second-language writers, especially, need the opportunity to review and monitor their own work. By writing drafts, you can try out various ways of presenting your ideas and you will get responses from your instructor and from your classmates. You will be working gradually toward a polished essay, exploring your own ideas and organization through the writing that you do. You will, therefore, have many opportunities—not just one—to make your essay as good as possible.

Because this section focuses intensively on writing drafts of an essay, separate journal assignments are not included in each chapter. However, you can continue to use the journal section of your notebook to explore any issues or questions that seem important. You can then use excerpts from your journal in the drafts of your essay.

CHAPTER 9

Plan and Write a First Draft

A reader of English generally expects writing to be direct and clear. A well-written piece states its point explicitly, so that the reader knows the writer's point of view without any doubt. Also, a reader looks for a clear presentation of that point of view early in the piece of writing; the writer does not keep the reader guessing. But just stating the point is not enough. The reader now expects to read more about it—more detail, explanation, or support. The reader also expects the supporting details to be concrete and specific, so that they convey the writer's own knowledge and experience. When you write, then, you must think about how and where to state your main point, and how you will support it: that is, with examples, explanations, definitions, comparisons, analyses, or stories and descriptions.

Of course, as you write, *you are the boss.* Remember that. No one is forcing you to write in a particular way or to use a difficult sentence. You can change direction whenever you want. You can throw out an idea and start again with a new one. Keep a stack of paper close by you as you work, and be prepared to use a lot of it.

Individual Assignments

1. To get all your material fresh in your mind, review the ideas you have had so far. Carefully read through all the notes in your notebook. Then, once again turn to all the materials in Part III that are connected with your subject: look at all the pictures and skim the reading selections. Now you are ready to make a plan for an essay and to establish some "signposts" to help you.

2. The following list expands on the purposes you worked with in Chapter 3. Choose one of them, and adapt it if necessary so that it fits your chosen topic.

My purpose is to:

tell my readers a story that is interesting because _____.
give my readers information about _____.
explain to my readers why _____.

persuade my readers that _____.
persuade my readers to _____.
describe _____ to show my readers _____.
compare _____ with _____ to show my readers _____.
point out similarities between _____ and _____ in order to _____.
express an opinion about _____ and show my readers why I hold that
    opinion.
analyze _____ into (how many?) _____ parts to show my readers _____.
define a problem (state what it is) and show my readers how to solve it
    by _____.

For your first signpost, complete the following sentence, and write it on a 4-by-6-inch index card:

My purpose in writing is to _____.

3. For your next signpost sentence, complete the following, and write your completed sentence on another index card:

The main point I want to get across to the reader is _____

_____.

Copy your two signpost sentences into section 2 of your notebook, the section reserved for drafts. Write them on a new right-hand page, facing an empty left-hand page.

4. Now, following the two signpost sentences in your notebook, make a plan for your draft by listing the supporting points you would use (e.g., examples, facts, stories, accounts of experience or reading, comparisons, analyses, descriptions) to develop your main point, as expressed in your second signpost sentence.

Your supporting points should be more specific than your main point. (If you have chosen as a main point an idea that is so limited that it does not need development or support, then it will be hard for you to list supporting points. In that case, you probably need to revise your main point.) Imagine a reader looking at your plan; this person will read your main point and then ask, "What makes you think that?" The reader now expects to be told more; you should supply the specific images, experiences, and knowledge you have that enable you to make your point.

The following plan was produced by a teacher as she wrote along with her class:

My purpose in writing is to describe my great-aunt's room in detail to show
    how much we can learn about people—and what we can't find out—
    from their rooms.

The main point I want to get across to the reader is that you can tell a lot
about people's lives and values from the way their rooms look.

Supporting points:

a. Background: place, setting, time. First impressions and general layout of
   my great-aunt's room: size, furniture, ornaments, trophies, and so on. (Refer to some of the pictures and readings in Part III.)
b. Photographs tell us about family, friends, and ambitions. (Refer to "From
   Minor Characters" by Joyce Johnson on p. 224.)
c. The dishes from different places tell us about her vacations and dreams.
d. Her trophies tell us about her husband.
e. The "mystery corner" hints at a secret in her life.
f. Lots of letters and cards show that she has helped many people.

---

5. For each of your supporting points, write down opposite it, on the left-hand
page, any details that might interest a reader and help support your point. Remember the pictures you looked at and the selections you read. You might be able to
use some of this material as a source of examples and to support your point.

The teacher who made the preceding plan added the following details on the
left-hand page. Note how they are all concrete and emerge from the writer's
specific knowledge and experience.

a. Overstuffed with furniture and trinkets; a lifetime of accumulation. Obviously a collector; she keeps everything. Every surface covered with
   photographs, ornaments, etc. A bed, couch, two chairs, a small desk and
   chair, and a round table. I could refer to "Lure of Possessions" by Barbara Lang Stern on p. 214 and the photograph by Walker Evans on p. 205
   and make connections.
b. Photograph of Great-aunt Anna when she was young and beautiful and
   wanted to go on the stage; lots of photographs of stage stars—her idols. I
   could refer to "From *Minor Characters*" by Joyce Johnson on p. 224 and
   particularly to the photograph mentioned there. Photograph of great-aunt
   with her family all around her—a really big family. Photograph of Anna
   with a handsome young man.
c. Dish from Niagara Falls: she can't remember if it was from her honeymoon or her tenth wedding anniversary. Tell the story about that. Different dishes, all from Florida, where her son goes every year.
d. Great-uncle Joseph was a runner and a swimmer, and all over the room
   are the silver cups and trophies he won. All are brightly polished, even
   though he died ten years ago. One big silver cup, the one he was the
   most proud of, is in the center of the round table: it is for a 10-mile road
   race he won when he was 50!
e. In one little corner of the room, on one shelf, there are objects she won't

talk about: the photograph of the young man, a glass jar, a string of beads, one cuff link, an old theater program, a pressed flower, and a letter which none of us has read.

f. Great-aunt Anna always helped neighbors when they were sick or their children were in trouble. She has saved all the letters and cards and gifts that they sent. Many of the cards are displayed around the room. One, in particular, is a big card with red roses and a big *Thank You* on it. Inside, it says, "We couldn't have managed without your help. You really are a wonderful person. With love, Your second family."

Now, count the number of concrete images this teacher recorded.

Even if you are planning to write on an abstract topic, concrete details and examples will help you to make your point convincing to a reader. How many concrete details have *you* included?

6. With the plan before you now, you have some guidelines for the major part of your essay. If you find beginnings difficult, write the body of your essay first and then write the introduction later. Or you can include a few notes in your plan for your introduction and your conclusion. The teacher who wrote the preceding plan did this:

Introduction: "Snapshot" scenes of a variety of rooms, real and imaginary, like pictures in a magazine. My inferences about the people who live in them. Statement of my main point. Quote from "Lure of Possessions" by Barbara Lang Stern, p. 214. Mention Walker Evans photograph (p. 205) and George Plimpton's "An Interview with Ernest Hemingway" (p. 210).

Conclusion: Summary of what all this tells us about my great-aunt as a person. Quote from Csikszentmihalyi and Rochberg-Halton's article about a research survey, "Object Lessons," on p. 217. Tell readers to look critically at their own rooms and possessions. What conclusions will an observer draw about his or her life and personality?

The teacher who wrote this plan tried to capture the reader's attention with a series of descriptions, making the reader wonder, What is all this leading up to? Then, she told the reader exactly what it was leading up to: her point of view about how rooms reveal a life and a personality. She decided to end with a summary of her great-aunt as revealed by the room and to direct the readers to look at themselves and their own rooms.

Details about what writers often do in their introductions and conclusions are included in Chapter 12.

7. Now you are ready to write. You have your two cards with your signposts on them; you have your plan and your list of details to support your main idea; and you have your notes in section 1 of your notebook, containing all the ideas you

---

WRITING A DRAFT

1. Find a quiet place to work—and a clear desk or table.
2. Have pens, pencils, and a stack of paper on hand.
3. Make sure you have a block of uninterrupted time. Don't let phone calls, visits, mealtimes, or family duties take you away from your writing.
4. Give yourself lots of space on the paper as you write your draft. Leave wide margins, and double-space between lines.
5. Place your signpost cards in front of you, and refer to them as you write.
6. In one sitting, try to write down everything you want to include, but don't worry about the order you write it in. Remember, you can always rearrange the ideas, add more content, and fix the grammar and spelling later.
7. Don't waste time recopying your draft to make it look neater, unless it is illegible to your instructor and classmates.

---

have been talking about, reading about, and writing about as you worked through the earlier chapters of the book. In all, you have a lot of material to help you write your draft. As you write, you might find it helpful to follow the guidelines presented in the accompanying box.

Write on right-hand pages that you can insert into your notebook following your plan in section 2 of your notebook. Make a photocopy of your draft, or use carbon paper as you write or type, so that you will have an extra copy. Then give your instructor your draft. Since you have a copy, you can continue to refer to the draft while your instructor is reading it and making suggestions for revision. (Your instructor might also recommend two or three chapters for you to review in Part II, "Twenty-One Troublespots," so that you know what to look for when you check your second draft for correctness. Write any assigned exercises or notes on spelling and grammar in section 4 of your notebook.)

CHAPTER 10

Look at the Draft

It is important for writers to learn how to read their own work critically and to assess its strengths and weaknesses in preparation for revising. Chapter 10 provides an example of a draft and offers some systematic ways (1) to examine a piece of writing and (2) to assess how well it fits the writer's intentions.

Classroom Activities

1. Read the following draft that developed from the plan and lists of details written by the teacher in Chapter 9.

Everything is white and tidy, with not much furniture, just a couch, a small table, and one picture. We wonder who lives here, and think that it could be a designer or an architect. Certainly it is someone who is more attracted to the present than the past. Now look at another room. This one is dark, wood-paneled, filled with books, pictures, antiques, objects, rugs, and pottery. Almost every surface is covered. This could be the home of a potter, a collector, or just someone with good taste and money to spend on it. Rooms are not just objects. They tell us a lot about the lives of the people who inhabit them. Often we can reconstruct quite accurately the lifestyle and values of a stranger just by seeing where he or she lives. Walker Evans must have known, when he photographed something as simple as a dresser, that he would be showing us something more than a piece of furniture. Hemingway's room could hardly have belonged to a city person (Plimpton 183–185). It had to be the home of a passionate big-game hunter. Rooms show us, too, not only what someone does but what the person's values are. As Dr. Stuart Asch observes: "What we do with our possessions reflects our philosophical/psychological view of the world: how much do I value a remembrance of things past? How much do I plan ahead for the future?" (Stern 240).

My great-aunt Anna lives in a small town in Virginia. I usually visit her briefly every summer, and, even though I have never really had enough time to get to know her personally, I feel as if I know a lot about her life from her room. After her husband died, she moved her bed and all her belongings to what used to be the dining room. Now she leaves this room only to go to the kitchen, the bathroom, or out into the garden. The first impression of this room is that it is very, very full. It is a mass of furniture, rugs, books, pictures, trinkets. Rugs cover the floor, and on them stand her bed, a long velvet-covered couch, two armchairs, a desk and chair, a round table covered with a dark cloth, and everywhere, on all the surfaces, lots of ornaments, plates, photographs, books, papers, and trophies my great-uncle Joseph won, including one for winning a road race when he was fifty years old. A lifetime is collected here. This room says "old age" as clearly as a desk with a computer, goldfish bowl, hamster cage, baseball, football helmet, and milk and cookies says "youth."

The main thing that captures attention is the photographs. They are everywhere. Many of them are photographs of stage stars. Anna once wanted to be an actress, and one photo shows her when she was performing in a play. A framed photograph on the round table shows her with her large family all around her. One photograph I always look at is one of her at a party with a handsome young man. I wish I knew who it was, but I never dared to ask.

Dishes are everywhere, too. Anna has collected them her whole life, and many of them are souvenirs of places that tell her a story. She often looks wistfully at the dish from Niagara Falls, though the colors are a little faded now. It bothers her that she can't remember if it was from her honeymoon or her tenth wedding anniversary, when she and Joseph went back to Niagara for a second honeymoon. A lot of the dishes are from Florida. Her son goes there every year and brings her back another dish. She often talks about how she would like to live there.

It would be hard for her to move. Her roots are here. She knows all the neighbors and has cared for many of them and their children at various times, visiting them, shopping for them, cooking for them, and buying them presents. All around the room on the shelves are cards of thanks from all these neighbors. One has red roses and a big *Thank You* on it; inside, it says, "We couldn't have managed without your help. You really are a wonderful person. With love, Your second family."

She shows visitors some of the cards and objects. However, on a shelf in one corner (we call it her "mystery corner"), there is a little space cleared around a group of objects she won't talk about, one of them being the photo of her and the young man. There is a glass jar, a string of beads, one cuff link, a theater program, a pressed flower, and a letter which nobody has read. I've heard that every day she looks at these objects and dusts them lovingly.

This to me is not just any elderly person's room. It is the home of someone caring and involved with family and friends, someone who likes to have around her reminders of episodes of her life. This, as a 1974 study of the relationship between people and objects noted, does not imply materialism but the cherishing of things "for the information they convey[ed] about the owner and his or her ties to others" (Csikszentmihalyi and Rochberg-Halton 84). She is loving and loved. Certainly for her, attachment to things seems "to go hand in hand with attachment to people" (Csikszentmihalyi and Rochberg-Halton 84). But all is not open. Although she shares a lot, there is some mystery to her, something she keeps to herself as a secret. Still, there is little sense here of "gratifications deferred," as with Joyce Johnson's mother's room (13–14). Rather, this is the room of someone who has lived a very full life. I wonder if people will say that about me when I am her age. Look at your room with a critical eye; what will someone say about you and your life and values as they look at it?

The writer did not make up a bibliographic list of references until she wrote her final draft, although she did include the page numbers of the original sources here. See Chapter 12, p. 62, for the form she used to cite her references.

Note how the writer included the part about the trophies in the general description of the room, instead of making it a major point of the paper. She did this because, as she thought about it, she realized that the trophies told more about her great-uncle than her great-aunt. Note, too, how she changed the order of the points she had listed. She wrote about the mystery corner last, before the conclusion, instead of about the letters and cards. Why do you think she did this?

2. Form a group of three or four students. Together discuss the preceding draft by answering the questions in the box on the facing page.

3. With the same group of students, look at the draft again. Take each paragraph one at a time, and summarize in one sentence what each paragraph is about. Write the sentences on a right-hand page in section 1 of your notebook. You should now have an outline of seven sentences, one for each paragraph.

4. Each member of the group should write on a piece of paper the first sentence of the draft he or she wrote in Chapter 9. Pass the pieces of paper around, and read each other's sentences. Then, taking one sentence at a time, the students in the group should discuss (1) what questions that sentence raises in a reader's mind and (2) what they as readers expect to read in

    a. the next sentence
    b. the rest of the piece of writing

RESPONSE QUESTIONS

1. What main idea is the writer trying to express in this draft?
2. Does all the information in this draft relate directly to the main idea? If not, which parts do not?
3. Which part of the draft do you like best? Why?
4. Are there any places where you would like more explanations, examples, or details?
5. Did you at any point lose the thread of the writing or find any places where the writer seemed to jump too suddenly from one idea to another?
6. Did the introduction capture your attention and make you want to read on? Why or why not?

5. Read your draft aloud to your group, or pass it around so that the other students can read it. The students in your group will respond to your draft by answering the six Response Questions above.

Individual Assignments

1. Read the following outline that one group of students wrote for the draft at the beginning of this chapter.

1. Our rooms and possessions tell people about our lives and about our values.
2. Great-aunt Anna lives in a room cluttered with the possessions of a lifetime.
3. She has a lot of photographs.
4. She collects dishes from different places.
5. She loves her neighbors and saves all their "Thank You" cards.
6. There are a few objects she won't talk about.
7. The room shows us she loves to collect and display her possessions to reflect her full and generous life.

Now, compare this outline to the one you wrote in Classroom Activity 3.

2. Next, see how one reader responded to the same first draft, using the six Response Questions above.

1. The main idea is that your great-aunt's room shows her values and her warm and generous life.
2. Some parts do not relate directly to that idea: for example, the two descriptions at the beginning, and the fact that Anna now occupies what

was once the dining room. Also, the descriptions of the photographs, dishes, and the mystery corner don't refer directly to Anna and her values.

3. I like the part that says: "She looks at these objects and dusts them lovingly." I would like to hear more about Anna herself.

4. I'd like to read more details about the objects in the mystery corner.

5. The movement from paragraph 3 to 4, 4 to 5, and 5 to 6 is abrupt. You seem to be just describing here, without telling us *why* those details are important to your main idea.

6. The beginning is a bit confusing. I wasn't sure what *everything* was in the first sentence. It also took a long time to get to the subject of the piece: Anna herself.

3. In section 2 of your notebook, on a left-hand page opposite your draft, make an outline (one sentence for each paragraph) of what you have written in your own draft. Now look at the outline. Is there a logical development of ideas from paragraph to paragraph?

4. Using the information that your classmates provided in Classroom Activities 4 and 5, answer *from their point of view* the six Response Questions about your own draft. Write your answers on a left-hand page in section 2 of your notebook.

Journal Assignment

It is interesting for student writers to find out how their classmates approach a writing task. When people write, they go about doing it in many different ways. Ernest Hemingway, for example, always wrote standing up.

In the journal section of your notebook, describe what *you* did when you wrote your draft. For example: How long did it take you? Where did you write? Did you write in silence, in a noisy atmosphere, with music playing? Was your writing interrupted? How often? (For instance, did you stop to get something to eat or drink?) What difficulties or writing blocks did you have? When did writing seem to be easiest? Give this entry to a few classmates and to your instructor to read.

CHAPTER 11

Explore Alternatives

To make effective changes in a piece of writing, you need to know what your options are. In Chapter 11, you will be looking at some methods of organization that writers of English commonly employ. You can then compare them to the organizational patterns you used in your draft and judge whether you should try some alternatives.

Individual Assignments

1. Carefully read the following examples of methods writers commonly use to support their point of view in an essay. Note that, for the most part, the support they provide is concrete and specific. They do not just make statements and express opinions and expect us to accept them. Instead, they provide us with the evidence they have for making those statements. How do writers do this?

    a. *They provide examples, illustrations, definitions, clarifications, or facts (from reading, research, or personal experience).*
        Russell Baker's description of Morrisonville (p. 198) could have ended after " . . . no city child would ever hear." Most of the second paragraph elaborates upon the idea expressed in its second sentence, which tells the reader that there were a lot of natural noises in the silence of the country. How many examples of sounds does Baker give? Note how these examples support what he means when he writes that an "orchestra of natural music" exists, even in the silence. He does not leave us to guess what this "orchestra" means; instead, he gives us precise examples. Without the examples, we might wonder what he means, or simply disagree that such an "orchestra" is possible and reject his ideas.
        Joan Costello states in "Treasures" (p. 212) that "often cherished objects serve as visible links to loved ones, events, or traditions of the past." Then she shows us *why* she feels she can make such a statement, by giving an example from her own experience: "For example, I treasure an ancient ebony necklace I found among my grandmother's possessions after she died."

In the excerpt from *Blooming* (p. 237), Susan Allen Toth gives six examples of high-school students' summer jobs that offered "preparation for life." The examples, more than the idea itself, make this particular passage lively and interesting.

The following expressions are used to introduce examples, illustrations, definitions, clarifications, or facts: *for example, for instance, indeed, in fact, in addition, again,* and *furthermore.*

b. *They describe exactly what happened or exactly what something or someone looks, sounds, smells, or feels like.*

In the excerpt from *The Diary of a Young Girl* (p. 187), Anne Frank tells us all the details about the Secret Annexe, so that we can have in our minds an accurate picture of it. How does she organize her description of the three floors of rooms? Where does she begin and end? In what order does she include all the information? What other ways would be possible?

George Plimpton, in "An Interview with Ernest Hemingway" (p. 210), tells us that Hemingway "prefers to work in his bedroom" and then gives a detailed description of the bedroom to show us why.

Useful expressions to denote chronological sequence or spatial relationships include *first, second, third . . . , next, finally, meanwhile, on the right, on the left, to the right, to the left, in front of, behind, beside, above,* and *below.*

c. *They compare one person, thing, or idea to another.*

In "Dulling of the Sword" on p. 239, David Ahl helps us to understand the changes in the Japanese attitude to work by comparing them to changes in love and marriage.

Russell Baker compares jobs "not so long ago" to jobs nowadays. In doing so, he makes a point about jobs today, which is the main point of the excerpt from *Poor Russell's Almanac* on p. 241.

Some useful expressions for comparing and contrasting are *similarly, just as, in the same way, but, however, on the other hand, in contrast,* and *yet.*

d. *They analyze or classify something (such as an object, a concept, or a group of people) by dividing it into different parts or types.*

Cherlin and Furstenberg, in their article on p. 267, look at American families in the year 2000. They organize the discussion by classifying and dividing them into three kinds: families of first marriages, single-parent families, and families of remarriages. Then, each type is discussed in turn.

In "Object Lessons" on p. 217, Csikszentmihalyi and Rochberg-Halton examine the complicated subject of people and their possessions by classifying both the types of objects people keep and the reasons people give for keeping them.

Useful expressions for analysis and classification include *one, another, first, second, third . . .* , and *most important.*

e. *They examine the causes and effects of something.*

Susan Allen Toth, after describing summer and after-school jobs, discusses the effects of those jobs on the students' skills and sense of values ("From *Blooming*," p. 237).

Julia Kagan examines a survey of rewards that make workers feel more satisfied, as well as rewards that motivate them to work harder ("Work in the 1980s and 1990s," p. 245). The result of the survey, she points out, is that companies should "pay attention to designing jobs to create maximum levels of intrinsic interest and to provide financial and nonfinancial rewards for those who put in maximum effort."

Some useful expressions that show cause and effect are *because, since, as a result, so, consequently, therefore, then.*

f. *They examine what others have said about an issue or a problem.*

Julia Kagan's survey of work in the 1980s and 1990s (p. 245) cites the views of others to support the main point of her article: that giving workers what they want will not necessarily make them want to work harder.

William Novak, in "What Do Women Really Want?" uses quotations from interviews with single men to present the point of view that some women have unrealistic expectations about their relationships with men (p. 281).

Useful expressions for citing what others have said include *as X says, X observes that . . .* , *according to X, in X's opinion, in X's view, X's opinion on this is . . .* , *X has pointed out that . . .* , *as X found . . .* , and *in a study of . . .* , *X found that . . . .*

2. Now look at each of these methods of support in turn, comparing them to evidence you have provided in your draft. Doing this will show you what combination of methods you have used, and it might also suggest some effective new methods you could include. In section 2 of your notebook, on a new right-hand page, write answers to the following questions:

Have you included any specific examples, illustrations, or facts? Can you think of some that would be good to include?

Have you described an incident or story to help support your point of view? If not, would doing this help to make your essay less general and more specific, one that only you, with your knowledge and experience, could have written? If you have used a supporting incident or story, did you present it in the order in which the events happened? Would it be possible to tell the story any other way?

Have you described what something looks, sounds, feels, or smells like? If not, ask yourself: (1) Is your reader going to know what images you

have in your head as the basis for your point of view? and (2) Should
you describe those images? If you *have* used description, *how* did you
describe the picture in your mind? From right to left, left to right,
clockwise, from the top down . . . ? Would any other way be possible?
Could parts of your essay benefit from more description so that your
readers will be able to see exactly what you have in mind?

Have you included, or could you include, an account of what others have
said about your topic? You might gather material from readings, interviews, television shows, or from your own conversations. Write the account if you need to. (For how to write reported speech, see Troublespot 19 in Part II.)

Have you included any analysis or classification, either of an object or of a
concept? Have you discussed each division or group separately? How
did you arrange the parts? Which ones came first and last? Why? For
example, which is first, the most important point or the least important
point? If you have not included any analysis, would it be useful to do
so?

Have you presented any analysis of causes and effects? If not, would it be
appropriate to do so? If you decide to include causes and effects, in
which order should you choose them?

Have you made use of comparison or contrast to develop your point? If so,
how did you organize it—block-by-block or point-by-point? (See the
next activity for help with organizing comparison or contrast.)

3. You are always making choices when you write, and it is useful for you to know
the full range of your options. As an example of this range, let us look at the
options open to a writer who has decided to write a comparison of two houses.

First, read the following writer's notes for his piece of writing (adapted from
Ann Raimes, *Techniques in Teaching Writing* [New York: Oxford University Press,
1983], pp. 136–138):

Main idea: Houses that look alike from the outside are often very different
on the inside.

The Warrens' house
Number of rooms: eight (and two bathrooms)
Position of kitchen: first floor
Stairs: at side of house; solid wood
Furniture: antiques
Front door: heavy wood

The Peppers' house
Stairs: central, spiral, metal
Number of rooms: four (and four bathrooms)
Garden: huge
Furniture: modern, white
Position of kitchen: second floor

When the writer sat down to write his draft, he chose to present his material in two blocks, as you can see in his outline:

1. The Warrens' house:
   a. rooms
   b. kitchen
   c. stairs
   d. furniture

2. The Peppers' house:
   a. rooms
   b. kitchen
   c. stairs
   d. furniture

Note how the writer used a block organization, arranging the points within each block to correspond with each other. Also, note that he left out the points (the garden and the front door) that did not contribute to a comparison of the two houses.

In planning this piece of writing though, the writer had another option. He could also have organized his comparison point-by-point, like this:

1. Number of rooms
   a. Warrens' house
   b. Peppers' house

2. Position of kitchen
   a. Warrens' house
   b. Peppers' house

3. Stairs
   a. Warrens' house
   b. Peppers' house

4. Furniture
   a. Warrens' house
   b. Peppers' house

Which type of organization (block or point-by-point) do you think is easier for the writer to write? Which type is easier for the reader to read and to see the differences clearly?

4. Give your answers to the questions in Individual Assignment 2 to your instructor for comments and advice.

CHAPTER 12

Rewrite

Your first draft has now been tested out on readers. You have your instructor's responses and your classmates' comments to help you decide what changes to make in your next draft. Chapter 12 will help you use the readers' responses to plan and write the second draft of your essay.

Classroom Activities

1. If you are not satisfied with your introduction, find a partner who wants to work on introductions too. (If you are pleased with the beginning of your draft, move on to Classroom Activity 3 in this chapter.) Discuss with your partner other ways you could begin your piece of writing. Remember, the introduction is what captures a reader's attention, so you should do your best to make the reader want to keep on reading.

The following list presents some devices that writers use in the first paragraph of an essay in order to capture the reader's attention:

> Ask a question (Kagan, p. 245; Mays, p. 292).
> Tell briefly about an interesting, funny, or startling incident (Brody, p. 264;
>   Shreve, p. 286).
> Provide historical or environmental background (Baker, p. 198; Didion,
>   p. 290).
> Quote something relevant or interesting (Gordon, p. 192; Stern, p. 214).
> Present factors or figures (Cherlin and Furstenberg, p. 267; Schnack, p. 279).
> Present two or more sides of a controversial issue (Kagan, p. 245; Beer,
>   p. 284).
> Show the reader why the topic needs to be discussed (Baker, p. 241; Cetron,
>   p. 243).

For examples of these devices, turn to the page numbers indicated (in Part III, "Materials"), and read the opening paragraph of each passage. Note that some of the introductions use more than one device.

2. Put your draft away. Now, as quickly as you can, on a new right-hand page of section 2 of your notebook, write a new opening paragraph. Do everything you can

to make your reader interested in what you are going to write. Try to be as clear as possible in expressing your ideas. When you have finished, exchange notebooks with your partner, and read each other's new introduction. Which introduction—the old or the new—makes you want to read on? Which one states clearly the main idea and connects directly to the body of the essay? Which of your partner's two introductions do you prefer? Why?

3. For your essay, invent two or three titles that are relevant to the content and that capture a reader's attention. Write them on a right-hand page. Ask your partner to comment, on the opposite page, on which title he or she likes best, and why.

4. Now look at the conclusion of your first draft. Does it fit into one of the following common devices for conclusions? If not, would one of these devices suit your purpose better than your current conclusion does?

> Do you give a fresh summary of the points you made and a strong restate-ment of your main point?
> Do you state your main point for the first time (your whole essay has led up to this)?
> Do you recommend action based on your main idea?
> Do you ask a question about the future?
> Do you present here the final point in a chronological or spatial sequence?

Your conclusion should be strong, leaving the reader with a good impression. It should be a real conclusion to the essay—a rounding off—and not just an abrupt stop. Do not include any apologies about lack of time or information. And you certainly do not have to begin with the stale phrase, "In conclusion . . . ." In fact, it's better not to.

If you would like to try a new conclusion, write one on a new right-hand page. Show your new conclusion to your partner.

5. Read the second draft composed by the teacher who wrote about her great-aunt Anna in Chapter 10.

Trinkets and Mysteries: The Story of a Life

As I sit at home, turning the pages of a glossy magazine, I can't help thinking of my great-aunt Anna, even though the magazine has pictures of houses and rooms, not of people. The picture on the cover, for instance, shows a room where everything is white and tidy, with not much furniture, just a couch, a small table, and one picture. Who lives here? A designer? An architect? Certainly, it is someone who is more attracted to the present than the past. Turn a page, and just inside we see another glossy picture, another room. This time the room is dark, wood-paneled, filled with antiques, objects, rugs, and exquisite Mexican pottery. Is this the home of an artist? A potter? A collector? Certainly, it is someone who appreciates shape, color, and texture, someone with expensive tastes and the money to indulge them.

We infer all this about these people because we know that rooms are not just background. They reveal a lot about the lives of their inhabitants. When Walker Evans photographed something as simple as a dresser, he must have known that he would be showing us more than a piece of furniture. Hemingway's room, too, with its leopard skin, bullfight journals, animal teeth, shotgun shells, carved animals, animal toys, and buffalo horns, could hardly have belonged to a city person (Plimpton 183–185). It had to be the home of a passionate big-game hunter. But rooms reveal more than a person's life. They tell us also about the person's values. As Dr. Stuart Asch observes, "What we do with our possessions reflects our philosophical/psychological view of the world: how much do I value a remembrance of things past? How much do I plan ahead for the future?" (Stern 240).

So I thought of my great-aunt Anna as I looked at the magazine because her room certainly reflects her views and values. This room, in a simple little house in a small town in Virginia, would never be featured in a magazine as fashionable as the one I am thumbing through. Anna has spent all of her life in that town. I usually visit her briefly every summer, and, even though I have never really had enough time to get to know her personally, I feel as if I know a lot about her past—and present—life from her room. It is a mass of furniture, rugs, books, pictures, and trinkets. The room is about 14 feet long and 12 feet wide, with big velvet-draped windows on one wall and shelves on the other three—all full of ornaments, plates, photographs, books, papers, and the trophies my great-uncle Joseph won for swimming and running. Dusty-colored rugs cover the floor. On one side is her bed; opposite the bed is a long velvet-covered couch. Completing a circle of furniture are two armchairs, a desk and chair, and right in the middle of the room is a round table covered with a dark cloth and more trinkets and trophies. The room, with its musty, dusty smell of lavender, says "old age" as clearly as a desk with a computer, goldfish bowl, hamster cage, baseball, football helmet, and milk and cookies says "youth." However, to me it says more. To me it says "Anna."

The photographs that seem to dominate the room, faces of stage stars smiling out of them, show Anna's ambitions. She once wanted to be an actress, and obviously she had some talent because one photo shows her, a young and beautiful woman in a feathered hat, perform-ing in a play. The ambition tó go on the stage was probably overtaken by the desire to have a family, for to do both was unthinkable in her time. A large framed photograph on the round table is testimony to that latter ambition: it shows her glowing with pleasure and pride with her family all around her. I once counted twenty-seven people in the picture!

She shows visitors most of these photographs. However, in one corner of the room, on a shelf, there is a little space cleared around a group of objects she has never talked about—to anyone. In the center is a photograph of her at a party with a handsome young man, tall and dashing, who looks down at her in admiration. Nobody knows who he is. Grouped around the picture is a collection of objects: an empty glass jar, a string of coral beads, one ornate silver cuff link, a theater program from the early 1940s, a pressed flower—probably a rose—and a letter which nobody has read. The letter is all yellow and crumbling now. I've heard that every day she looks at these objects and dusts them lovingly.

The sense of dreams unfulfilled that this corner conveys is matched by the dishes propped up on display. Anna's travels are confined to this collection of souvenir plates, showing exotic scenes from around the world. Each one recalls the person who gave it to her and the story of the trip that accompanied it. But the only place she ever actually visited was Niagara Falls. She often looks wistfully at the gold-edged plate, the blue of the waterfall now somewhat faded. It bothers her that she can't remember if it dates from her honeymoon or her tenth wedding anniversary, when she and Joseph went back to Niagara for a second honeymoon. A large number of the dishes say *Florida* on them. Her son goes there every year and brings one back to her. She goes there, too, in spirit, as she looks at them and thinks of the stories he used to tell. She often talks about how she would like to live there, under the palm trees.

She knows, though, that it would be hard for her to move. Her roots—her present and future as well as her past—are here. She knows all the neighbors, and has cared for many of them and their children at various times in their lives, visiting, shopping, cooking, and buying presents. We see her selflessness in all the cards of thanks from all these neighbors. One, next to her husband's big silver cup that he won for a 10-mile road race when he was fifty, has red roses and a big *Thank You* on it; inside, it says, "We couldn't have managed without your help. You really are a wonderful person. With love, Your second family." I've seen her pick that card up often and wipe away a tear.

Yet this room does much more than reflect and look back sentimentally to the past. There is little sense here of "gratifications deferred," as with Joyce Johnson's mother's room (13–14). Even though some dreams were not fulfilled, a sense of accomplishment shines out. This room shows the pride of someone who has lived and continues to live a full life. It reveals to us someone caring, involved with family and friends, while preserving the past, knowing how it affects the present and the future. The geographical space of her life may have been confined to this town with only two trips away, but it is unconfined in its generosity and warmth of feeling. Certainly, attachment to her things seems "to go hand in hand with attachment to people" (Csikszentmihalyi and Rochberg-Halton 84). But despite all the room reveals, it also hints at an untapped part of her, a mystery that she keeps to herself as a secret. I like her more for that.

As I turn the pages of the glossy magazine, I wonder about my own life, about my room, and about what my family and friends will say about me when I am old. And you? If we come and look at *your* room with a critical eye, what will it tell us about *you* and your life and values—and your secrets?

WORKS CITED

Csikszentmihalyi, Mihaly, and Eugene Rochberg-Halton. "Object Lessons."
    Psychology Today December 1981: 78–85.
Johnson, Joyce. *Minor Characters.* Boston: Houghton Mifflin, 1983.
Plimpton, George. "Interview with Hemingway." *Writers at Work: the Paris
    Review Interviews, Second Series.* London: Secker and Warburg, 1963.
Stern, Barbara Lang. "Lure of Possessions: Do You Cling to Objects or Throw
    Away Your Past?" *Vogue* March 1983: 240.

Note how the writer has now cited the exact source of the materials she referred to. For an example of the format to use for documentation, see Troublespot 18, "Quoting and Citing Sources."

6. With a small group of students, list the ways in which this draft differs from the first one (pp. 48–50). (For example: How has the introduction changed? How did the writer change the organization? Why do you think she made those changes? Has she added or taken out any material?) Do you think this draft is better than the first? Why or why not?

7. With your group, briefly tell each other the following:

What I've done so far in my draft is ————————————————.

What I think I'll do next is ————————————————————.

The members of the group should point out anything that does not seem to follow a logical development of ideas. In addition, the group should discuss whether further reading or research might be of use to each writer. For instance, you may want to suggest that the writer interview someone or read a particular book or article.

Individual Assignments

1. After you have done any additional research, write your plan for your second draft. (Start on a new left-hand page facing an empty right-hand page in section 2 of your notebook.) First, consider who you want your readers to be:

  a. Specific people whom you name?
  b. The students in your class?
  c. A newspaper or magazine (name it)?
  d. Experts who know about your topic?
  e. People who are interested in your topic but who are not experts?

For the pieces of writing you do for this course, your readers will include your classmates and your instructor. You can designate them as the only readers, or they can act as advisers and editors to help you prepare your essay for a larger audience. Then, consider a few possible titles. The writer of the draft you have just read considered these four titles before she chose the last one:

Rooms and Values
Anna's Life Revealed
What Rooms Say
Trinkets and Mysteries: The Story of a Life

Which title do you prefer? Why? Do you like the choice the writer made? Note the form of the title: it does not have to be (and usually isn't) a sentence. It is not surrounded by quotation marks or underlined. Most words are capitalized; articles *(a, an, the)*, connecting words, and short prepositions *(in, on, to, etc.)* are not capitalized unless they begin the title.

Write your new plan like this:

Title: _____

My reader(s): _____

My point is _____

In which paragraph will I make this point? _____

  Write your outline like this:

  Introduction: What will the content be? How will I introduce my reader to the topic and to my particular focus and point?
  Body paragraphs: What am I going to say about my point? How am I going to develop it for a reader? What examples will I use? What personal

experience, knowledge, or reading will I refer to? How many paragraphs will I need? List the main idea and details of each paragraph.

Conclusion: What will the content of my conclusion be? How will I leave the reader—with a strong restatement of my main idea, with a recommendation or question, or with a summary of the points I have made?

2. When you have a long period of free time outside class, find a quiet place; assemble all your notes and plans and the responses to the first draft; and supply yourself with pens, pencils, and a stack of paper. Make as many notes as you want on your first draft. If you want to move sections around, have scissors and tape on hand.

Use as much of your first draft as you want, refer to your new plan, and write your second draft (on right-hand pages). Again, do not worry about grammar and spelling. Instead, concentrate on making your ideas clear and interesting. You will have the opportunity to fix errors soon.

If you can, make a photocopy or keep a carbon of your draft so that, when you hand it in to your instructor in Chapter 13, you will have a copy for yourself.

3. When you have completed the draft, look at it again, and examine its structure using the same methods that you employed in Chapter 10: that is, by making a paragraph-by-paragraph outline and answering the Response Questions (p. 51). You can also ask another student to read your essay and outline it for you. If you have referred to any other writers, use Troublespot 18 ("Quoting and Citing Sources") or a handbook to check the form of your documentation and list of references. In addition, if you want to improve any sections, do so before you submit your new piece of writing as your final draft.

Once you are satisfied with the ideas you have on the page and the organization of those ideas, you will be ready to pay attention to correctness of grammar, sentence structure, word choice, and spelling. These items are the subjects of the rest of Part I and of Part II.

Editing

Until now, you have been concentrating on putting your ideas down on paper so that they will be clear and interesting to your readers, including your instructor, your classmates, and any other readers you selected. You have been thinking about the whole piece of writing, its content, and its shape.

Readers comprehend the content and the shape of the whole essay by reading your words and sentences, which must conform to conventions. Otherwise, readers will be distracted by errors. In the drafts you have written so far, you have been urged not to worry about grammar, sentence structure, or spelling, because you would have the opportunity to work on them later. The next four chapters give you that opportunity.

In these chapters, you will work mainly on editing (that is, correcting and improving) your second or third draft. You will get help from your classmates and instructor, just as you did in the previous chapters. You will look closely at grammar, spelling, style, and vocabulary, and you will be directed to chapters in Part II, "Grammar: Twenty-One Troublespots," that deal with specific grammatical problems.

Because you are writing in a second language, you are bound to make mistakes. Some mistakes you will have to learn to recognize one by one because they derive from areas of the language where there are very few rules to help you. So, you have to learn, one at a time, new words, prepositions, and idioms. Other mistakes you will be able to correct systematically, by applying the rules by which written English operates. Part II of this book is devoted to specific points of the grammatical system that cause trouble for students who are writing English as a new language. As you edit, remember to ask for help whenever you need it.

CHAPTER 13

Discover and Correct Errors

Your instructor and your classmates will help you find the grammatical errors that you need to correct in the last draft of your paper. To find ways to apply rules and correct your errors, Part II will be useful; you can use it to apply grammatical concepts to your own writing in a concrete way. You need to get into the habit of examining your own writing systematically for errors.

Classroom Activities

1. With a partner, examine the following paragraph from the first draft of a paper written by a student from Zaire. The instructor has underlined errors and indicated omissions. Decide how the writer should correct the errors.

It is true, as Toth shows us, that the fact of working make children feel like adults. But in some countries, students don't work. In my country, for example they don't work for two principal reason. The first one is that there are not enough jobs for everybody, and it's quiet impossible for a student to get a job. The second reason is that university keeps you busy full time, sometimes even while you're on vacation. In Toth's book, the fact of working is idealized, because in this country you cannot live without a job. That is why work is so important to people. In my country, you have to work to earn a living, but if for some reason you can't the group take care of your necessities. We are helpful to each other even in big cities. So there are no worldwide generalizations we should make about work. We can only examine it country by country and culture by culture. We can learn a lot about the status of work in society if we compare work here in the U.S.A. to work in my country.

---

2. Exchange one copy of your latest draft with a partner. Read each other's draft, and when you come across a sentence or a word that needs correction, underline it. Now give the paper back. Explain to each other what troubled you about the places you underlined. If you need more assistance, ask your instructor for help.

ERROR SYMBOLS

Symbol	*Error in or problem with*	*Troublespot no.*
adj	use of adjective	13
adv	use of adverb	14
agr	agreement in number (singular or plural)	9
art	article missing or wrong	12
cap	capitalization of noun	6
cond	conditional sentence form	17
coord	sentence coordination	2
frag	sentence fragment	1
-ing	*-ing* form	15
neg	negation	5
n. pl	noun plural	6
p	punctuation	1, 2, 3, 18, 21
part	participle form	15
pass	use of the passive	10
poss	use of possessive and apostrophe	20
pron	pronoun form	11
q	question form	4
quot	quotation form and punctuation	18
ref	pronoun and its referent	11
rel	form for a relative clause	16
rep. sp.	reported speech or paraphrase	19
ss	sentence structure or sentence boundaries	1
sub	combining independent and subordinate clauses	3
vf	verb form	8
vt	verb tense	7

OTHER SYMBOLS

id	idiom (This is not how we would express the idea in English.)
sp	spelling
wc	word choice
wf	word form (e.g., *success/successful/succeed*)
∧	omission
⌒⌣	word order (e.g., *the old big house*)
?	Sentence does not work. (I'm not sure what you want to say here.)

Individual Assignments

1. Carefully read through your latest draft. Pay special attention to any of the "troublespots" your instructor alerted you to in your first draft. Make any necessary corrections.

2. Now hand in the corrected draft to your instructor. Make the corrections on your own copy too.

Your instructor will indicate errors and comment on the changes you have made in your second draft. When your instructor returns your paper, work alone or with a partner to review the appropriate troublespots in Part II and to correct any errors in your draft. Use section 4 of your notebook (the spelling and grammar section) to do any of the exercises your instructor assigns from Part II or to write down your own corrected sentences.

3. If your instructor wants to tell you what type of error you have made, then you should both agree on a set of symbols. In the box on p. 67, you will find error symbols which correspond to the troublespots in Part II.

CHAPTER 14

Improve Style

While your instructor is reading your second draft, you can be working on your own copy of the same draft. Look at your writing critically to see if you can improve sentence variety, transitions between sentences and paragraphs, and cohesive links between sentences and paragraphs. Chapter 14 describes in detail what you can look for.

Classroom Activities

1. Read through your essay with this question in mind: Is there a series of short or repetitive sentences that could be combined? Pari, a student from Iran, found this passage in her piece of writing:

I have two friends. They are twins. Both of them are girls. They are very different in the way they think and the way they behave. One of them likes white. The other one likes red. Even the way they dress is different.

They are sharing a bedroom. They have a very big bedroom. They have divided the bedroom between them.

There are no grammatical errors here, but it is obvious that the style of the passage could be improved.

With a partner, decide which ways some of these short sentences can be combined into longer sentences, so that you preserve the meaning but cut out unnecessary words. You can, of course, add coordinating and subordinating words whenever necessary. If you need to review the ways to coordinate and subordinate, see Troublespots 2 and 3 in Part II. When you have listed all the possible ways of combining Pari's sentences, discuss which way you like the best, and why.

2. Working with your partner, decide which ways can be used to combine any short sentences in your own essay. If you cannot decide which way would be best, ask your instructor for advice.

3. One student found this passage as she read through her essay:

Even though many people oppose a free education policy because
they feel that they will end up supporting people who do not like to
work and use education as an escape from work, in my opinion will
benefit most families.

The sentence is certainly very long and complicated. In fact, the writer herself got lost in it! Some instructors would indicate a "sentence structure" error
here, but that would not point out to the writer what to do to correct the error.
Can you discover what went wrong? And can you devise ways to fix the sentence?
If you have trouble with this, review Troublespots 1 and 3.

Now read through your own essay again, with this question in mind: Do any
sentences seem so long and complicated that they might be difficult for a reader
to understand?

4. If you discovered any long, difficult sentences, show them to your partner. Try
to explain what you were trying to say in each sentence. Then work with your
partner to make each sentence more manageable. Aim at achieving variety in the
length and structure of the sentences. Some long sentences work well, particularly
if they are surrounded by short sentences, and you will not need to change them.

5. Now read through your essay again to examine links between paragraphs or
sentences. Links are made in a variety of ways. Here are some of them:

Sometimes a repeated word will make the link between the end of one
paragraph and the beginning of the next:

. . . This incident showed me how important possessions can be for children.

Childhood possessions can mean as much to adults as they do to children . . . .

(Note the repetition of *possessions* and *children.*)

Sometimes a phrase will refer the reader back to a previous word or idea:

. . . Then he walked out and slammed the door.

This incident made me question the notion that women are more emotional and show their feelings more openly than men do. . . .

(Note how the phrase *this incident* forms a link between the ideas of the
two paragraphs.)

Sometimes a linking word indicates a transition—that is, a movement from
one idea to another:

. . . In some ways, then, work is nothing but drudgery.

However, some people are lucky enough to look at work another way . . . .

(Note that the word *however* provides a transition from one idea to another by pointing out a contrast.)

The following words are frequently used to signal a transition from one idea to the next—from sentence to sentence or from paragraph to paragraph: *however, then, therefore, on the other hand, in addition, first, second, finally, meanwhile, similarly, thus,* and *for this reason.* For a chart of these linking words, see Troublespot 2, "Combining Sentences: Coordinating," as well as Chapter 11, "Explore Alternatives," in Part I. Underline any links you find in your draft, and write *link* in the margin if you think you need to supply a link.

6. If you found any places that were missing a connecting link, rewrite those sections of your essay to supply one. If you need advice, confer with your partner or with your instructor.

7. Read "The Old Man and His Grandson" on p. 258. In it, draw a circle around all the pronouns (e.g., *he, they, them*) and possessive adjectives (e.g., *his, their*). If you need to review these parts of speech, see Troublespot 11, "Pronouns."

Next, draw a line connecting the words you have circled to the noun phrases they refer to. Can you find all the nouns that they refer to? (See Answer Key, p. 297.)

Now read your draft, and do the same thing. If at any point you cannot make the connection in your own essay, examine the passage closely. Are you sure that you have made clear for the reader what each pronoun refers to?

Individual Assignment

Make any changes on your copy of the draft. When your instructor returns the original, see whether he or she has suggested any of the stylistic changes you are considering. If your ideas do not agree, show your instructor your proposed changes before incorporating them into your final copy.

CHAPTER 15

Use a Dictionary

When you get your paper back from your instructor, you can begin fixing any errors. For most of the grammatical errors indicated, you can turn to Part II for help. If your instructor has indicated any problems with word choice, word form, or spelling, the first tool for you to use is a dictionary.

Classroom Activities

1. With a group of students, read the following passage, which is taken from the first draft of a student's uncorrected essay.

---

possessions | A way of telling about personality is by looking at the number of things people have collected for themselves. Some people like the bare necessities and no special objects but others like an excess of material things. I have a friend who loves to buy nice things and store them in a closet. His roommate wants more space for his own things. He always says, "Why can't you throw some of this junk away?" My friend just walks out of the room when he says things like that.

What words could be used in place of the circled ones? For example, the first *things* has been replaced by *possessions*. Use a dictionary to check spelling whenever necessary.

2. Now read through your draft again. If any words are repeated too often, or are not concrete enough, underline them. The list below shows some alternatives for overused, vague words, some of which are marked in the passage in Classroom Activity 1.

thing   *object, possession,* or a more specific word like *jewelry* or *shoe*

nice	*pleasant, cheerful, tasty* (food), *delicious* (food), *kind*
walk	*hurry, limp, stagger, creep, tiptoe, stride*
good	*excellent, honest, delicious* (food), *well-cooked* (food), *loyal* (friend), *exciting, interesting* (book)
say	*exclaim, state, announce, complain, emphasize, threaten*
situation	*celebration, argument, business meeting, dilemma,* or any more specific item

Look at the following list of words:

thing
implement
sharp tool
knife
kitchen knife
12-inch carving knife

Note how they progress from the general to the specific. If you read about someone holding a silver "thing," you might imagine something very different from what the writer had in mind. The last one—"12-inch carving knife"—conveys to the reader precisely what the writer sees in his or her mind.

Individual Assignments

1. Has your instructor indicated any "word form" or "word choice" problems in your draft? If so, try to find replacements for incorrect and inappropriate words. Use your dictionary to check both the meaning and the spelling of any word that your instructor has marked with *sp, wc,* or *wf*. Often, a dictionary definition will suggest other words to you; some dictionaries also provide words of similar meaning (that is, *synonyms*) that you might want to use.

To help you understand a dictionary and use it efficiently, the definitions of the words *knife* and *implement* are given on p. 74 as they appear in *The American Heritage Dictionary of the English Language, New College Edition* (New York: Houghton Mifflin, 1976). Explanations of some parts of the entries are provided. Note how much information you can get from one short dictionary definition.

2. Replace any problem words in your paper. If you need more help than a dictionary provides, you may want to consult a thesaurus. If you need assistance with making a word choice and you don't know how to find it in a dictionary or thesaurus, ask your instructor for help.

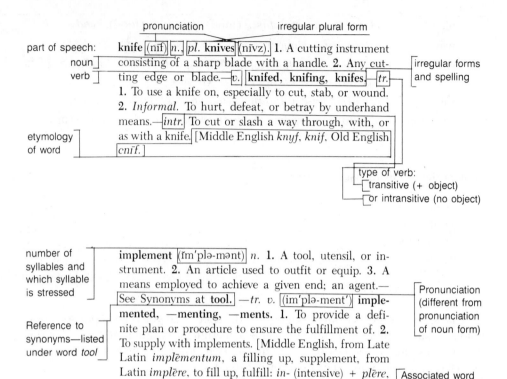

pronunciation   irregular plural form

part of speech: knife (nīf) *n.*, *pl.* knives (nīvz). **1.** A cutting instrument
noun   consisting of a sharp blade with a handle. **2.** Any cut-
verb   ting edge or blade.—*v.* **knifed, knifing, knifes,** *tr.*
               1. To use a knife on, especially to cut, stab, or wound.
               2. *Informal.* To hurt, defeat, or betray by underhand
               means.—*intr.* To cut or slash a way through, with, or
etymology   as with a knife. [Middle English *knyf, knif,* Old English
of word   *cnīf.*]

irregular forms
and spelling

type of verb:
transitive (+ object)
or intransitive (no object)

number of   **implement** (ĭm′plə-mənt) *n.* **1.** A tool, utensil, or in-
syllables and   strument. **2.** An article used to outfit or equip. **3.** A
which syllable   means employed to achieve a given end; an agent.—
is stressed   See Synonyms at **tool.** —*tr. v.* (im′plə-ment′) **imple-**
                 mented, —**menting,** —**ments. 1.** To provide a defi-
Reference to   nite plan or procedure to ensure the fulfillment of. **2.**
synonyms—listed To supply with implements. [Middle English, from Late
under word *tool* Latin *implēmentum,* a filling up, supplement, from
                 Latin *implēre,* to fill up, fulfill: *in-* (intensive) + *plēre,*
                 to fill]—**im′ple-men-ta′tion** *n.*

Pronunciation
(different from
pronunciation
of noun form)

Associated word
forms, with stress
and syllables

CHAPTER 16

Prepare Final Copy and Proofread

First, you did a lot of reading, writing, and discussing, and then you planned, wrote, and revised your essay. Others read your drafts and commented on them, giving you advice on content, organization, and correctness. You edited your last draft for grammar, sentence structure, style, and vocabulary. Now, you are ready to present to a reader a polished version of the ideas you have developed. This means that you are ready to write or type your final version and then proofread it (that is, check it carefully once more) to make sure that what you present to your reader has no mistakes.

Individual Assignments

1. Write all necessary changes and corrections directly on your most recent draft. If you rewrite a section in order to make it more legible, write it on a separate sheet. Use scissors to cut it to fit, and use tape to insert it into your draft.

2. To prepare for writing your final draft, provide yourself with 8½-by-11-inch paper, a pen with dark ink (or a typewriter or printer with a dark ribbon), your last corrected draft, a dictionary, a clear surface, and lots of time.

3. As you write your final copy, follow the guidelines given in the box at the top of p. 76.

4. You have taken a great deal of trouble with this piece of writing, so you will want to be sure that your finished version is as perfect as you can make it. Read through it once again to make sure you did not make any mistakes. You need to proofread carefully by checking every single word and grammatical ending.

   Practice by carefully reading the following passage from a student's essay. How many proofreading corrections does the writer need to make? What are they? (See Answer Key, p. 298.) In your next class session, compare your answers with those of your classmates.

GUIDELINES FOR FINAL COPY

1. Put your name and date at the top of the first page. (Or, if your instructor prefers, include these on a title page.)
2. Put the title at the top of the first page or on the title page. Capitalize the first letter of all words except articles, short prepositions, and connecting words. Do not underline the title or put it in quotation marks. Leave a space of one line under the title.
3. Begin numbering the pages on page 2. Put the page number in the center of the bottom of the page or in the top right-hand corner.
4. Write on one side of the paper only, and leave margins of about 1 inch at the top, bottom, and on each side.
5. Indent each paragraph—that is, begin each paragraph about 1 inch (or five type-written spaces) in from the margin so that a reader can see clearly where paragraphs start.
6. Be as careful as you can so that you do not have to cross out or erase. If you decide to change something you have written and you do not have time to recopy the whole essay, then make the change very neatly. For example:

   They ~~where~~ *went* to the beach every day.

7. If you are unsure about the spelling of a word, check your dictionary.

When women take on too much work, they injure there families. Gradually, the job they have lose it's glamour for them and they find that it is not exciting any more. They find themselves more and more torn between home and work, particularly when they have to do all the traditional women's jobs around the house as well as their full-time job. A single male dentist can open a can. But when does a woman dentist plan what to give her family for dinner? In a busy day, there isn't enough time for that.

Some women could have made a good salary in a job instead of staying home and doing housework, they decide that it is better for the family not to work for a few years. They think their family life will be improve. A mother of three children that I once knew very well told me that she is happy at home now with her children and doesn't miss her advertising job at all. She doesn't know why she ever decided to work in the first place. Her children happiness come first for her.

---

5. In reading through your own final copy, it is useful to slow down your reading so that you do not miss anything. After all, you know the content of this essay very well by now, so your eye might skip over a mistake that another reader would notice. Here are a few ways to slow yourself down:

    a. Put a pencil point on each word, and say the word aloud as the pencil touches it.

    b. Read the last sentence first, and work your way, sentence by sentence, backward through the essay. This way, your eye will not be carried forward by the content, and you will be able to look at the words in each sentence more carefully.

    c. If you can, put the essay away for a day or more, and then proofread it when the content is less immediate and familiar.

    d. Ask a friend to read your final copy aloud to you as you check it by reading the corrected draft you worked from.

6. Finally, hand your completed final copy in to your instructor. You are finished!

To explore another subject through the process of writing about it, return to Chapter 1 and choose a different subject area. Then, follow the same steps of getting started, finding ways in, writing, rewriting, editing, and proofreading. Use your notebook and your journal again to help you explore your subject.

PART II ✳

GRAMMAR ✳
Twenty-One
Troublespots

Part II gives you help with twenty-one grammatical troublespots. It is not intended to be a complete review of English grammar, nor is it meant to cover everything you need to know to correct all errors in a piece of writing. Rather, Part II concentrates on rules, not exceptions, so it will help you learn general principles. You will find explanations of some conventions of standard written English—areas of the language that operate systematically, according to rules. These explanations are accompanied by exercises (an Answer Key is included at the back of the book) and by questions, in the form of a flowchart, that you can ask about each troublespot as you examine a piece of your own writing. These questions will focus your attention on the problem. Sometimes, such focusing is precisely what a writer needs to find—and correct—errors.

The editing advice frequently suggests that you seek help—in a dictionary or grammar reference book, from a classmate, or from your instructor. Experienced writers often seek advice, so make sure to use the resources around you.

When your instructor identifies a grammatical point that is causing you trouble, he or she will tell you to work on a particular chapter in Part II. Review that chapter along with a piece of your own writing. Write any notes, questions, grammar exercises, or corrected versions of your own sentences in section 4 of your notebook (the "grammar and spelling" section). Whenever possible, work through the troublespot with a partner. Your instructor might assign a classmate who has little difficulty with this problem area to guide you. Or, he or she might assign you a partner who is having difficulties similar to the ones you are having; you can then try to help each other understand the problem and fix your errors.

Sentence Structure and Boundaries

> **Question:** What makes up a sentence, and where does a sentence begin and end?

A. Which of the following are standard sentences in written English? Which are not?

1. the sun came out.
2. When the sun came out, we all went to the beach.
3. The beach looked lovely
4. The waves splashing on the sand.
5. We playing games.
6. Ate our picnic.
7. Ham sandwiches ate we.
8. Ate too we cake chocolate.
9. We stayed there for four hours, sunbathing and swimming.
10. Because we were having such a good time.

In section 4 of your notebook, list how these sentences should be written. You can correct the grammar or punctuation, or combine one sentence with the sentence that comes before or after it. (See Answer Key, p. 298.) When you have finished, list what you consider the requirements of a sentence to be.

B. Each of the following examples contains one group of words that is *not* a sentence, even though it has a capital letter and end punctuation. It is only part of a sentence (that is, a *sentence fragment*).

1. The little girl saw a spider. A great big black one.
2. She screamed loudly. To try to scare the spider.
3. Because she was frightened. She ran into another room.
4. She sat down next to her mother. Her legs still shaking.

Determine which is the fragment, and why, according to the list of sentence requirements you made in Item A. Decide how you could turn the sentence fragment into a complete sentence or include it in another sentence. Write your new sentences in your notebook. (See Answer Key, p. 298.)

C. Sentences can be long or short, simple or complex. This is a simple sentence:

The man bought a new car.

It contains one independent clause (a sentence that makes sense alone and can stand alone). This independent clause has a verb, *bought,* and a subject for the verb, the person who did the buying, *the man.* In addition, it has an object, telling us what the man bought—*a new car.* However, we can add other information, too, and the sentence will still have only one independent clause. It will just be a longer sentence. We can add information at several points within the sentence, and that information can take the form of different grammatical structures:

1. *Add information at the beginning.*
   Last week, the man bought a new car.
   Because he felt adventurous, the man bought a new car.
   Although his wife hated the idea, the man bought a new car.
   Wanting to look prosperous, the man bought a new car.
   Bored with his life in the city, the man bought a new car.
   To try to impress his friends, the man bought a new car.

2. *Expand the subject.*
   The rich man bought a new car.
   The man who got a raise last week bought a new car.
   The man who works in my office bought a new car.
   The man working in my office bought a new car.
   The man and his wife bought a new car.
   The man with an old Cadillac bought a new car.

3. *Insert some additional information in the middle.*
   The man in my office, Joseph Moran, bought a new car.
   The man, wanting to impress his friends, bought a new car.
   The man, proud and excited about his raise in salary, bought a new car.

4. *Expand the verb.*
   The man bought and sold a new car.
   The man bought a new car and sold it.

5. *Expand the object.*
   The man bought a fancy new red car.
   The man bought a new car and a computer.

The man bought his wife a new car.
The man bought a new car for his wife.

6. *Add information at the end.*
   The man bought a new car last week.
   The man bought a new car because he felt adventurous.
   The man bought a new car when he could afford it.
   The man bought a new car to try to impress his friends.
   The man bought a new car even though his wife didn't approve.

Note that in each of the preceding sentences, there is only one clause (a subject and verb combination) that can stand alone—the independent clause.

D. Try to expand the following sentence by adding information in different places. See how many different variations you can invent. Refer to Item C for examples of structures that you might add.

The doctor prescribed some pills.

E. Compare your list of the requirements of a sentence (Item A) to the requirements shown in the box below. How many of these requirements did you write down in your list in Item A?

Editing Advice

Use the following flowchart with a piece of your writing to examine any sentences that you think might have a problem in structure. Begin with the last sentence of your draft and work backward. In this way, you can isolate each

---

REQUIREMENTS OF A SENTENCE

– A sentence needs a capital letter at the beginning.
– A sentence needs a period, a question mark, or an exclamation point at the end.
– A sentence needs a subject.
– A sentence needs a finite verb (a complete verb phrase—that is, the auxiliaries, such as *is, were, has, had, will, can, might, should have,* and *will be*—along with the verb forms used to form the verb phrase). See Troublespot 8, "Verb Forms."
– A sentence needs standard word order. In English, the regular sequence is SVO (Subject-Verb-Object), with insertions possible at several points in the sequence.
– A sentence needs an independent "core" idea, which can stand alone. This is known as a *main clause* or, as we call it in this book, an *independent clause.*

sentence from its context and examine it more objectively. Ask these questions for each problematic sentence:

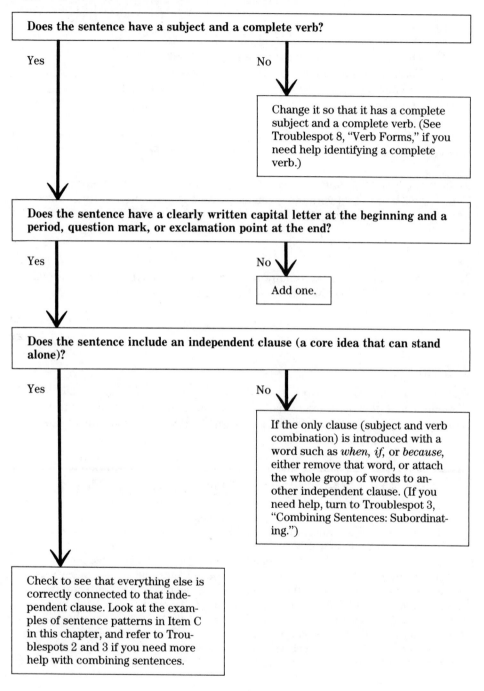

Does the sentence have a subject and a complete verb?

Yes   No

Change it so that it has a complete subject and a complete verb. (See Troublespot 8, "Verb Forms," if you need help identifying a complete verb.)

Does the sentence have a clearly written capital letter at the beginning and a period, question mark, or exclamation point at the end?

Yes   No

Add one.

Does the sentence include an independent clause (a core idea that can stand alone)?

Yes   No

If the only clause (subject and verb combination) is introduced with a word such as *when, if,* or *because,* either remove that word, or attach the whole group of words to another independent clause. (If you need help, turn to Troublespot 3, "Combining Sentences: Subordinating.")

Check to see that everything else is correctly connected to that independent clause. Look at the examples of sentence patterns in Item C in this chapter, and refer to Troublespots 2 and 3 if you need more help with combining sentences.

Combining Sentences: Coordinating

> ***Questions:*** **How do I connect one sentence to another? What options do I have to connect (coordinate) sentences to make the ideas equally important?**

A. You can connect complete sentences together to form a coordinate sentence that will contain two or more independent clauses of equal importance (that is, core ideas). There are several ways to do the following:

$$S+V \qquad\qquad S+V$$

(subject + verb) + (subject + verb)

Which way you choose will depend on what seems to fit best the content and context of your piece of writing. So, consider all the options, in context, before you choose.

1. When sentences are closely connected and their structure is similar, you can connect them by using a semicolon:

   The man bought a new car; he gave it to his wife as a surprise birthday present.
   Her mother took care of the children; her father earned the money.
   (Shreve, p. 286)

2. You can also indicate *how* two independent clauses are related in meaning within a sentence if you coordinate the two clauses by using a comma followed by one of these seven *connecting words:*

$$S+V, \quad \left\{ \begin{array}{l} \text{and} \\ \text{but} \\ \text{or} \\ \text{nor} \\ \text{so} \\ \text{for} \\ \text{yet} \end{array} \right\} \quad S+V$$

Examples:

The man bought a new car, *but* his wife didn't know about it.

Our bees provide us with honey, *and* we cut enough wood to just about make it through the heating season. (Doherty, p. 193)

Important: To connect two independent clauses, a comma is not enough. You need a comma and a connecting word, or you need a semicolon. The following sentences are *not* acceptable English (the asterisk indicates an ungrammatical sentence):

*The man bought a new car his wife didn't know about it. (There is no connecting word between these two independent clauses, nor is there any punctuation to separate them. This is called a *run-on sentence.*)

*The man bought a new car, his wife didn't know about it. (The two clauses are separated only by a comma, yet a period or semicolon is needed. This is called a *comma splice.*)

B. Two independent clauses with the same subject can be condensed into one sentence:

The man bought a new car.
The man changed his job.

These can be condensed as follows:

The man bought a new car and changed his job. (No comma separates the two verbs when they have the same subject.)

C. There are also many *linking expressions* that help to point out how sentences are joined according to meaning. Even if you use one of these words, you still need to separate your sentences with a period or with a semicolon at the end of your first independent clause. For example:

The little girl had always hated spiders. *In fact,* she was absolutely terrified of them.
or   The little girl had always hated spiders; *in fact,* she was absolutely terrified of them.
or   The little girl had always hated spiders. She was, *in fact,* absolutely terrified of them.
or   The little girl had always hated spiders. She was absolutely terrified of them, *in fact.*

Linking words and phrases are set off from the rest of the sentence by commas. A list of some of the most frequently used linking expressions is shown in the box below. The expressions are not necessarily interchangeable. The context determines which is appropriate. If you want to use a linking expression but are not sure which one to use, ask your instructor.

D. On p. 267, look at the reading entitled "The American Family in the Year 2000." Starting with the paragraph that begins "Although joint custody . . . " on p. 268, examine the use of the linking expressions throughout the rest of the article. List them, and write down the author's purpose in employing them. What ideas do they link? What kind of meaning do they signal between the two ideas? Use the box below to help you. (See Answer Key, p. 299.)

E. Connect the following pairs of sentences by using punctuation, connecting words, or linking expressions. Remember, you need to determine the relationship between the two sentences before you can choose a connecting word or a linking expression. Write your new, combined sentences in your notebook.

1. Hemingway had some individual peculiarities as a writer.
   He always wrote standing up.

2. Hemingway was a gifted journalist, novelist, and short-story writer.
   He was an active sportsman.

3. Hemingway mostly did his writing in pencil on onionskin typewriter paper.
   He shifted to his typewriter when the writing was easy for him, such as writing dialogue.

4. Hemingway's room looked untidy at first glance.
   He was a neat person at heart.

LINKING EXPRESSIONS

Writer's purpose	*Linking words and phrases*
To add an idea:	in addition, furthermore, moreover
To show time or sequence:	meanwhile, first, second, then, next, later, finally
To contrast:	however, nevertheless, though, in contrast, on the other hand
To show result:	therefore, thus, consequently, as a result
To emphasize:	in fact, of course, indeed, certainly
To provide an example:	for example, for instance
To generalize or summarize:	in general, overall, in short

5. Hemingway was a sentimental man, keeping his possessions all around him.
   He hardly ever threw anything away.

6. Hemingway always did a surprising amount of rewriting of his novels.
   He wrote the ending to *A Farewell to Arms* thirty-nine times.

7. Hemingway wrote his short story "The Killers" in one morning.
   After lunch, he wrote "Today Is Friday" and "Ten Indians."

8. Hemingway often wrote all through the afternoon and evening without stopping.
   His landlady worried that he wasn't eating enough.

(See Answer Key, p. 299.)

F. The following passage contains some sentences that are not correctly connected and others that would benefit from the addition of a linking expression. Rewrite the passage in your notebook, avoiding faulty sentence structure and combining sentences by using connecting words or linking expressions.

> My grandfather could speak three languages well. He grew up in Poland during the German occupation. His parents took him to the United States in 1946, the family spoke Polish at home most of the time, but my great-grandparents also spoke German because they wanted my grandfather to remain bilingual. Now my grandfather no longer speaks Polish or German at home, he speaks only English. His children don't speak Polish at all. They understand it a little.

(See Answer Key, p. 299.)

Editing Advice

If you feel unsure about how a sentence you have written is connected to the ideas surrounding it, ask yourself these questions:

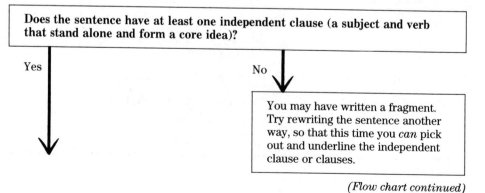

Does the sentence have at least one independent clause (a subject and verb that stand alone and form a core idea)?

Yes

No

> You may have written a fragment. Try rewriting the sentence another way, so that this time you *can* pick out and underline the independent clause or clauses.

(Flow chart continued)

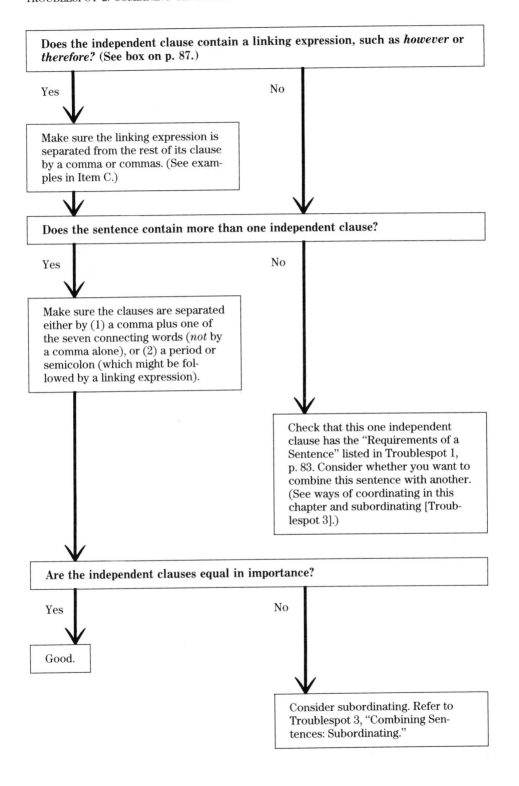

Does the independent clause contain a linking expression, such as *however* or *therefore*? (See box on p. 87.)

Yes | No

Make sure the linking expression is separated from the rest of its clause by a comma or commas. (See examples in Item C.)

Does the sentence contain more than one independent clause?

Yes | No

Make sure the clauses are separated either by (1) a comma plus one of the seven connecting words (*not* by a comma alone), or (2) a period or semicolon (which might be followed by a linking expression).

Check that this one independent clause has the "Requirements of a Sentence" listed in Troublespot 1, p. 83. Consider whether you want to combine this sentence with another. (See ways of coordinating in this chapter and subordinating [Troublespot 3].)

Are the independent clauses equal in importance?

Yes | No

Good.

Consider subordinating. Refer to Troublespot 3, "Combining Sentences: Subordinating."

TROUBLESPOT 3

Combining Sentences: Subordinating

> *Question:* **How are sentences put together to make one idea subordinate to another?**

A. You can combine two simple sentences by using connecting words or linking expressions; the result is two independent clauses (see examples in Troublespot 2). You also have the option of making one of your independent ideas subordinate to, that is, dependent on, the other.

Look at these two simple sentences:

Hemingway was a sentimental man.
He hardly ever threw anything away.

One way to combine these ideas is to coordinate the sentences (Troublespot 2) as follows:

Hemingway was a sentimental man, so he hardly ever threw anything away.
Hemingway was a sentimental man. In fact, he hardly ever threw anything
away.

In the preceding example, the two clauses have equal weight and, therefore, equal importance in the reader's mind. One way to change the emphasis is to subordinate one idea to the other: make the most important idea the independent clause and make the less important idea a *condensed phrase*, attaching it to the core idea. The following examples include condensed phrases:

Hemingway, *a sentimental man*, hardly ever threw anything away.
Being sentimental, Hemingway hardly ever threw anything away.
For sentimental reasons, Hemingway hardly ever threw anything away.

B. The two clauses can also be combined by keeping them as full clauses (subject + verb) and (subject + verb), but making one of them subordinate to the other by introducing it with a *subordinating word.* For example:

Hemingway, *who was a sentimental man*, hardly ever threw anything away.
Because Hemingway was a sentimental man, he hardly ever threw anything away.

The dependent clause of each of these two sentences is in italics. Note that it
cannot stand alone. It has been made subordinate to the independent clause and
is now dependent on it for meaning.

C. The accompanying box shows both the relationships that allow one sentence
to be subordinated to another (type of clause) and the subordinating words used
to begin dependent clauses.

DEPENDENT CLAUSES

Type of clause	*Examples of subordinating words*
Relative	that, who, whom, which, whose (*that, whom, which* are some-times omitted as the object of the clause) The man *who* won the lottery bought a new car.
Time	when, before, after, until, since, as soon as *When* he won the money, he decided to buy a car.
Place	where, wherever She drove *wherever* she wanted.
Cause	because, as, since She got a parking ticket *because* she parked illegally.
Purpose	so that, in order that He drove fast *so that* he could get to work on time.
Result	so . . . that, such . . . that He drove *so* fast *that* he got a speeding ticket.

Condition	if, unless
	    If she hadn't won the lottery, she would have been very
	        unhappy.

Concession	although, even though
	    Although she thought she was a good driver, she got a lot of
	        tickets for speeding.

Included statement *or* question	that (sometimes omitted), what, why, how,
	where, when, who, whom, which, whose, whether, if
	    He knows *why* he gets so many tickets.
	    He knows [that] his business will be successful.

D. Short sentences can thus be combined to make longer sentences by coordinating clauses, subordinating clauses, or by condensing core ideas into phrases. Combine the following short independent clauses into longer sentences, by using coordinating or subordinating words, or by condensing ideas. Find as many ways as you can, and write your new sentences in your notebook.

> Jack wanted to make a good impression.
> Jack wore a suit.
> The suit was new.
> The suit belonged to his brother.
> Jack was our administrative assistant.
> The suit was big for him.
> The pants kept falling down.

(See Answer Key, p. 299.)

E. Read the way one student found to combine these seven sentences into one:

> Wanting to make a good impression, Jack, our administrative assistant, wore his brother's new suit, but the suit was so big for him that the pants kept falling down.

Examine the structure of this new sentence by answering these questions:

1. How many independent clauses are there? What are they?
2. What is the subject and verb of each independent clause?
3. If there is more than one independent clause, how are the independent clauses connected?
4. How many subordinate clauses (a subject + verb combination preceded by a subordinating word) are there?
5. How have other core ideas been attached to the independent clause(s)?

(See Answer Key, p. 300.)

Examine the structure of some of the new sentences you formed by asking the same questions.

F. In a similar way, long sentences can be broken down into their short, core parts. This breakdown is a useful way for you to check the structure of any long sentences you write. The following long sentence is from "From *Minor Characters*" by Joyce Johnson on p. 224:

> Her picture as a young woman, placed on the polished lid [of the piano] that's never opened except when the piano tuner comes, is in a heavy silver frame of ornate primitive design brought by my uncle from Peru.

To examine which ideas Johnson combined and how she combined them, separate the sentence into short sentences (like the ones in Item D). That is, break the sentence down into its basic set of core ideas (expressed in a series of independent clauses), so that all the ideas in the sentence are included. Begin like this:

Her picture is in a heavy silver frame.

(See Answer Key, p. 300.)

G. Find as many ways as you can to combine each of the following sentence groups into one sentence. Include all the ideas that are there, but collapse sentences into words or phrases, if you want. You can also add words (subordinating words, for example, or connecting words like *and* and *but*) that will help you to combine the ideas. Use the chart of subordinating words in Item C to help you, too.

1. I watched a little girl.
   She was carrying a big shopping bag.
   I felt sorry for her.
   I offered to help.

2. My family was huge.
   My family met at my grandparents' house every holiday.
   There were never enough chairs.
   I always had to sit on the floor.

3. Computers save time.
   Many businesses are buying them.
   The managers have to train people to operate the machines.
   Sometimes they don't realize that.

4. All their lives they have lived with their father.
   Their father is a politician.
   He is powerful.
   He has made lots of enemies.

5. She wanted to be successful.
   She worked day and night.
   She worked for a famous advertising agency.
   Eventually she became a vice president.

6. He really wants to go skiing.
   He has decided to go to a beach resort in California.
   His sister lives in the beach resort.
   He hasn't seen her for 10 years.

(See Answer Key, p. 300.)

Which sentence of each group did you select as the independent clause of your new sentence? Why did you select that one? How does the meaning of your sentence change if you choose a different independent clause?

Editing Advice

1. If you find any groups of sentences in your essay that seem short and need some variation, ask these questions:

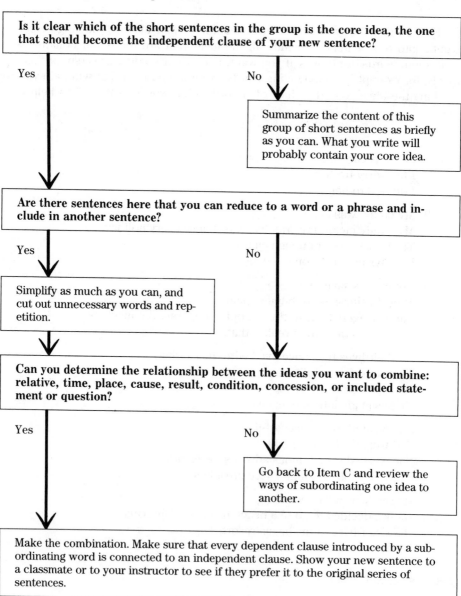

Is it clear which of the short sentences in the group is the core idea, the one that should become the independent clause of your new sentence?

Yes

No

Summarize the content of this group of short sentences as briefly as you can. What you write will probably contain your core idea.

Are there sentences here that you can reduce to a word or a phrase and include in another sentence?

Yes

No

Simplify as much as you can, and cut out unnecessary words and repetition.

Can you determine the relationship between the ideas you want to combine: relative, time, place, cause, result, condition, concession, or included statement or question?

Yes

No

Go back to Item C and review the ways of subordinating one idea to another.

Make the combination. Make sure that every dependent clause introduced by a subordinating word is connected to an independent clause. Show your new sentence to a classmate or to your instructor to see if they prefer it to the original series of sentences.

2. Now look for sentences that seem a bit too involved and complicated for a reader to figure out. Ask the following:

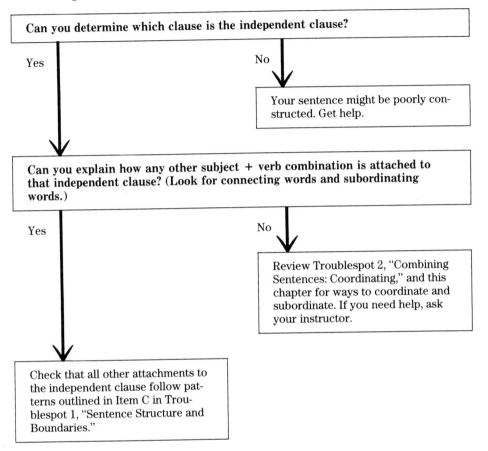

Can you determine which clause is the independent clause?

Yes

No

Your sentence might be poorly constructed. Get help.

Can you explain how any other subject + verb combination is attached to that independent clause? (Look for connecting words and subordinating words.)

Yes

No

Review Troublespot 2, "Combining Sentences: Coordinating," and this chapter for ways to coordinate and subordinate. If you need help, ask your instructor.

Check that all other attachments to the independent clause follow patterns outlined in Item C in Troublespot 1, "Sentence Structure and Boundaries."

TROUBLESPOT 4

Questions

> *Question:* **What do I need to know about questions when I edit my writing?**

A. In English, we indicate a question (1) by putting a question mark at the end of the sentence and (2) by putting an *auxiliary verb* (i.e., a helping verb) in front of the subject.

They are living in New York.	*Are* they living in New York?
They have a lot of money.	*Do* they have a lot of money?
They can buy whatever they want.	*Can* they buy whatever they want?
They like fast cars.	*Do* they like fast cars?
They bought a Porsche last week.	*Did* they buy a Porsche last week?
They could have bought a Rolls-Royce.	*Could* they have bought a Rolls-Royce?

B. Sometimes a question is used to draw a reader's attention to an issue; the writer does not expect the reader to actually answer the question. Such a question is simply a *rhetorical* device that lets a reader know that the writer will answer the question. Look at the following examples from the reading passages in Part III:

But what's happening when we feel overwhelmed, rather than consoled, by too many objects that we nonetheless don't want to part with and continue collecting? (Stern, p. 215)

What did I actually learn from all my summer and after-school jobs? (Toth, p. 238)

How can he possibly envision anyone analyzing a system or researching a market? (Baker, p. 241)

What do these people do? (Baker, p. 241)

Is this gap responsible for the declining growth rate of the nation's productivity? (Kagan, p. 245)

Why don't fringe benefits, lack of stress, and good working conditions produce motivation to work hard? (Kagan, p. 274)

Who teaches us this instinct? Where does the habit come from? (Mays, p. 292)

Questions are also used as titles:

> Are Women Bosses Better? (Schnack, p. 279)
> What Do Women Really Want? (Novak, p. 281)

C. When a question is reported within a statement, it no longer functions as a question. Both the word order and the final punctuation become the same as in a statement.

> *Direct question:* She often asks, "What do I need to do next?"
> *Reported question:* She often asks what she needs to do next.

> *Direct question:* He wants to know, "What did she say?"
> *Reported question:* He wants to know what she said.

See also Troublespot 19, "Reporting and Paraphrasing."

D. Choose one of the pictures in Part III, and write five questions about it. Imagine that you are going to write an essay about the picture, and that you will provide answers to the questions in the essay.

E. Look at the answers you wrote in Chapter 2, Individual Assignment 1 (p. 13); they were in response to the Preview Questions accompanying the set of materials you chose in Part III. (You will find these answers in section 1 of your notebook.) Now, without looking at Part III, try writing the *questions* to the answers you gave. Then, check what you wrote here against the Preview Questions.

F. Read through another student's journal entries, and write down on the left-hand pages three questions you want to ask the writer about the pieces of writing.

Editing Advice

If you have problems writing questions, look at your essay and ask the following questions:

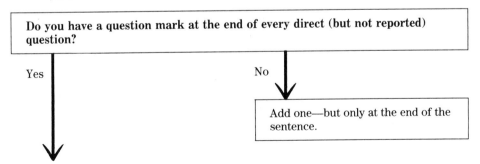

(Flow chart continued)

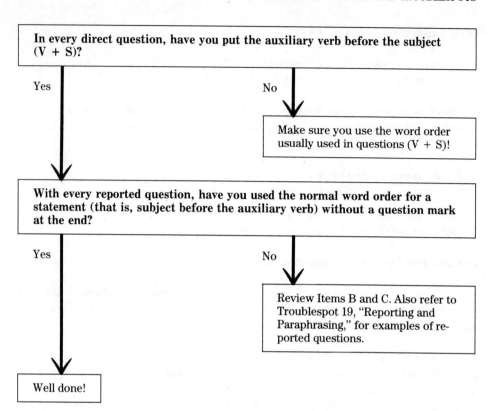

In every direct question, have you put the auxiliary verb before the subject (V + S)?

Yes   No

Make sure you use the word order usually used in questions (V + S)!

With every reported question, have you used the normal word order for a statement (that is, subject before the auxiliary verb) without a question mark at the end?

Yes   No

Review Items B and C. Also refer to Troublespot 19, "Reporting and Paraphrasing," for examples of reported questions.

Well done!

Negatives

> *Question:* **What do I have to check when I use a negative in a sentence?**

A. In some languages, the negative can occur in various positions in a sentence. In English, the adverb *not* comes after the first verb in the clause.

Sally has *not* been to London.
She is *not* planning to go this year.

B. *Not* can be contracted with some auxiliary verbs. However, contractions are usually used only in informal writing, such as in letters and journals. Contractions are generally not used in more formal writing, such as essays or textbooks. (When you write an essay, ask your instructor if contractions are acceptable.) Examples of contractions include: *isn't, aren't, wasn't, weren't, doesn't, don't, didn't, hasn't, haven't,* and *can't.* Note that the contraction for *will not* is *won't.*

C. English uses only *one* negative in a clause. For instance:

She did*n't* do anything.
She did *nothing.*

A double negative is incorrect.

*She did*n't* do *nothing.*

D. Alternative ways of expressing negation are shown in the following lists.

Regular form	*Alternative form*
not a	no
not any	no
not any of	none of
not anyone	no one
not anybody	nobody
not anything	nothing
not anywhere	nowhere
not ever	never
not either	neither

Examples:

Researchers find that workers do*n't* have *any* real incentive.
Researchers find that workers have *no* real incentive.
He ca*n't* justify *any* of his expenditures.
He can justify *none* of his expenditures.
She ca*n't* explain *either* of her decisions.
She can explain *neither* of her decisions.

E. You can give special emphasis to the negative *never* by placing it first in the sentence. In such a case, however, the first auxiliary verb must come *before* the subject.

I *have never* seen such a sloppy piece of work.
Never have I seen such a sloppy piece of work!

The first place in the sentence also provides emphasis for the expression *not only . . . but also.*

The couple *not only took care* of the housework *but also* tended the garden.
Not only did the couple *take care* of the housework, *but* they *also* tended the garden.

Note the word order (and the verb form) when *not only* is placed first in the sentence.

F. *Neither* can be used as a sentence negative. Its meaning is equivalent to *not . . . either,* but it is more emphatic.

The mother doesn't have much free time. The children do*n't either.*
The mother doesn't have much free time, and *neither* do the children.

Note also how *either . . . or* and *neither . . . nor* are used:

The children don't have *either* a full-time mother *or* father at home.
or   The children have *neither* a full-time mother *nor* father at home.

Neither the mother *nor* the children have much free time.
or   *Neither* the children *nor* the mother has much free time.

What is the difference between the verb forms in the last two sentences? What could account for the use of the plural form *(have)* and the singular form *(has)*? (See Answer Key, p. 300.)

G. Rewrite the underlined sections in the following passage, using an alternative way of expressing negation. Refer to the lists in Item D.

> "Workaholics" are people who are addicted to work. They <u>don't have any time</u> for their family. They <u>don't think anything</u> is as important as their job and doing well in that job. Workaholics <u>can't ever really relax;</u> they are always tense, anxious, and irritable about finishing a project. They <u>will go nowhere</u> unless they take work along with them. One workaholic has been seen adding columns of figures while trying to sail a boat in a storm! Often, on a weekend away, workaholics <u>will talk to nobody</u>, except, of course, when they call their office, which they usually do a few times a day.

(See Answer Key, p. 301.)

H. Write a paragraph about a sports fan you know or about someone with a passionate hobby or interest. Use some of the structures discussed in this chapter. Underline the negatives you use.

Editing Advice

If you have been having problems with negatives, examine each negative form in your essay and ask the following questions:

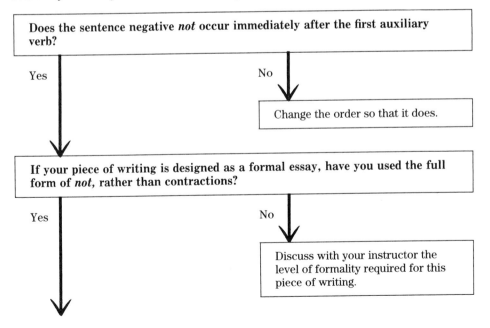

(Flow chart continued)

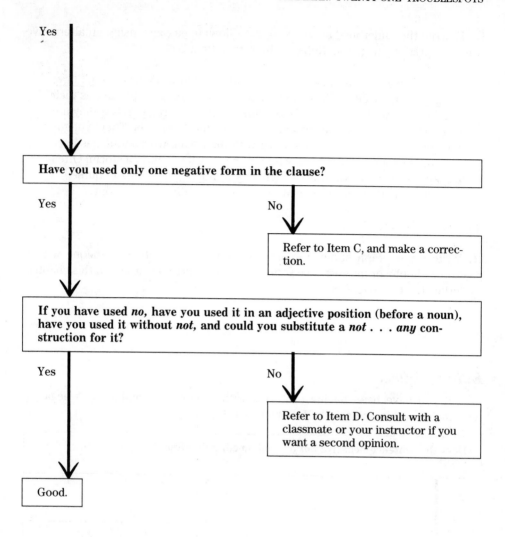

Yes

Have you used only one negative form in the clause?

Yes

No

Refer to Item C, and make a correction.

If you have used *no,* have you used it in an adjective position (before a noun), have you used it without *not,* and could you substitute a *not . . . any* construction for it?

Yes

No

Refer to Item D. Consult with a classmate or your instructor if you want a second opinion.

Good.

Nouns

Question: What do I need to know about nouns to edit my writing?

A. Nouns can be classified as follows:

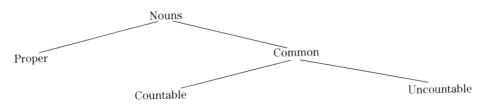

B. The two major classes are *proper* and *common* nouns.

1. Proper nouns include, for instance, names of specific people, countries, cities, rivers, languages, places, buildings, schools, months, and days of the week. They begin with capital letters. (See also Items A and D in Troublespot 12, "Articles.") For example:

   My birthday is in *January.*
   The *River Thames* runs through *London,* past the *Houses of Parliament.*
   Henry Wright went to *Columbia University* last *September* to study *French.*

2. If a noun is not a proper noun, it is a common noun. For example, names of objects and animals are common nouns. These nouns do not begin with capital letters. In addition, they are often preceded by one or more *determiners,* as listed below:

   - articles: *a, an, the* (See Troublespot 12, "Articles.")
   - demonstrative adjectives: *this, that, these, those* (See Troublespot 11, "Pronouns.")
   - possessive adjectives: *my, his, our,* etc. (See Troublespot 11, "Pronouns.")
   - possessive nouns: *Sally's, the group's,* etc.

- quantity words: *some, many, much, a lot of,* etc. (See Item E.)
- numerals: *one, two, seventeen,* etc.

C. *Countable nouns* form one of the two classes of common nouns. Note the following:

1. Countable nouns have a plural form:

   The little *girls* sat down on the grass. They ate some *cookies.*

2. The most common way to form a plural of a countable noun is to add *-s* or *-es.* Add it even when there is a numeral included to tell the reader there is more than one. Note that the ending *-y* changes to *-ies* when *-y* is preceded by a consonant.

one girl	two girls
a box	some boxes
one match	a lot of matches
a party	three parties

   Some words do not use *-s* for the plural. For example:

one man	two men
a child	many children
that tooth	those teeth

   Use your dictionary to check any plurals that you are not sure of.

D. *Uncountable nouns* form the second of the two classes of common nouns. In the context of the sentence we used previously, there is an uncountable noun:

The little girls sat down on the *grass.* They ate some cookies.

Grass is here an uncountable, mass noun, meaning *lawn.* (However, in another context, *grass* can be a countable noun, and its plural is *grasses.*)

 Countable and uncountable nouns vary from language to language. In English, some nouns do not have a plural form because they are considered essentially uncountable: *advice, enjoyment, equipment, furniture, happiness, homework, information, knowledge,* and *luggage.*

Examples:

I asked for some *information.*
He gave me a lot of *information.*

She took a lot of *luggage* on her trip.
She took ten pieces of *luggage* on her trip. (*Luggage* has no plural form;
  pieces indicates the plural.)

    There are other mass nouns that can be considered as countable or uncount-
able, depending on the context:

UNCOUNTABLE: *Chocolate* is fattening. (all chocolate: mass noun)
COUNTABLE: He ate a *chocolate*. (one piece; one serving in a box of choco-
    lates: countable)
Then he ate four more *chocolates*.

E. Note the use of quantity words with nouns. Some quantity words (e.g., *some, a
lot of, lots of, no, not any*) can be used with either **countable** plural nouns or
uncountable nouns. Others (e.g., *many, several, a little*) can be used with only
one of the two. Use the accompanying box, "Quantity Words," to help you if you
are in doubt.

F. Identify the nouns in the following eight sentences in "From *Growing Up*" by
Russell Baker on p. 295 and categorize them as (1) common *(C)* or proper *(P)*; (2)
countable *(count)* or uncountable *(unc);* and (3) if countable, as singular *(s)* or

QUANTITY WORDS

With uncountable nouns (e.g., luggage, information, happiness)	*With countable plural nouns (e.g., girls, cookies, children, luxuries)*
not much	(not) many
a little	a few
(very) little	(very) few
a great deal of	several
less	fewer

The following quantity words can be used with both uncountable and countable
nouns:

some
any
a lot of
lots of
no
not any

plural *(pl)*. Write the nouns and the identifying abbreviation in your notebook. For example:

James bought a dozen eggs, some rice, and a melon.

James: P
eggs: C, count, pl.
rice: C, unc.
melon: C, count, s.

1. I was enjoying the luxuries of a rustic nineteenth-century boyhood, but for the women Morrisonville life had few rewards.
2. Both my mother and grandmother kept house very much as women did before the Civil War.
3. They had no electricity, gas, plumbing, or central heating.
4. For baths, laundry, and dishwashing, they hauled buckets of water from a spring at the foot of a hill.
5. They scrubbed floors on hands and knees, thrashed rugs with carpet beaters, killed and plucked their own chickens, baked bread and pastries, patched the family's clothing on treadle-operated sewing machines . . . .
6. By the end of a summer day a Morrisonville woman had toiled like a serf.
7. [The men] scrubbed themselves in enamel basins and, when supper was eaten, climbed up onto Ida Rebecca's porch to watch the night arrive.
8. Presently the women joined them, and the twilight music of Morrisonville began.

(See Answer Key, p. 301.)

G. Decide where the student who wrote the following paragraph made mistakes with noun capitals and plurals. Be careful: *some, any,* and *a lot of* can be used with uncountable as well as countable nouns, as in *a lot of money* and *a lot of books* (see Item E). How would you explain to the student what was done wrong and what must be done to correct the errors?

When I saw my two ancient suitcase, I knew it was time to buy some new luggage. I looked in the windows of all the store in the center of the Town. But all I saw was clothing. I tried on three dress but didn't buy any. At last, I saw a wonderful leather bag made in spain, but it was too expensive.

(See Answer Key, p. 302.)

Editing Advice

Look at any noun in your draft that seems problematic, and ask these questions:

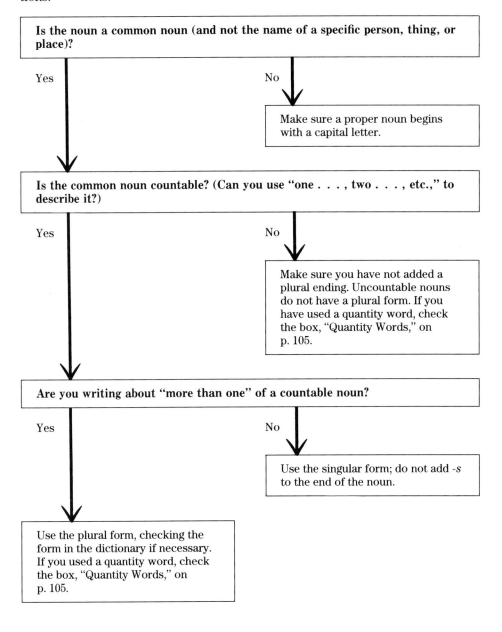

Is the noun a common noun (and not the name of a specific person, thing, or place)?

Yes

No

Make sure a proper noun begins with a capital letter.

Is the common noun countable? (Can you use "one . . . , two . . . , etc.," to describe it?)

Yes

No

Make sure you have not added a plural ending. Uncountable nouns do not have a plural form. If you have used a quantity word, check the box, "Quantity Words," on p. 105.

Are you writing about "more than one" of a countable noun?

Yes

No

Use the singular form; do not add -*s* to the end of the noun.

Use the plural form, checking the form in the dictionary if necessary. If you used a quantity word, check the box, "Quantity Words," on p. 105.

TROUBLESPOT 7

Verb Tenses

Question: How do I decide which verb tense to use?

A. When you write, there are two main things to consider about verb tense: (1) appropriateness and (2) consistency. First, how do you choose the appropriate verb tense? For the most commonly used active-voice verbs, use the following tables and example sentences to help you establish which of four time relationships you want to express. (For the passive voice, see Troublespot 10.)

Time Relationship Expressed: Simple Time

Past	Present	Future
She wrote.	She writes.	She will write.
		She is going to write.

Examples:

She *wrote* a story yesterday. (Completed in definite and known past time: e.g., last week, a month ago, in 1984.)

She *writes* every day. (Repeated action or habit in present time: e.g., once a week, whenever she can, often.)

She *will write* a novel next year. (Future time stated or implied: e.g., in the next six months, before she is thirty.)

Note: In clauses beginning with *when, before,* or *as soon as,* use the present and not the future tense for simple time. For example:

When she *arrives,* we'll begin the meeting.

Time Relationship Expressed: In Progress at a Known Time

Past	*Present*	*Future*
She was writing.	She is writing.	She will be writing.

Examples:

She *was writing* when I called her at 8 P.M. last night. (Happening and
    continuing at a known or stated time in the past: I interrupted her; she
    probably continued afterward.)

She *was writing* all day yesterday. (Happening continuously over a period
    of time in the past.)

She *is writing* at this moment. (Happening in the present, right now.)

She *will be writing* when you call her at 8 P.M. tonight. (Happening continu-
    ously at a known or stated time in the future: she will probably con-
    tinue writing after you call.)

Note: The *-ing* form is not used for verbs expressing states of mind (*believe, know,
understand, want, hate, seem, need,* etc.); senses (*taste, smell,* etc.); or possession
(*have, own,* etc.). The simple forms are used instead.

Time Relationship Expressed: Completed *Before* a Known Time or Event

Past	*Present*	*Future*
she had written	she has written	she will have written

Examples:

She *had* already *written* one story when she started high school. (Two past
    events are indicated: an activity was completed by a stated time in the
    past. She wrote the story when she was twelve; she started high school
    when she was fourteen.)

She *has* (already, just) *written* two stories. (An activity was completed
    some time before the present. The main point is not *when* she actually
    wrote them, but that she *has written* them at some time in the past,
    with the effect being relative to present time.)

She *will* (already) *have written* three stories when she graduates from high
    school next year. (Two future events are indicated: an activity will be
    completed by a stated time in the future. First she will write the stories;
    then she will graduate.)

Time Relationship: In Progress for a Stated Length of Time and up to a Known and Specific Time or Event

Past	*Present*	*Future*
She had been writing.	She has been writing.	She will have been writing.

Examples:

She *had been writing* for three hours before all the lights went out. (One event was interrupted by the other; both the length of time and the end of the action in the past must be stated.)

She *has been writing* a novel for two years. (Length of time is stated or implied and continues until the present: she will probably continue; she has not finished the novel yet. Often used with *for* and *since*.)

She *will have been writing* for six hours by the time the party starts at 8 P.M. tonight. (An event in the future interrupts or indicates the end of the action; both length of time and final event must be stated or clear from the context.)

B. Consistency of tenses is important. Usually, the verb tenses a writer uses in a passage will fit consistently into one of two time zones: (1) Past or (2) Present/Future. The accompanying box summarizes the four tense/time relationships described in Item A, and divides them into two time zones:

TENSE/TIME RELATIONSHIPS

Time relationship	*Past zone*	*Present/Future zone*	
simple	wrote	writes	will write
in progress	was writing	is writing	will be writing
completed	had written	has written	will have written
in progress for . . . and up to	had been writing	has been writing	will have been writing

Auxiliaries other than *has/had* and *is/was* show the time zone distinction, too (see Item B in Troublespot 8 for list of auxiliaries):

Past zone	*Present/Future zone*
did	does/do
would	will
could	can
should	shall
might	may
had to	must

C. Do not surprise or confuse your reader by switching from one zone to another in the middle of a paragraph, unless you have a good reason. In the following paragraph, for instance, the time zone switches from Present/Future to Past at the point marked with an asterisk, but the reader is not surprised. Why not? What does the writer do to prepare us for the switch?

I think that big families can offer their members a lot of support. When a child has done something wrong, there is always someone to turn to. Or if a child feels upset about a fight with a friend, even if the child's mother isn't at home, an aunt or a grandmother will be able to comfort him or her and offer advice. *Once when I was six years old, I fell off my bicycle. I had been riding very fast around the block in a race with my friends. My father was working and my mother was out shopping. But the house was still full of people: my aunt bathed my knees, my grandmother gave me a glass of milk and a cookie, and my uncle drove me to the doctor's office.

(See Answer Key, p. 302.)

D. Read the following passage from "Mr. Doherty Builds His Dream Life" by Jim Doherty on p. 193.

We love the smell of the earth warming and the sound of cattle lowing. We watch for hawks in the sky and deer in the cornfields.
   But the good life can get pretty tough. Three months ago when it was 30 below, we spent two miserable days hauling firewood up the river on a toboggan. Three months from now, it will be 95 above and we will be cultivating corn, weeding strawberries and killing chickens. Recently, Sandy and I had to reshingle the back roof. Soon Jim, 16, and Emily, 13, the youngest of our four children, will help me make some long-overdue improvements on the privy that supplements our indoor plumbing when we are working outside. Later this month, we'll spray the orchard, paint the barn, plant the garden and clean the hen house before the new chicks arrive.

Now, underline each complete verb phrase, and identify (1) which time zone (Past, Present, or Future) it fits into, (2) what time is expressed, and (3) what signals, if any, Doherty gives for any switches. Write the verbs and your identifications in your notebook. For example: *love:* Present/simple present

(See Answer Key, p. 302.)

E. Choose another passage from Part III or an article in a newspaper or magazine. Underline the verbs, and identify what time is expressed according to the boxes in Item B.

Editing Advice

If you are having problems with verb tenses, look at all the active voice verbs in your draft, one paragraph at a time, and ask these questions:

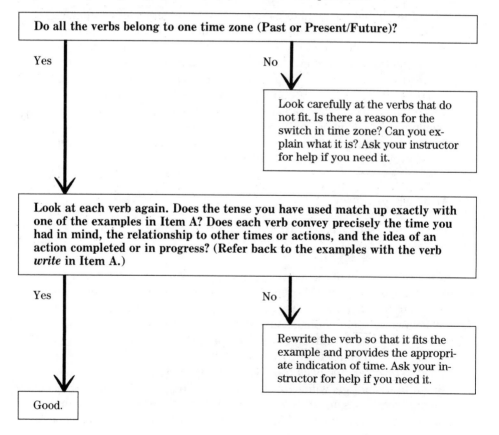

Do all the verbs belong to one time zone (Past or Present/Future)?

Yes

No

Look carefully at the verbs that do not fit. Is there a reason for the switch in time zone? Can you explain what it is? Ask your instructor for help if you need it.

Look at each verb again. Does the tense you have used match up exactly with one of the examples in Item A? Does each verb convey precisely the time you had in mind, the relationship to other times or actions, and the idea of an action completed or in progress? (Refer back to the examples with the verb *write* **in Item A.)**

Yes

No

Rewrite the verb so that it fits the example and provides the appropriate indication of time. Ask your instructor for help if you need it.

Good.

Verb Forms

Question: How do I know which verb form goes with which auxiliary?

A. Look at these verb forms:

Simple (no -s)	-s	-ing	Past	Participle
paint	paints	painting	painted	painted
sing	sings	singing	sang	sung
take	takes	taking	took	taken

There are regular rules about which verb forms are used with which auxiliary verbs to form a complete (or *finite*) verb in a clause or sentence. There are no exceptions. So, choose which verb form to use according to the helping verb you use. The chart given in Item B will help you.

B. In the accompanying chart, note that *only* the forms checked are possible after the helping verbs listed in the left-hand column.

Verb Forms

I. Verb form used after an auxiliary

	Simple (no -s)	-s	-ing	past	participle
DO does/do did	✓				

(Chart continued)

	Simple (no -s)	-s	-ing	past	participle
WILL will would can could shall should may might must	√				
HAVE has/have had will have would have can have could have shall have should have may have might have must have					√
BE am/is/are was/were has been/ have been had been will be would be can be could be shall be should be may be might be must be will have been would have been can have been			√		√ Passive (see p. 122)

	Simple (no -s)	-s	-ing	past	participle
BE could have been shall have been should have been may have been might have been must have been					
BEING am/is/are being was/were being					✓ Passive (see p. 122)

II. Verb form used with no auxiliary

	Simple (no -s)	-s	-ing	past	participle
Simple time (past)				✓	
Simple time (present) (*he, she, it* forms as subject)		✓			
Simple time (present) (*I, you, we, they* forms as subject)	✓				

You see from the chart that, for most auxiliary sequences, the form of the verb after an auxiliary is fixed. You do not have to guess which form to use. Only with the *be* forms do you have a choice: you need to determine whether you want an active or a passive form before you decide whether to use the *-ing* or the participle form.

C. In the following two passages from the readings in Part III, underline each complete (finite) verb phrase. As you do so, look at the preceding chart, and note where each verb phrase fits into the chart.

1. About half of the children whose parents had divorced hadn't seen their father in the last year; only one out of six had managed to see their father an average of once a week. If the current rate of divorce persists, about half of all children will spend some time in a single-parent family before they reach 18.

Much has been written about the psychological effects on children of living with one parent, but the literature has not yet proven that any lasting negative effects occur. One effect, however, does occur with regularity: women who head single-parent families typically experience a sharp decline in their income relative to before their divorce. Husbands usually do not experience a decline. (Cherlin and Furstenberg, pp. 268–269)

2. In the common everyday job, nothing is made any more. Things are now made by machines. Very little is repaired. The machines that make things make them in such a fashion that they will quickly fall apart in such a way that repairs will be prohibitively expensive. Thus the buyer is encouraged to throw the thing away and buy a new one. In effect, the machines are making junk. (Baker, p. 241)

(See Answer Key, p. 302.)

D. Choose a reading from Part III, a newspaper, a magazine, or from your own or a partner's journal, and examine each verb as you did in Item C.

Editing Advice

Look at all the complete verbs you have written in your draft, one paragraph at a time. Ask these questions:

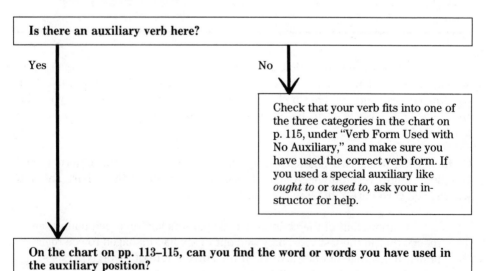

Is there an auxiliary verb here?

Yes

No

Check that your verb fits into one of the three categories in the chart on p. 115, under "Verb Form Used with No Auxiliary," and make sure you have used the correct verb form. If you used a special auxiliary like *ought to* or *used to*, ask your instructor for help.

On the chart on pp. 113–115, can you find the word or words you have used in the auxiliary position?

(Flow chart continued)

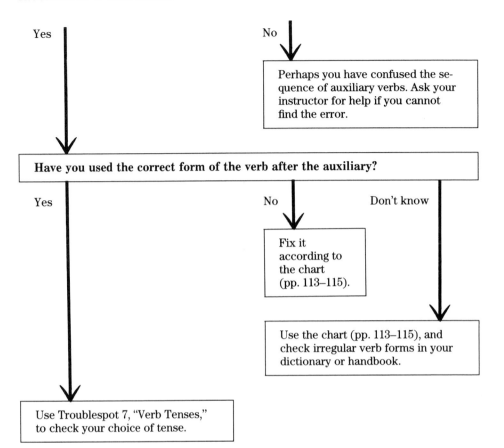

Yes | No

Perhaps you have confused the sequence of auxiliary verbs. Ask your instructor for help if you cannot find the error.

Have you used the correct form of the verb after the auxiliary?

Yes | No | Don't know

Fix it according to the chart (pp. 113–115).

Use the chart (pp. 113–115), and check irregular verb forms in your dictionary or handbook.

Use Troublespot 7, "Verb Tenses," to check your choice of tense.

TROUBLESPOT 9

Agreement

> **Question:** How can I solve problems of agreement in my writing?

A. In a clause or a sentence in the present tense, make sure that the verb agrees in number with its subject—specifically, with the head noun (i.e., the most important noun) of its subject.

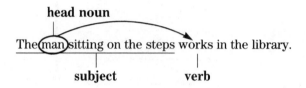

head noun

The man sitting on the steps works in the library.

subject   **verb**

If the head noun is a *he/she/it* form, use the third person singular form (*-s* ending) of the verb. If the head noun is a *they* form, use the plural form of the verb (i.e., the simple form with no *-s* ending).

Determining singular or plural endings can be confusing because an *-s* ending on a noun indicates plural (i.e., *they* form), while an *-s* ending on a verb indicates singular (i.e., *he/she/it*) form.

> The dog bark*s* every night. (*Dog* = "it," so the verb is singular.)
> The dog*s* bark every night. (*Dogs* = "they," so the verb is plural.)

B. Read the following excerpt from "Mr. Doherty Builds His Dream Life" (p. 194).

> Sandy, meanwhile, pursues her own hectic rounds. Besides the usual household routine, she oversees the garden and beehives, bakes bread, cans and freezes, chauffeurs the kids to their music lessons, practices with them, takes organ lessons on her own, does research and typing for me, writes an article herself now and then, tends the flower beds, stacks a little wood and delivers the eggs.

Underline all the verbs. How would the passage change if the writer were telling us not just about Sandy but about Sandy and her sister? Begin with "Sandy and her sister, meanwhile, pursue," and write the new version in section 4 of your notebook. (See Answer Key, p. 303.)

C. Agreement in number occurs not only with simple present verbs but also with the following auxiliaries: *am/is/are; was/were; does/do; has/have.* Look at these examples from "Mr. Doherty Builds His Dream Life" (pp. 193–197):

The river *was* thawing.
The buildings *were* in good shape.
My wife Sandy and I *have* finally found contentment here in the country.
I*'m* not making anywhere near as much money as I did when I *was* employed full time, but now we *don't* need as much either.

The verb agrees with the head noun of the subject even when the sentence contains additional information between the head noun and the verb.

The crime reported on the front page of all the newspapers last week *was* never solved.
The crimes reported on the front page of all the newspapers last week *were* never solved.

D. Some pronouns that regularly require a singular verb are troublesome to second-language students: *everyone, everybody, someone, somebody, anyone, anybody, no one, nobody,* and *something.*

Examples:
Everybody *has* left.
Everyone *wants* to be liked.
Somebody who *is* standing over there *wants* to speak next.

Look for examples of these words when you read, and note the verb form used.

E. When a sentence starts with *There* plus a form of *be*, the verb agrees with the head noun of the noun phrase that follows the verb. For example:

There *is* one *bottle* on the table.
There *are* two *bottles* on the table.
There *is* some *juice* on the table.
There *is* a *vase* of flowers on the table.

Note how the head noun determines agreement in sentences with *a lot of:*

There *are* a lot of *people* in the room.
There *is* a lot of *money* in my bag.

Decide whether to use *is* or *are* in the following sentences:

1. There _____ some apples in the bowl on the table.
2. There _____ some money in my wallet.

 3. There _____ a carton of milk in the refrigerator.
 4. There _____ a box of books in the basement.
 5. There _____ a lot of voters in rural regions.
 6. There _____ a lot of food on the shelves.
 7. There _____ a few coffee cups in the dishwasher.
 8. There _____ no knives in the drawer.
 9. There _____ no furniture in the room.
 10. There _____ many serious problems that the voters in this
     district have to face.

(See Answer Key, p. 303.)

F. When a sentence has a *compound subject* (i.e., more than one subject), the
verb must be plural in form:

> My sister *visits* me every year. (subject: sister)
> My aunt and my sister *visit* me every year. (compound subject: aunt and
>   sister)

G. When you write a relative clause beginning with *who, which,* or *that,* look for
its *referent*—the word that *who, which,* or *that* refers back to. The referent determines whether the verb should be singular or plural. For example:

> The *people* in my class *who are* studying English *do* a lot of extra reading.

> The *student* in my class *who is* sitting in the corner usually *does* a lot of
>   extra reading.

See also Troublespot 16, "Relative Clauses."

H. For pronoun agreement (when to use *this/these, his/her,* and so on), see
Troublespot 11, "Pronouns."

Editing Advice

If you have a problem with agreement of subject and verb, look at each
troublesome verb you have written and ask the following questions:

> **Is the verb a present-tense form (*-s* form or "no *-s*" form), or does the verb
> phrase begin with one of the following auxiliaries: *does/do, has/have, am/are/
> is,* or *was/were*?**

(Flow chart continued)

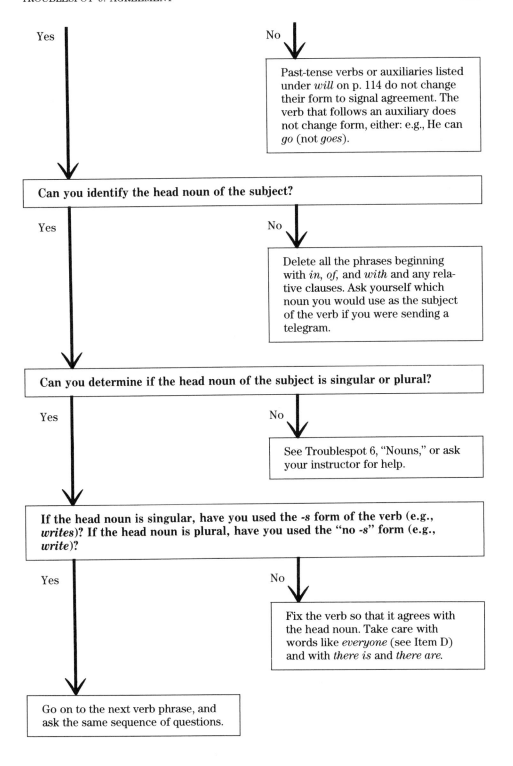

Yes   No

Past-tense verbs or auxiliaries listed under *will* on p. 114 do not change their form to signal agreement. The verb that follows an auxiliary does not change form, either: e.g., He can *go* (not *goes*).

Can you identify the head noun of the subject?

Yes   No

Delete all the phrases beginning with *in*, *of*, and *with* and any relative clauses. Ask yourself which noun you would use as the subject of the verb if you were sending a telegram.

Can you determine if the head noun of the subject is singular or plural?

Yes   No

See Troublespot 6, "Nouns," or ask your instructor for help.

If the head noun is singular, have you used the *-s* form of the verb (e.g., *writes*)? If the head noun is plural, have you used the "no *-s*" form (e.g., *write*)?

Yes   No

Fix the verb so that it agrees with the head noun. Take care with words like *everyone* (see Item D) and with *there is* and *there are*.

Go on to the next verb phrase, and ask the same sequence of questions.

Active and Passive

> **Question:** How do I decide when to use a verb in the passive voice, and what must I remember about how to use it?

A. The following sentence has a verb in the active voice:

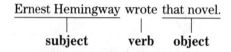

Ernest Hemingway wrote that novel.

    subject   **verb** **object**

We can change the emphasis by rewriting the sentence like this:

That novel was written by Ernest Hemingway.

Note what we have done:

> We have made the original subject, *Ernest Hemingway*, less important in the sentence.
> We have reversed the order of the subject and object of the original sentence.
> We have changed the verb form to a form of *be* followed by the participle (see also Troublespot 8, "Verb Forms").
> We have added *by* before the original subject.

B. Sometimes writers overuse the passive voice, which makes their writing flat and dull. But there are times when the passive is necessary to convey your meaning. Use the passive when it is not important to emphasize or even mention the doer of the action (the *agent*). For example:

Good! The garbage *has been collected.*
He *was promoted* to vice-president a month ago.
When gold *was discovered* in the area, new towns sprang up overnight.
Her performance *is being watched* very closely.
These tomatoes *were grown* in New Jersey.
I *was told* to send the form to you. [The writer doesn't want to say who did the telling.]

If the agent is important, the active voice is usually preferable:

Two prospectors discovered gold in the area.

Not

Gold was discovered in the area by two prospectors.

C. The passive occurs frequently in the following instances:

   1. In scientific writing:

      The experiment was performed in 1983.

   2. In journalism, or other writing, when the writer cannot or does not want to identify the agent:

      Jewelry worth five hundred thousand dollars was stolen from the Hotel Eldorado late last night.

   3. When the action is more important than who did it. For example, see the sentences of paragraph 7 in "From *Poor Russell's Almanac*" by Russell Baker on p. 241.

      In the common everyday job, nothing is made any more.
      Very little is repaired.
      The buyer is encouraged to throw the thing away.

      In these sentences, *who* makes, repairs, or encourages is not what is important.

   4. In a sentence with the same subject as the previous clause, when the flow of the sentences makes the passive acceptable. Look again at paragraph 7 of the selection by Russell Baker on p. 241:

      In the common everyday job, nothing is made any more. Things are now made by machines.

      Things forms a link with *nothing* in the previous sentence, and thus gives the two sentences more cohesion than if a new subject had been introduced, as in the sentence:

      Machines now make things.

D. The form and sequence of passive verbs is often a problem for students writing in a second language. Look at the examples in the following list.

Active	*Passive*
They paint the house every three years.	The house *is painted* every three years.
They painted the house last year.	The house *was painted* last year.

Active	*Passive*
They will paint the house next year.	The house *will be painted* next year.
They are painting the house now.	The house *is being painted* now.
They were painting the house all last week.	The house *was being painted* all last week.
They have just painted the house.	The house *has just been painted.*
They had just painted the house when the roof collapsed.	The house *had just been painted* when the roof collapsed.
They will have painted the house by next Tuesday.	The house *will have been painted* by next Tuesday.

Note that in all the passive sentences, we use a form of *be* plus a participle. In addition, a *be* form can be joined by other auxiliaries.

The house *should be painted.*
The house *might have been painted* last year: I'm not sure if it was.

E. Read the following four selections from the readings in Part III. Write down all the verbs in your notebook, and indicate which verbs are active and which are passive.

> 1. Consider the typical twelve-story glass building in the typical American city. Nothing is being made in this building and nothing is being repaired, including the building itself. Constructed as a piece of junk, the building will be discarded when it wears out, and another piece of junk will be set in its place. (Baker, p. 241)
> 2. None of us will ever forget [our] first winter. We were buried under five foot of snow from December through March. (Doherty, p. 194)
> 3. One thing is certain about tomorrow's job markets: dramatic shifts will occur in employment patterns. These changes are going to affect how we work and how we are educated and trained for jobs. (Cetron, p. 243)
> 4. The essence of Japan's problem is that . . . 20% of the entire work force will retire at 80% of their base pay for the rest of their lives. Japan was forced to go robotic to remain competitive. The United States, too, will be filling many of today's blue-collar jobs with robots. (Cetron, pp. 243–244)

(See Answer Key, p. 303.)

F. In the journal section of your notebook, write an entry for your instructor describing what you were taught about the English language and about writing in your previous schools. After you have written your entry, look carefully at the verbs you used. Did you use the passive or the active? Why did you make the choices you made?

Editing Advice

When you want to examine closely whether you have correctly used a verb in the passive voice, ask these questions:

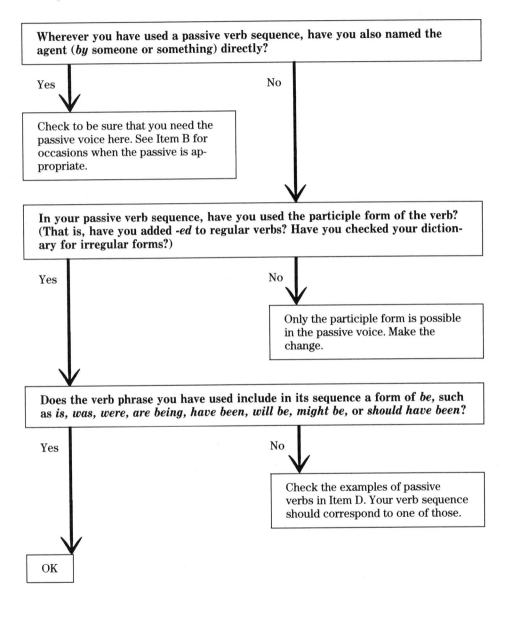

Wherever you have used a passive verb sequence, have you also named the agent (*by* someone or something) directly?

Yes

No

Check to be sure that you need the passive voice here. See Item B for occasions when the passive is appropriate.

In your passive verb sequence, have you used the participle form of the verb? (That is, have you added *-ed* to regular verbs? Have you checked your dictionary for irregular forms?)

Yes

No

Only the participle form is possible in the passive voice. Make the change.

Does the verb phrase you have used include in its sequence a form of *be*, such as *is, was, were, are being, have been, will be, might be*, or *should have been*?

Yes

No

Check the examples of passive verbs in Item D. Your verb sequence should correspond to one of those.

OK

TROUBLESPOT 11

Pronouns

> *Question:* **How do I know which pronoun to use?**

A. The forms of pronouns are rule-governed; that is, which forms to use are determined by specific rules. The box below shows the rule-governed forms of the personal pronouns. No other forms are possible. Note carefully the form *its.* Even though it indicates possession, there is no apostrophe. Do not confuse *its* with *it's,* which is the contracted form of *it is.*

B. In English, a pronoun agrees in gender (male, female, or neuter) with the noun it refers back to (its *referent*) and not with the noun following it:

My father never visits *his* aunt.

My mother often visits *her* uncle.

C. Other troublesome forms are demonstrative pronouns or adjectives. These are used to point out (or "demonstrate") what you are referring to. (See p. 127.)

Look at the following four examples from the readings in Part III. In section 4 of your notebook, answer the question that follows each passage.

1. One would expect people to cherish paintings because of their beauty and originality, or because of the artist's skills; in short, for aesthetic rea-

PERSONAL PRONOUNS

Subject pronoun	*Object pronoun*	*Possessive adjective (+ noun)*	*Possessive pronoun*	*Reflexive pronoun*
I	me	my	mine	myself
we	us	our	ours	ourselves
you	you	your	yours	yourself
you	you	your	yours	yourselves
he	him	his	his	himself
she	her	her	hers	herself
it	it	its	–	itself
they	them	their	theirs	themselves
one	one/him/her	one's	–	oneself

126

Demonstrative Adjectives or Pronouns

Singular	*Plural*
this	these
that	those

---

sons. Yet only 16 percent of the time were any of *those* characteristics mentioned. (Csikszentmihalyi and Rochberg-Halton, p. 220)

Which characteristics does the author mean?

2. If someone wore shoes with run-over heels, or shoes that had not been shined for a long time, or shoes with broken laces, you could be pretty sure *this* person would be slovenly in other things as well. (Connell, p. 260)

Which person is the writer referring to?

3. Most of all, though, I worried about facing my mother. Even as I write *that* sentence, I feel it sounds unfair. (Toth, p. 262)

Which sentence is she referring to?

4. Right now, women still hold only 6 percent of middle-management positions and one percent of jobs in upper management. But *this* will change, says one female executive . . . . (Schnack, p. 280)

What does *this* refer to?

(See Answer Key, p. 303.)

D. In the following selection from "Treasures" by Joan Costello on p. 212, circle any personal pronouns or demonstratives that you find. (Turn to p. 212 if you need explanations of any of the vocabulary.) Then decide what word in the passage each pronoun refers to. Draw a line from the circled pronoun to its referent—that is, the word (or words) to which it refers. Note the use of *it is* to begin a sentence and to direct the reader's attention to what comes next. Do not circle that use of *it*. Finally, note that the word *that* can also be used to introduce clauses (see Troublespot 3, "Combining Sentences: Subordinating").

Children form attachments to objects at an early age. Most children select a

blanket or toy animal to cherish. Usually it is one that they have nearby as

they fall asleep. Typically the object evokes a sense of comfort and its soothing qualities may substitute somewhat for the attention of loved ones. As children grow, their early attachments to blankets or teddy bears fade and they invest other objects with special meanings. It is often unclear why they choose certain objects over others; nor is it clear even to them precisely what these things mean.

(See Answer Key, p. 304.)

Editing Advice

Look at each problematic pronoun in your essay, and ask these questions:

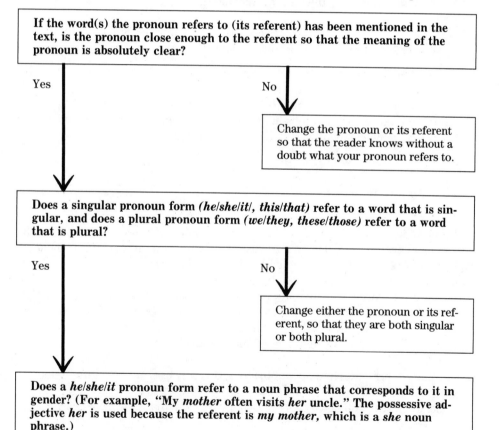

If the word(s) the pronoun refers to (its referent) has been mentioned in the text, is the pronoun close enough to the referent so that the meaning of the pronoun is absolutely clear?

Yes   No

Change the pronoun or its referent so that the reader knows without a doubt what your pronoun refers to.

Does a singular pronoun form (he/she/it/, this/that) refer to a word that is singular, and does a plural pronoun form (we/they, these/those) refer to a word that is plural?

Yes   No

Change either the pronoun or its referent, so that they are both singular or both plural.

Does a he/she/it pronoun form refer to a noun phrase that corresponds to it in gender? (For example, "My mother often visits her uncle." The possessive adjective her is used because the referent is my mother, which is a she noun phrase.)

(Flow chart continued)

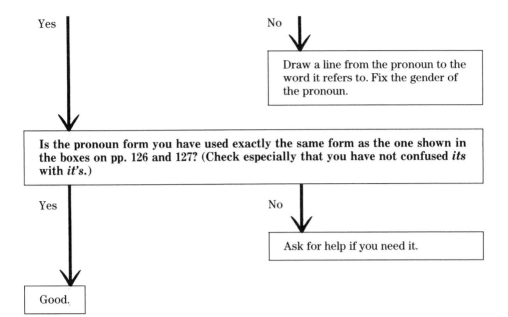

Yes   No

Draw a line from the pronoun to the word it refers to. Fix the gender of the pronoun.

Is the pronoun form you have used exactly the same form as the one shown in the boxes on pp. 126 and 127? (Check especially that you have not confused *its* with *it's*.)

Yes   No

Ask for help if you need it.

Good.

Articles

> *Question:* **When do I use *a, an, the,* or no article at all?**

Other languages do not use articles the way that English does, so some second-language writers find articles to be troublesome. While there are rules to help you, there are also a lot of exceptions and a lot of fine distinctions to be made. You should not expect to learn a rule, apply it, and then never make another error again. Learning how to use articles correctly takes a long time. You need to read a lot, notice how articles are used, and make notes in section 4 of your notebook. You should also study and refer to the explanations, examples, and charts that follow.

A. The article you use depends on the noun it modifies, so you have to begin by looking at the noun and making the following distinctions (see also Troublespot 6, "Nouns"):

1. Is it a *common* or *proper* noun? A proper noun is the name of a specific person, place, or thing (e.g., *James Raimes, Hunter College, England*). All proper nouns begin with a capital letter. Other nouns are common nouns (e.g., *man, school, country*). For the most part, singular proper nouns are not preceded by an article (however, see Item D in this chapter). Plural proper nouns are preceded by *the*, as in *the Great Lakes* and *the United States.*

2. If the noun is a common noun, is it *countable* or *uncountable* in the sentence in which you want to use it? Examples of countable nouns are:

   chair (a chair, two chairs)
   meal (one meal, three meals)
   machine (a machine, some machines)

   Uncountable, or mass and abstract nouns, include, for example:

furniture	information
rice	gravity
machinery	pollution
equipment	satisfaction
advice	

   (See also Items C and D in Troublespot 6, "Nouns.")

Difficulty with articles occurs with common nouns because what is considered countable and uncountable varies from language to language. In Spanish, for example, the equivalent of *furniture* is a countable word; in English, *furniture* is always uncountable. It has no plural form, and we cannot say **a furniture*.

Most grammar books list nouns that are regularly uncountable in English. However, someone else's list is never as useful to you as your own. As you continue to read and write in English, keep a list in your notebook of any uncountable nouns you come across.

B. Next, decide whether a common noun, in your sentence context, has a specific or a nonspecific reference for the writer and the reader.

1. A *specific* reference is known by the writer and by the reader as something unique, specific, or familiar, or previously identified to the reader.

   Example A: My daughter is looking after *the dog* this week.

   The writer here expects the reader to know precisely which dog is meant: the family's dog, or a dog the writer has previously identified and perhaps described.

   Example B: My neighbor bought *a dog*. My daughter is looking after *the dog* this week.

   Here the dog is identified as the specific dog that the neighbor bought.

   Example C: *The dogs* that belong to the bank manager have been trained to attack.

   The reader knows specifically which dogs: the ones that belong to the bank manager.

2. A *nonspecific* reference is not identified by the writer and by the reader as something known, unique, or familiar.

   Example A: My daughter is looking after *a dog* this week.

   Here the writer does not expect the reader to know about the dog in question. It could be any dog—a neighbor's dog, a schoolmate's dog, a poodle, a spaniel, or a sheepdog.

   Example B: *Dogs* are friendly animals.

   Here the writer is making a generalization about all dogs everywhere.

   Example C: *Some dogs* can be trained to be attack dogs.

   Here the writer is not making a generalization about all dogs, but limiting the statement with a quantity word.

C. Once you have made these distinctions about the noun in the context of the meaning of your sentence, you can then apply some general rules about article use. But beware! Article use is complex. The accompanying box offers only general guidelines to help you decide which articles to use with common nouns. There are many cases that you just have to learn one by one. So, use your notebook whenever you find an exception to a rule.

Note: The important things to remember as you work with the box are:

1. A countable singular noun *must have an article (a/an* or *the)* or some other determiner (e.g., *this, her, every)* in front of it. A countable singular noun *never stands alone;* that is, in a sentence, *book* by itself is not possible. So, you must write:

   a book
   the book
   this/that book
   my/his/etc., book
   every/each book

2. Uncountable nouns are *never* used with *a/an.* Therefore, forms such as **a furniture, *an advice,* or **an information* are not possible. To express the concept of amounts of these uncountable nouns, we have to use expressions such as *two pieces of furniture, several types of food, three teaspoons of sugar, some items of information,* or *a piece of equipment.* (See also Troublespot 6, "Nouns.")

3. Some nouns can be determined as countable or uncountable only in the context of the sentence in which they are used. For example:

ARTICLES WITH COMMON NOUNS

Type of noun	Reference for writer and reader	
	Specific	*Nonspecific*
Countable singular	the	a/an
Countable plural	the	Quantity words (*some, a few, many,* etc.). See p. 105 in Troublespot 6, "Nouns." *or* No article with a generalization.
Uncountable	the	Quantity words (*some, a little,* etc.). See p. 105 in Troublespot 6, "Nouns." *or* No article with a generalization.

>
> *Life* can be hard when you are old. (Here *life* is generic and uncountable; the writer is making a generalization.)
>
> My grandmother lived *a happy life*. (Here *life* is countable; the writer sees different types of lives: *a happy life, an unhappy life, a useful life*, etc.)

So, what you intend as you write determines the category of countable/uncountable. Only occasionally is it fixed within the word itself.

D. Note some word groups that cause difficulties:

>
> Unique objects: *the earth, the sun, the moon,* but *Earth*
>
> Places: *France, Central Park, San Francisco, Mount Vesuvius, McDonald's,*
>
> but *the United States of America, the United Kingdom, the Sahara (Desert), the Hague, the Statue of Liberty*
>
> Oceans, rivers, seas, and lakes: *the Pacific, the Amazon, the Mediterranean, the Great Lakes,* but *Lake Superior*
>
> Diseases and ailments: *a cold, a headache, the flu,* but *pneumonia, cancer*
>
> Destination: *to go to the store, to go to the post office, to go to the bank, to go to school, to go to church, to go to bed, to go home*
>
> Locations: *at home, in bed, in school, in college*
>
> Expressions of time: *in the morning, in the evening* (but *at night*), *all the time, most of the time* (but *sometimes, in time, on time*)

When trying to decide whether to use an article, ask for help if you need it. Every time you learn a new use of an article, record it in your notebook.

E. Examine the first paragraph of "Object Lessons" on p. 217. Underline all the nouns, and examine the articles or other determiners (see Item B in Troublespot 6, "Nouns"). Try to fit each article or determiner + noun into one of the categories in the box on p. 132. Write down in your notebook the categories to which you would assign the articles and nouns:

>
> Countable or uncountable?
>
> If countable, singular or plural?
>
> Specific or nonspecific reference?

(See Answer Key, p. 304.)

F. Read a short passage in English every day for a few days. Underline all the nouns and articles, and try to explain why the writer chose to use that form. This close examination will help you understand the relationships between articles and the concepts they express.

Editing Advice

If you have problems deciding on *a/an/the* or no article at all, look at each troublesome noun phrase and ask the following questions:

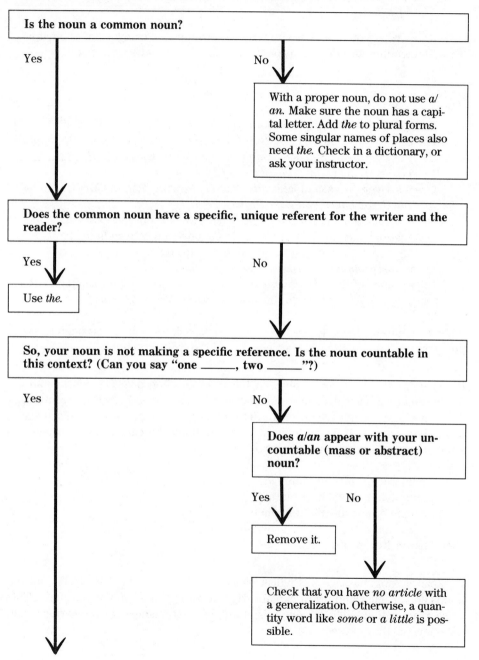

Is the noun a common noun?

Yes / **No**

With a proper noun, do not use *a/an*. Make sure the noun has a capital letter. Add *the* to plural forms. Some singular names of places also need *the*. Check in a dictionary, or ask your instructor.

Does the common noun have a specific, unique referent for the writer and the reader?

Yes / **No**

Use *the*.

So, your noun is not making a specific reference. Is the noun countable in this context? (Can you say "one _____, two _____"?)

Yes / **No**

Does *a/an* appear with your uncountable (mass or abstract) noun?

Yes / **No**

Remove it.

Check that you have *no article* with a generalization. Otherwise, a quantity word like *some* or *a little* is possible.

(Flow chart continued)

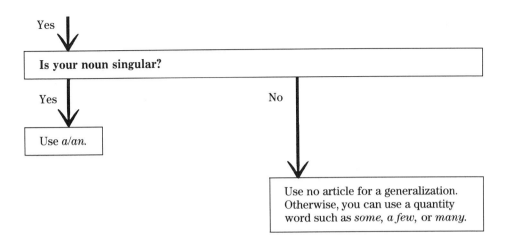

Yes

Is your noun singular?

Yes   No

Use *a/an*.

Use no article for a generalization.
Otherwise, you can use a quantity
word such as *some, a few,* or *many.*

TROUBLESPOT 13

Adjectives

> *Question:* **What do I need to know about adjectives to edit my writing?**

A. In English, adjectives have no plural form. Look at the adjective *important* in the sentences below. Note the position of the adjective in the sentence, and the form of the adjective and of the noun it modifies.

> An *important* politician attended the conference.
> Some *important* politicians attended the conference.
> The politicians who attended the conference are *important.*

B. We add endings to short adjectives when we form comparatives or superlatives:

> Sally is smart and witty. She is smart*er* and witt*ier* than her sister.
> She was the smart*est* in her class, but not the witt*iest.*

C. But when the adjective is long (i.e., three syllables), we use *more* for the comparative and *the most* for the superlative:

> She was *more serious* about her work than other students, and she was *the most ambitious* student in her class.

D. Adjectives expressing nationality always have a capital letter:

> a *French* film
> a *Chinese* restaurant

E. Adjectives in a series tend to occur in a certain order, as indicated in the box on p. 137. However, there can be frequent exceptions.

F. Look carefully at each of the following noun phrases, and determine which category in the following box each word belongs to:

1. that sophisticated young Italian model
2. his comfortable white velvet couch
3. two middle-aged Catholic bishops
4. their charming little wood cabin

Determiner	Opinion	Physical description				Nationality	Religion	Material	Noun	Head noun
		Size	*Shape*	*Age*	*Color*					
three	beautiful			old						houses
my			long		blue			silk	evening	gown
a	delicious					French				meal
her		big		old		English		oak	writing	desk
Lee's	charming						Catholic			teacher
several		little	round					marble	coffee	tables

(See Answer Key, p. 304.)

G. Read the last paragraph of "An Interview with Ernest Hemingway" on p. 211. Examine the following *adjective + noun* sequences, and determine the category of each adjective according to the box above.

1. bookcase top
2. wood beads
3. a little cast-iron turtle
4. a Venetian gondola
5. a little tin model
6. a circular straw place mat
7. three buffalo horns

Do the same with this sequence from the article "Treasures" by Joan Costello on p. 212:

8. an ancient ebony necklace

(See Answer Key, p. 305.)

H. Some adjectives used after a verb phrase *(predicate adjectives)* are regularly used with prepositions:

I am *afraid of* ghosts.
I confess that I am *proud of* winning the race.

Whenever you come across a *predicate adjective + preposition* in your reading, write the whole sentence in which it appears in section 4 of your notebook. Here are some to start off your list:

aware of   interested in
suspicious of   different from

fond of   full of

satisfied with   jealous of

happy about

Editing Advice

If you are unsure about your use of an adjective at any point in your essay, ask these questions:

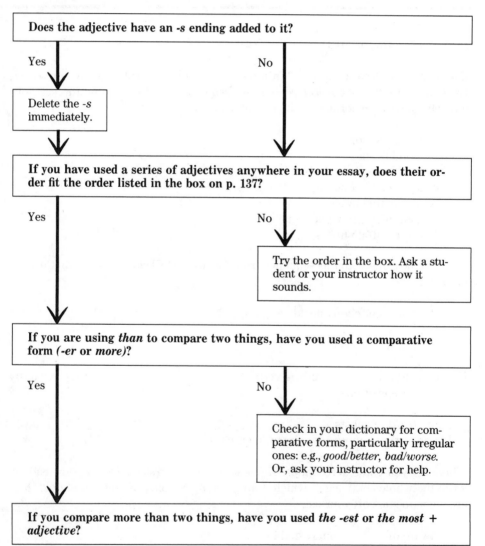

Does the adjective have an *-s* ending added to it?

Yes

No

Delete the *-s* immediately.

If you have used a series of adjectives anywhere in your essay, does their order fit the order listed in the box on p. 137?

Yes

No

Try the order in the box. Ask a student or your instructor how it sounds.

If you are using *than* to compare two things, have you used a comparative form *(-er* or *more)*?

Yes

No

Check in your dictionary for comparative forms, particularly irregular ones: e.g., *good/better, bad/worse.* Or, ask your instructor for help.

If you compare more than two things, have you used *the -est* or *the most +* *adjective*?

(Flow chart continued)

Yes

No

Check in your dictionary for the form of the superlative, especially irregular forms like *the best* and *the worst*. Ask for help if you need it.

Good.

TROUBLESPOT 14

Adverbs

Question: **How can I tell whether to use an adjective or an adverb, and how do I use an adverb in a sentence?**

A. Adjectives tell us about nouns:

The *comfortable* chair is in the corner.

The chair in the corner $\begin{Bmatrix} \text{looks} \\ \text{seems} \\ \text{is} \end{Bmatrix}$ *comfortable.*

Comfortable tells us *what kind of* chair it is.

Adverbs tell us about verbs:

He was sitting *comfortably.*

Comfortably tells us *how* he was sitting.

Adverbs also tell us about adjectives:

She was *conspicuously* silent.

The adverb tells us *in what way* she was silent.

They were *noticeably* angry.

The adverb tells us *in what way* they were angry.

B. A common adverb ending is -*ly.* Occasionally, however, -*ly* will be found on words that are *not* adverbs, such as *friendly* and *lovely,* so be careful.

C. In section 4 of your notebook, write down the adverb forms of the following adjectives: *happy, simple, careful, successful, fortunate, basic, angry, possible.* If necessary, use your dictionary to help you.

140

(See Answer Key, p. 305.)

D. Adverbs that tell us how an action occurs can appear in different positions in a sentence. Note the following:

Adverb	Subject	Adverb	Verb + Object	Adverb
Systematically,	the teacher		reviewed the tenses.	
	The teacher		reviewed the tenses	systematically.
	The teacher	systematically	reviewed the tenses.	

But while an adverb can be moved around in a sentence, it can *never* be placed between the verb and a short object. The following sentence is not acceptable in English:

*The teacher reviewed *systematically* the tenses.

E. Another type of adverb that can be moved around in a sentence is one that tells us about the whole sentence: for example, *fortunately, actually, obviously, certainly,* and *recently.*

Certainly, he is very intelligent.
He is *certainly* very intelligent.
He is very intelligent, *certainly.*

F. Many adverbs of frequency tell us about the whole sentence and not just about the verb. They do not always end in *-ly* and can be placed in different positions in the sentence. These adverbs include *always, sometimes, often, seldom, usually,* and *frequently.* For example:

She is *always* tactful. (after single *be* verb)
She *always* behaves tactfully. (before single verb)
She has *always* spoken tactfully to her boss. (after first auxiliary verb)

G. Underline the adverbs used in the first two paragraphs of "From *Househusbands*" by William R. Beer on p. 284. (See Answer Key, p. 305.) Then use the same words in sentences of your own. Write the sentences in section 4 of your notebook.

Editing Advice

If you are worried about whether you have used an adverb correctly, ask yourself the following questions:

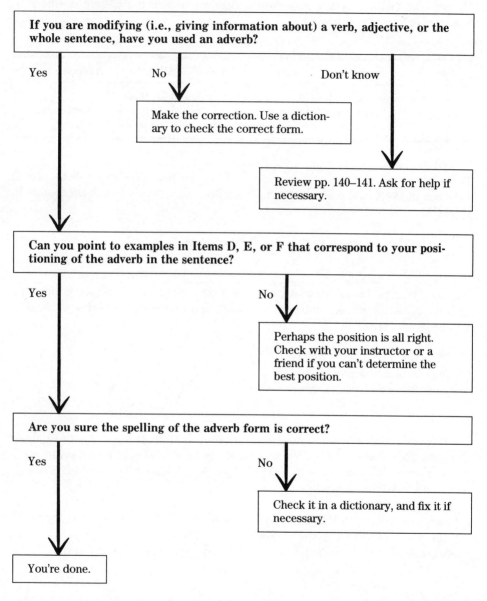

If you are modifying (i.e., giving information about) a verb, adjective, or the whole sentence, have you used an adverb?

Yes   No   Don't know

Make the correction. Use a dictionary to check the correct form.

Review pp. 140–141. Ask for help if necessary.

Can you point to examples in Items D, E, or F that correspond to your positioning of the adverb in the sentence?

Yes   No

Perhaps the position is all right. Check with your instructor or a friend if you can't determine the best position.

Are you sure the spelling of the adverb form is correct?

Yes   No

Check it in a dictionary, and fix it if necessary.

You're done.

-ing *and Participle Forms*

> *Question:* **How can I avoid errors with *-ing* forms and participle (*-ed/-en*) forms?**

A. Word forms that end with *-ing* are used in the following ways:

1. As part of a complete active verb phrase, with one or more auxiliaries:

   He is
   He was
   He will be   paint*ing* the house.
   He should be
   He has been
   etc.
   (See also pp. 109–110 in Troublespot 7, "Verb Tenses.")

2. To include additional information in the sentence:

   The woman *wearing* blue jeans is his sister.
   (The woman is wearing blue jeans.)

   Walking as quickly as I could, I managed to get out of sight.
   (I was walking quickly.)

   Hurrying along the street, I saw them get into their car.
   (I was hurrying.)

   I saw him *hurrying* along the street.
   (He was hurrying.)

   She left early, *promising* to return soon.
   (She promised to return.)

   Driving over the bridge, we admired the lights of the city.
   (We were driving.)

   But not *Driving over the bridge, the lights looked beautiful.
   (Why not? Because the lights weren't driving!)

   Note how all these *-ing* phrases express an active meaning.

143

3. As adjectives:

a *crying* baby (The baby is crying.)
an *interesting* movie (The movie interested us.)
The play was very *boring*. (The play bored us.)
The race was *exhausting*. (The race exhausted the runners.)

4. As nouns (*-ing* nouns are called *gerunds*):

a. As the subject of the sentence:

Swimming is good for you.
Driving on icy roads is dangerous.

b. As the object of certain verbs:

She *dislikes swimming*.
He *enjoys playing* tennis.
She *avoids driving* on icy roads.
He *finished cooking* dinner at 8 P.M.
The thief *denied having* taken the television.
They *postponed holding* the meeting.

There are other verbs regularly followed by the *-ing* noun form. Note them as you come across them in your reading.

c. After certain verb phrases with prepositions:

They *insisted on paying* for themselves.

Other verb phrases include:

approve of	get (be) used to
blame for	look forward to
complain about	suspect of
get (be) accustomed to	thank for

5. In idiomatic expressions with the verb *go:*

to go shopping	to go skating
to go fishing	to go swimming
to go dancing	to go sightseeing
to go bowling	

B. Participles (*-ed/-en* words) are used in the following ways:

1. As part of a complete active verb phrase with *have* auxiliaries:

He *has painted* the house.
They *had painted* the house before I arrived.

See also Troublespot 8, "Verb Forms."

2. As part of a complete passive verb phrase with *be/being* auxiliaries:

The house
{
is
is being
was
was being
will be
should be
has been
had been
might be
might have been
etc.
}
painted.

(See also Troublespot 10, "Active and Passive."

3. To add information to a sentence:

Confused by the people and traffic, Jack wandered around for hours before he found his sister's apartment building.
(Jack was confused.)

Begun five years ago, the building had never progressed beyond the foundations.
(The building was begun five years ago.)

When *depressed* by responsibilities, [the lawyer] retires to the basement and blows on the old trombone. (Csikszentmihalyi and Rochberg-Halton, p. 217)
(When the lawyer is depressed by his responsibilities, he . . . .)

The food *prepared* in that restaurant is very exotic.
(The food that is prepared by the chef in that restaurant is very exotic.)

Note how all the preceding participial phrases express a passive meaning.

4. As adjectives:

an *exhausted* swimmer
The swimmer was *exhausted* after the race.
The *exhausted* swimmer collapsed after the race.

C. Sometimes writers mix up the *-ing* and *-ed/-en* forms. Study these correct sentences:

Football *interests* a lot of people. (*Interests* is a verb.)

Football is an *interesting* sport.
Football is *interesting* to Pat's two children.
Pat's children are *interested* in football.
Interested in the match, the children stayed home from school to watch it.

D. Write as many sentences as you can using each of the following groups of words. Use the past-tense verb form, the *-ing* form, and the participle *(-ed/-en)* forms of the first word of each group. Add any other words you need.

1. annoy	Julie	the loud radio
2. confuse	the students	the difficult lecture
3. surprise	we (or) us	the end of the movie

(See Answer Key, p. 305.)

E. In the following passages from the readings in Part III, fill in the *-ing* or the participle form of the given verb:

1. Just as many of us are aware of *(save)* _____ special things to pre-

serve memories or enhance relationships, we've also felt that by *(get rid)*

_____ of gifts, photos, letters, we're *(mark)* _____ the end of

a period or relationship. (Stern, p. 215)

2. When I watch Emily *(collect)* _____ eggs in the evening, *(fish)*

_____ with Jim on the river or *(enjoy)* _____ an old-fash-

ioned picnic in the orchard with the entire family, I know we've *(find)*

_____ just what we were *(look)* _____ for. (Doherty, p. 197)

3. *(Construct)* _____ as a piece of junk, the building will be *(discard)*

_____ when it wears out, and another piece of junk will be *(set)*

_____ in its place. (Baker, p. 242)

4. Japan was *(force)* _____ to go robotic to remain competitive. The

United States, too, will be *(fill)* _____ many of today's blue-collar jobs

with robots. The *(displace)* _____ workers will have to learn the new

skills necessary to build and maintain the robots. (Cetron, p. 244)

5. What is clear is that few such men exist today, although women still seem

(surprise) _____ and *(disappoint)* _____ when they can't

find them. (Novak, p. 282)

(See Answer Key, p. 306.)

F. Rewrite the following pairs of sentences as one sentence by using an *-ing* or a participle phrase to include the first sentence in the second. Make the second sentence your new independent clause. For example:

He felt hungry.
He bought three slices of pizza.
New sentence: Feeling very hungry, he bought three slices of pizza.

  1. She wanted to get the job.
     She arrived early for the interview.

  2. The gray-haired man is wearing a blue coat.
     The gray-haired man is my father. (Begin with "The gray-haired man.")

  3. The movie excited us.
     We saw a movie last week.

  4. The student was confused by the examination questions.
     The student failed the exam.

  5. A painting was stolen from the museum yesterday.
     The painting was extremely valuable.

  6. The little boy was asked to share his toys.
     The little boy screamed and cried.

  7. She played in the tennis tournament.
     She twisted her ankle.

  (See Answer Key, p. 306.)

Editing Advice

If you have problems with *-ing* and participle forms, ask the following questions about each troublesome sentence:

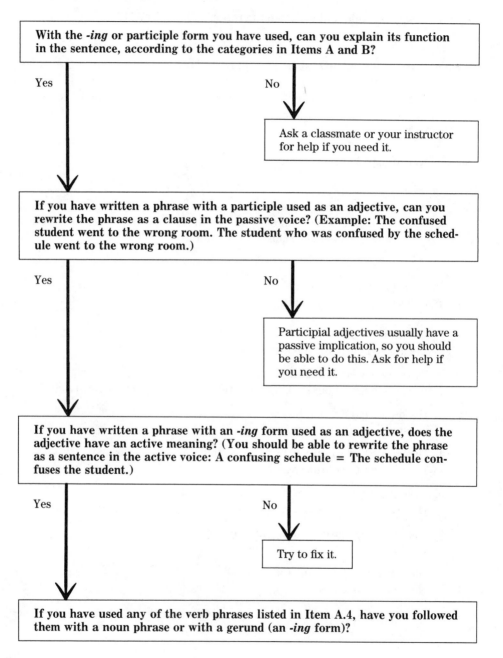

With the *-ing* or participle form you have used, can you explain its function in the sentence, according to the categories in Items A and B?

Yes   No

Ask a classmate or your instructor for help if you need it.

If you have written a phrase with a participle used as an adjective, can you rewrite the phrase as a clause in the passive voice? (Example: The confused student went to the wrong room. The student who was confused by the schedule went to the wrong room.)

Yes   No

Participial adjectives usually have a passive implication, so you should be able to do this. Ask for help if you need it.

If you have written a phrase with an *-ing* form used as an adjective, does the adjective have an active meaning? (You should be able to rewrite the phrase as a sentence in the active voice: A confusing schedule = The schedule confuses the student.)

Yes   No

Try to fix it.

If you have used any of the verb phrases listed in Item A.4, have you followed them with a noun phrase or with a gerund (an *-ing* form)?

(Flow chart continued)

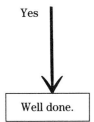

Yes

Well done.

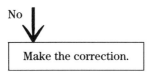

No

Make the correction.

Relative Clauses

> **Question:** What do I need to know about clauses with *who, whom, whose, which,* and *that?*

A. Relative clauses tell the reader more about a noun phrase:

The boy kept looking at his watch.
(The boy was waiting at the corner.)
The boy *who was waiting at the corner* kept looking at his watch.

The independent clause is *The boy kept looking at his watch.* The clause *who was waiting on the corner* tells the reader more about *the boy;* it tells the reader which boy we mean.

B. A relative clause is combined with (or *embedded in*) an independent clause in the following way, with the relative clause following its referent (the head noun it refers back to):

1. I bought a suit.
   (The suit made me look thinner.)
   I bought the suit *that made me look thinner.*
2. I bought a suit.
   (My mother liked the suit.)
   I bought the suit *that my mother liked.*
   or I bought the suit *my mother liked.*
   That can be omitted if the pronoun is the object of its own clause. See Item D.
3. The person was wearing the same suit. I took over the person's job.
   The person *whose job I took over* was wearing the same suit.

C. The relative pronouns *who, which,* and *that* can refer back to singular or plural noun phrases. When *who, which,* or *that* is the subject of its relative clause, the verb of that clause agrees with the noun phrase that the pronoun refers back to:

The *journalist who wants* to interview you *works* for a newsmagazine.

The *journalists who want* to interview you *work* for a newsmagazine.

Note that we do *not* repeat the subject of the sentence—*journalist(s)*—after the relative clause. The following sentence is *wrong* in English:

*The journalists who want to interview you *they* work for a newsmagazine.

They should be omitted here. The subject of the verb *work*—that is, *journalists*—has already been stated.

D. When the relative pronoun—*who(m)*, *which*, *that*—is the object of its own clause, it can be omitted:

I bought the suit that my mother liked. (My mother liked the suit.)
I bought the suit my mother liked.
I didn't buy the suit (that) I really liked!

E. Sentences that combine prepositions with relative pronouns require special attention.

The woman is a teacher.
(My friend is talking to the woman.)

There are five possible ways to combine these sentences:

1. The woman *whom* my friend is talking *to* is a teacher.
2. The woman *who* my friend is talking *to* is a teacher.
(Some people now accept the *who* form in the object position in the relative clause. Others, however, insist on the first version (with *whom*), which is more formally "correct." Ask your instructor which form you should use in your classes.
3. The woman *that* my friend is talking *to* is a teacher.
4. The woman my friend is talking *to* is a teacher.
5. The woman *to whom* my friend is talking is a teacher.

Note that you cannot use *that* as a relative pronoun immediately after a preposition. In the last example, *whom* is the only pronoun possible after *to*.

F. Use the box on p. 152 to help you determine which relative pronoun to use. You see from the box that you can use the word *that* as a relative pronoun in both subject and object positions. There are times, however, when you *cannot* use *that* as the relative pronoun in these positions:

1. When the relative clause gives additional information about a unique person, thing, or event. The clause does not define or restrict which person, thing, or event the writer means, but adds information about a person or

Position within clause	Relative pronoun refers to:	
	people	*things/concepts*
subject	who that	which that
direct object	who/whom that (omitted)	which that (omitted)
possessive	whose	whose of which

thing that has already been identified. Relative clauses like this use *who*, *whom*, and *which*; they also have commas around them, as in these sentences from the readings:

Sandy's folks, who live nearby, are a couple of chicken pluckers . . . . (Doherty, p. 195)
She's engaged to my father, who stands beside her in a dark suit. (Johnson, p. 224)
The girls absorbed these matters with greater facility than Douglas, who tended to ask the reason for everything . . . . (Connell, p. 260)

Note that in each case the referent is unique: *Sandy's folks, my father, Douglas.*
       If your referent is not a proper noun or a unique person or thing, then the relative clause is restrictive and you will not use commas (as in the examples in Items A through E). *When in doubt, leave the comma out.*

2. When the relative pronoun refers to the whole of the previous clause:

He moved to the country, which he had always wanted to do.

3. When the relative pronoun follows a preposition:

The controversy to which the author is referring has not yet been resolved.

G. Combine each of the following pairs of sentences into one sentence, using a relative clause. (Refer to the box in Item F if you need help.) Pay special attention to which of the two sentences you want to embed in the other. How does it change the sense of the sentence if you do it another way? Only one of these sentences will need commas around the relative clause. Which one is it?

1. The man was awarded a prize. The man won the race.
2. The girl is sitting in the front row. The girl asks a lot of questions.
3. The people are from California. I met the people at a party last night.
4. The house is gigantic. He is living in the house.
5. Ms. McHam lives next door to me. Ms. McHam is a lawyer.
6. The journalist has won a lot of prizes. You read the journalist's story yesterday.
7. The radio was made in Taiwan. I bought the radio.
8. She told her friends about the book. She had just read the book.
9. The man is a radio announcer. I am looking after the man's dog.

(See Answer Key, p. 306.)

H. Combine the following pairs of sentences by making the second sentence into a relative clause. Separate the clauses with a comma, because you are providing additional rather than necessary information. Introduce the relative clause with expressions like the following: *some of whom/which, one of whom/which, many of whom/which, none of whom/which, neither of whom/which, most of whom/which.* For example:

She has three sisters. None of them will help her.
She has three sisters, *none of whom* will help her.

1. At the lecture there were thirty-three people. Most of them lived in the neighborhood.
2. They waited half an hour for the committee members. Some of them just did not show up.
3. I sang three songs. One of them was "Singing in the Rain."
4. The statewide poetry competition was held last month, and she submitted four poems. None of them won a prize.
5. On every wall of his house, he has hundreds of books. Most of them are detective novels.

(See Answer Key, p. 306.)

Editing Advice

If you want to check that you have used a relative clause correctly, ask the following questions:

Can you identify both the independent clause and the relative clause in your sentence?

(Flow chart continued)

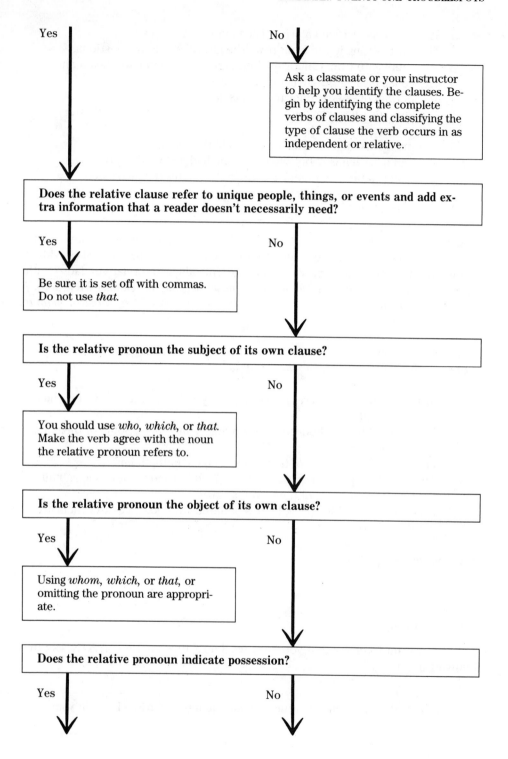

Yes

No

Ask a classmate or your instructor to help you identify the clauses. Begin by identifying the complete verbs of clauses and classifying the type of clause the verb occurs in as independent or relative.

Does the relative clause refer to unique people, things, or events and add extra information that a reader doesn't necessarily need?

Yes

No

Be sure it is set off with commas. Do not use *that.*

Is the relative pronoun the subject of its own clause?

Yes

No

You should use *who, which,* or *that.* Make the verb agree with the noun the relative pronoun refers to.

Is the relative pronoun the object of its own clause?

Yes

No

Using *whom, which,* or *that,* or omitting the pronoun are appropriate.

Does the relative pronoun indicate possession?

Yes

No

(Flow chart continued)

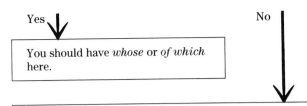

Yes

You should have *whose* or *of which* here.

No

Is the relative pronoun the object of a preposition?

Yes

Follow either of these patterns:

The apartment (that) she is living in is huge.
The apartment in which she is living is huge.

TROUBLESPOT 17

Conditions

> *Question:* **What do I need to be aware of when I write sentences with**
> ***if?***

A. There are four types of conditions you can express:

fact
future prediction
speculation about present or future
past speculation (contrary to fact)

The type of condition you write depends upon the meaning you want to express.

1. The following sentences express conditions of *fact:*

   If the roosters are not butchered, they gobble up a lot of feed. (Doherty, p. 195)
   If water freezes, it turns into ice.
   If you hear a quick "beep," it's the busy signal.
   If it's Thursday, I have to go to my exercise class.

2. The following sentences express conditions of *future prediction:*

   If the current rate of divorce persists, about half of all children will spend some time in a single-parent family before they reach eighteen. (Cherlin and Furstenberg, p. 268)
   If I get promoted, I will be very happy.
   She might take the job if she can work a shorter day.

3. The following sentences express conditions of *present-future speculation:*

   If either of us stopped working outside the home, the division of responsibility would certainly change. (Beer, p. 284)
   If I were a mommy, I'd be a doctor. (Shreve, p. 288)
   If the current recession were to end tomorrow, probably 1.2 million of the more than 11 million unemployed in the United States today would never be able to return to their old jobs. (Cetron, p. 243)
   If I had enough money, I would take a long vacation.
   If my grandparents were alive today, they would be shocked by that bathing suit.

When you write sentences like these, the reader should understand them in the following way:

If I had enough money—but I don't— . . . .
If my grandparents were alive today—but they aren't— . . . .

4. The following sentences express conditions of *past speculation* (contrary to fact):

If she had applied for the management training program last year, she would have learned about financial planning. (But she didn't apply, so she didn't learn about financial planning.)

She wouldn't have paid her employees such high salaries if she had known about financial planning. (But she didn't know about financial planning, so she paid them too much.)

B. We can summarize the patterns of conditional verb tenses as shown in the box below. Some other forms can be used, and you will probably come across them in your reading. However, for the purpose of correctness in your own writing, use the box as a guide.

C. To practice using conditional forms, write short journal entries on these topics:

1. If you had $1 million, what would you do?
2. Tell a reader about something you once did that you wish you had not

CONDITIONAL SENTENCES

Meaning	*If clause*	*Independent clause*
Fact	Same tense in both (usually present)	
Future prediction	present	*will* *can* *should* *might* } + simple form
Present-future speculation	past *(were)*	*would* *could* etc. } + simple form
Past speculation	*had* + participle	*would have* *could have* etc. } + participle

done. How would your life have been different if this had not happened?

3. Think of something that is likely to happen. Tell your reader what will happen as a result if this other event occurs.

D. Rewrite the following sentences, using a conditional clause with *if*:

1. I didn't see him, so I didn't pay him the money I owed him. (If I had seen him . . . .)
2. She doesn't spend much time with her children, so she doesn't know their friends.
3. He didn't lock the windows; a burglar climbed in and took his jewelry.
4. The woman wasn't able to find an ambulance, so her husband died on the street.
5. He doesn't have anyone to help him, so he won't finish the job on time.

(See Answer Key, p. 307.)

Editing Advice

If you have doubts about the accuracy of the tenses in a sentence with a conditional clause, ask the following questions:

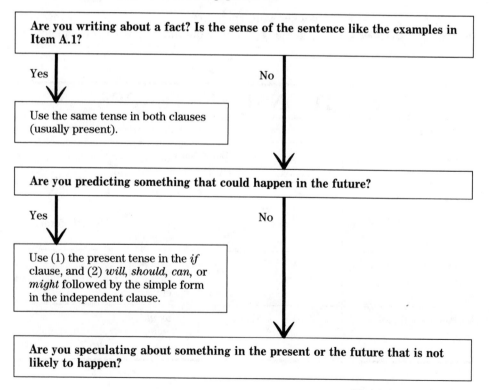

(Flow chart continued)

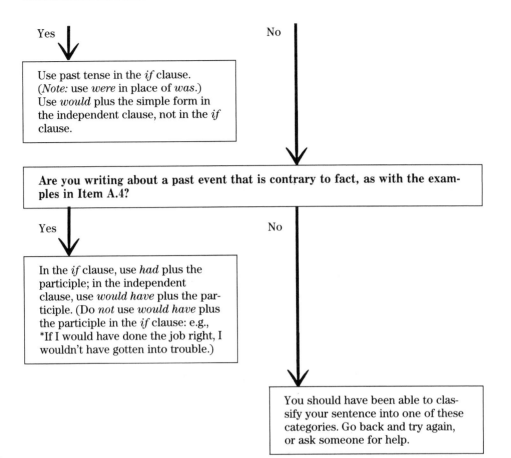

Yes

No

Use past tense in the *if* clause.
(*Note:* use *were* in place of *was*.)
Use *would* plus the simple form in
the independent clause, not in the *if*
clause.

Are you writing about a past event that is contrary to fact, as with the examples in Item A.4?

Yes

No

In the *if* clause, use *had* plus the
participle; in the independent
clause, use *would have* plus the participle. (Do *not* use *would have* plus
the participle in the *if* clause: e.g.,
*If I would have done the job right, I
wouldn't have gotten into trouble.)

You should have been able to classify your sentence into one of these
categories. Go back and try again,
or ask someone for help.

TROUBLESPOT 18

Quoting and Citing Sources

> *Question:* **When and how do I quote a speaker or writer?**

A. Look at the following passage:

>   Mrs. Stein, with her hat on, came back into the room, digging into her purse.
>   "Marilyn and I are going to that new Italian place," she said, "and I've lost the address. It's that real elegant place where they serve everything burning on a sword."
>   Priscilla started coughing.
>   "I think that cough is psychosomatic*," Lee said.
>   Priscilla put a handkerchief to her lips, and Mrs. Stein said, "What does that mean? Does that mean we'll all get it?"
>   "Probably," Lee said. "Probably."
>   "Ah, here it is," the woman exclaimed, snatching a piece of paper from her purse. "Priscilla, don't light another cigarette."
>   Priscilla was moving a hand around in the pocket of her mink coat.
>   "What's this?" she asked, pulling out a small box. "Lee, it's for you."
>   She handed him the box, which was from Tiffany's, and he opened it and found a pair of gold cuff links.

Answer the following questions about the passage. Write your answers in section 4 of your notebook.

1. How are quotation marks and capital letters used with the following: (a) part of a sentence, (b) a complete sentence, and (c) more than one sentence?
2. What is the relative position of quotation marks and end-of-quotation punctuation?
3. What punctuation separates an introductory phrase like "He said" from a quotation?
4. When is a capital letter used to introduce a quotation—and when isn't one used?

---

*psychosomatic: caused by state of mind
Source: Aubrey Goodman, *The Golden Youth of Lee Prince*. Greenwich, Connecticut: Crest Books, 1959, p. 312.

5. With dialogue, when are new paragraphs formed?

(See Answer Key, p. 307.)

B. In the preceding passage, which is from a novel, direct quotation is used to record the exact words of a conversation. When you want to record dialogue directly, use direct quotation. You may also want to quote directly when you are writing an essay. Try to quote directly only passages that are particularly noteworthy, or do a great deal to support the point you want to make. You can quote whole sentences or parts of sentences.

Look carefully at the type of material quoted and at the punctuation and capitalization used with the quotation in these examples from the readings:

1. That can have important implications for the kids. "In general, the more question-asking the parents do, the higher the children's IQ's," Lewis says. ("The Analysts Who Came to Dinner," p. 263)
2. Some men do help out, but for most husbands dinnertime remains a relaxing hour. While the female cooks and serves, Lewis says, "the male sits back and eats." ("The Analysts Who Came to Dinner," p. 263)
3. Dr. Entin believes that pictures often say more than words because "people do not guard their body language with the same vigor as their words." (Brody, p. 265)

How does the usage in these examples compare with the answers you gave to the questions in Item A?

C. Whenever you quote, you need to cite your source. That is, you need to tell your reader who said or wrote the words, where they appeared, and when. Sometimes, you might want to refer to an authority, but not quote exact words. In the following passage, the author does not quote directly but summarizes an expert's opinion on a controversial issue. However, the author still cites her source and lets us know where she found that opinion expressed:

In fact, based on interviews with hundreds of executives for her book *Paths to Power: A Woman's Guide From First Job to Top Executive* (Addison-Wesley, 1980), Ms. Josefowitz says that women are better managers than men. (Schnack, p. 279)

Here the author tells us the title of the book, the author's name, the publisher, and the date of publication. When you write academic essays, you usually do not give all this information in the text of your essay, but at the end. You need to give your readers all the information they need to locate the source, including the exact page where you found the information.

Various disciplines have certain guidelines for citing sources. If you have to write a paper for a psychology course, for instance, make sure you ask your instructor what form to use. For essays in the humanities, for example, the Modern Language Association (MLA) recommends that you give a brief reference in parentheses in your text, so that your reader knows the author's name and the page number. Then, at the end of the essay, you include a list (alphabetical by author) of Works Cited, with full bibliographical details of each source.

The following example is a passage from an essay that cites two readings from Part III.

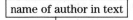
name of author in text

We have seen how children can form great passions for their favorite possessions. Costello points out how children are at first simply attached to treasures; then later, they form collections of objects that some adults regard as junk; these objects, however, serve the purpose of allowing children to "practice negotiation skills in acquiring and exchanging property" (108). Teenagers, of course, can also show disregard for small mundane possessions, throwing away a comb just because it is dirty (Connell 114).

author and page
numbers in parentheses

page numbers
in parentheses

At the end of the essay, a list of Works Cited would appear, containing, in alphabetical order, the following two entries:

WORKS CITED

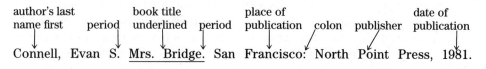

author's last   book title   place of   date of
name first   period   underlined   period   publication   colon   publisher   publication

Connell, Evan S. Mrs. Bridge. San Francisco: North Point Press, 1981.

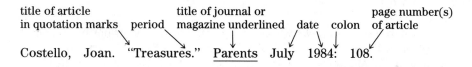

title of article   title of journal or   page number(s)
in quotation marks   period   magazine underlined   date   colon   of article

Costello, Joan. "Treasures." Parents July 1984: 108.

D. See also the example in Chapter 12 in Part I, pp. 59–62. Read "The Chrysler and the Comb" on p. 209. In one paragraph, summarize in your own words the conversation between Mrs. Bridge and her daughter. Include two direct quotations: one complete sentence and one part of a sentence. For practice, add a reference to your source in parentheses (for the reference for "The Chrysler and the Comb," see the Acknowledgments section), and list the novel in a Works Cited section at the end of your paragraph. Show your paragraph to your instructor, and explain why you chose your two direct quotations. What seemed special about them?

Editing Advice

If you have quoted directly in your piece of writing, ask these questions:

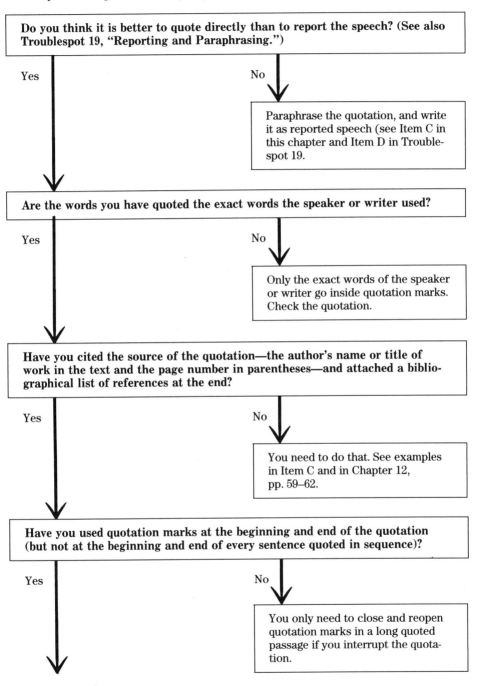

Do you think it is better to quote directly than to report the speech? (See also Troublespot 19, "Reporting and Paraphrasing.")

Yes   No

Paraphrase the quotation, and write it as reported speech (see Item C in this chapter and Item D in Troublespot 19.

Are the words you have quoted the exact words the speaker or writer used?

Yes   No

Only the exact words of the speaker or writer go inside quotation marks. Check the quotation.

Have you cited the source of the quotation—the author's name or title of work in the text and the page number in parentheses—and attached a bibliographical list of references at the end?

Yes   No

You need to do that. See examples in Item C and in Chapter 12, pp. 59–62.

Have you used quotation marks at the beginning and end of the quotation (but not at the beginning and end of every sentence quoted in sequence)?

Yes   No

You only need to close and reopen quotation marks in a long quoted passage if you interrupt the quotation.

(Flow chart continued)

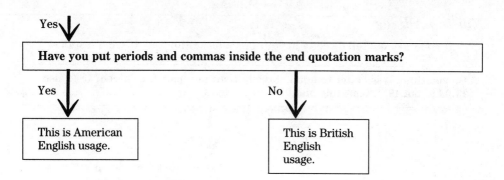

Yes

Have you put periods and commas inside the end quotation marks?

Yes

This is American
English usage.

No

This is British
English
usage.

Reporting and Paraphrasing

> *Question:* **How is reporting what I hear or read different from quoting directly?**

A. We use direct quotation when we are writing dialogue or when we are telling the reader exactly what somebody else said or wrote, word for word. We quote exact words when those words are particularly appropriate. If, however, we want to convey general ideas rather than exact words, we usually use reported speech. Note the difference in form:

The mayor asks, "How am I doing?"
The mayor asks how he is doing.

Here the introductory verb is in the present tense. With an introductory verb in the past, we would write this:

The mayor asked how he was doing.

Look closely at the two sentences below. Count the number of differences you can find between them.

The woman asked, "Where are my glasses?"
The woman asked where her glasses were.

(See Answer Key, p. 307.)

Sometimes, particularly when we report a long piece of speech or writing, it is better to paraphrase—that is, express in our own words the intention of the speaker or writer:

The mayor asked the people to assess his progress.
The woman wanted to find her glasses.

B. Look at the cartoon at the top of the next page. Write a description of each frame of the four-frame cartoon. First, quote directly what the characters Lucy and Charlie Brown say, using quotation marks. Begin like this:

© 1959 United Feature Syndicate, Inc.

One day Lucy was sitting and offering psychiatric help for five cents. Charlie Brown came along, sat down, and said, ". . . ."

(See Answer Key, p. 308.)

C. Now, rewrite your description of the cartoon. This time use reported speech. Keep the reported speech as close to the original quotations as possible. Observe the following conventions:

1. Do not use quotation marks.
2. Do not use a question mark at the end of a reported question.
3. In a reported question, use statement word order (subject + verb) and not question word order.
4. After an introductory verb in the past (like *said*), use past-tense verbs for the reported speech.
5. Pronouns like *I, we, you* change when you write reported speech.
6. *This* and *these* change to *that* and *those*.
7. Incomplete sentences usually have to be reworded slightly when they are reported.
8. Do not use the same introductory verb every time. Introductory verbs include *say, ask, tell someone to . . . , reply, complain, advise someone to . . . , want to know,* and others.

Begin like this:

> One day Lucy was sitting and offering psychiatric help for five cents. Charlie Brown came along, sat down, and said that . . . .

(See Answer Key, p. 308.)

D. Usually, when we report speech, we do not simply transform the original words into reported speech. Instead, we tell about the ideas that were expressed, using our own words. That is, we paraphrase. A paraphrased report might look like this:

> One day, when Lucy was offering psychiatric help for five cents, Charlie Brown visited her booth and complained of depression. He wanted advice on how to deal with it, but Lucy simply urged him not to be depressed—and charged him five cents anyway!

In an essay, always state where ideas come from. Even if you do not quote another writer exactly but just refer to and paraphrase his or her ideas, you still have to say where those ideas came from. You need to state the name of the author, the title of the work, the place and date of publication, and the publisher. You do this by mentioning the author or title and the page number (in parentheses) in your text and then giving the full bibliographic reference at the end of the paper. (See Item C in Troublespot 18 for examples.) Using another author's words or ideas as your own and not citing the source is *plagiarism.* This is *not acceptable* and could be illegal. For different methods of citing the sources of your ideas, consult your instructor or a handbook.

E. Look at the passage from *The Golden Youth of Lee Prince* on p. 160. With the book open in front of you, rewrite the passage, changing all the direct speech to reported speech. Use no direct quotation at all. Begin like this:

> Mrs. Stein told the people in the room that she and Marilyn were going to a new Italian restaurant . . . .

(See Answer Key, p. 308.)

Now, close the book, and write another account of the conversation you have just rewritten. This time rely on your memory. Paraphrase the passage, and do not use any direct quotation. Concentrate on conveying the main gist of the conversation. The reporting does not have to be an exact sentence-by-sentence replica of the original.

Editing Advice

If you have written about what somebody else said or wrote, ask these questions:

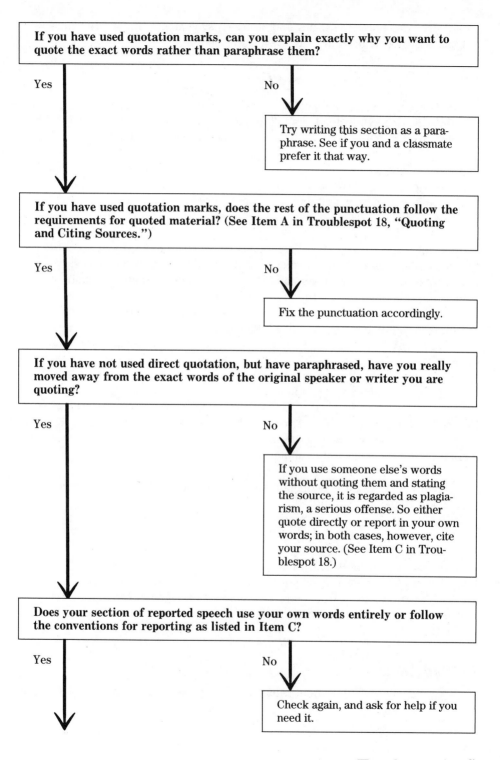

If you have used quotation marks, can you explain exactly why you want to quote the exact words rather than paraphrase them?

Yes | No

Try writing this section as a paraphrase. See if you and a classmate prefer it that way.

If you have used quotation marks, does the rest of the punctuation follow the requirements for quoted material? (See Item A in Troublespot 18, "Quoting and Citing Sources.")

Yes | No

Fix the punctuation accordingly.

If you have not used direct quotation, but have paraphrased, have you really moved away from the exact words of the original speaker or writer you are quoting?

Yes | No

If you use someone else's words without quoting them and stating the source, it is regarded as plagiarism, a serious offense. So either quote directly or report in your own words; in both cases, however, cite your source. (See Item C in Troublespot 18.)

Does your section of reported speech use your own words entirely or follow the conventions for reporting as listed in Item C?

Yes | No

Check again, and ask for help if you need it.

(Flow chart continued)

Yes

Now acknowledge the source of
your information briefly in the text
and then fully in a bibliographic reference at the end. (See Item D in
this chapter and Item C in Troublespot 18.)

TROUBLESPOT 20

Apostrophes for Possession

> *Question:* **How do I know whether to write *'s* or *-s'*?**

A. When we speak, -*'s* and *-s'* sound the same. But there is a difference in writing. Look at the following sentences:

1. a. The girl has a computer.   1. b. It is the girl's computer.
2. a. The girls have a computer.   2. b. It is the girls' computer.
3. a. The man has a computer.   3. b. It is the man's computer.
4. a. The men have a computer.   4. b. It is the men's computer.

What do you note about the four sentences labeled *b*? Why do you think sentence 2b looks different from the others? Write down an explanation. Look closely at the four sentences labeled *a* to help you find the answers. (See Answer Key, p. 308.)

B. Rewrite each of the following pairs of sentences as one sentence. Use an apostrophe to show possession. Make the italicized verb the verb of your new sentence. For example,

Their daughters took a vacation.
The vacation *was* wonderful.
New sentence: Their daughters' vacation was wonderful.

1. The baby has some toys.
   The toys *are* all over the floor.
2. The babies were crying.
   The crying *kept* everyone awake.
3. The house belongs to my family.
   The house *is* gigantic.
4. Ms. Johnson has a son.
   He *is* a lawyer.
5. The women have plans.
   Their plans *are* ambitious.
6. The politicians have plans.
   Their plans *are* ambitious.

(See Answer Key, p. 308.)

C. When you write two nouns together without an apostrophe and you want to check whether you need an apostrophe, see if you can reword the phrase using *of* or the idea of ownership:

*the girl computer = the computer of the girl *or,* the computer belonging to the girl

This phrase needs an apostrophe to show possession: *the girl's computer.*

If the idea of ownership does not work, as in *coffee shop,* you do not need an apostrophe. Also, if the first word of the two is the name of a building, an object, or a piece of furniture, you do not need an apostrophe: *hotel room, car door, table leg.*

Note: The possessive adjective *its* shows possession but is *never* used with an apostrophe. (The form *it's* means "it is.")

The college announced *its* new policy.
It's [it is] a good policy.

D. Rewrite the following phrases, using an apostrophe. For example:

the bone belonging to the dog
the dog's bone

1. the room belonging to their daughters (i.e., two daughters share a room)
2. the room belonging to their son (they have one son)
3. the advice of the president
4. the problems of the teachers
5. the efforts of Ms. Johnson
6. the toothbrush belonging to my brother
7. the house belonging to his mother-in-law
8. the decision made by my family

(See Answer Key, p. 309.)

Editing Advice

If you have trouble deciding when and where to put an apostrophe to show possession, look carefully at any two nouns that are together in your essay and ask these questions:

Is there an *of* or ownership relationship between the two nouns?

Yes ⬇   No ⬇

(Flow chart continued)

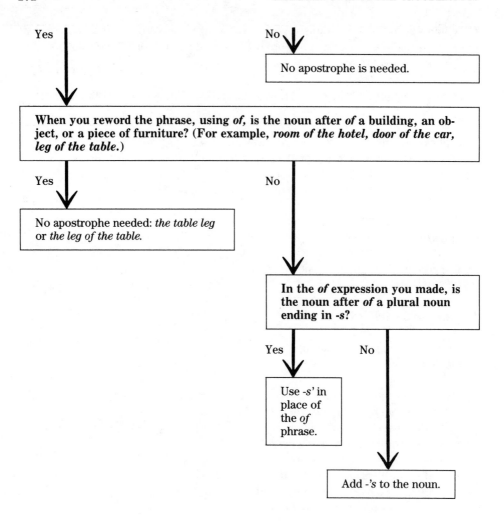

Yes

No

No apostrophe is needed.

When you reword the phrase, using *of,* is the noun after *of* a building, an object, or a piece of furniture? (For example, *room of the hotel, door of the car, leg of the table.*)

Yes

No

No apostrophe needed: *the table leg* or *the leg of the table.*

In the *of* expression you made, is the noun after *of* a plural noun ending in *-s*?

Yes

No

Use *-s'* in place of the *of* phrase.

Add *-'s* to the noun.

Commas

Question: What are the rules for using commas?

A. It is more common to overuse commas than to omit them when they are needed. So, you might be able to use the rule "When in doubt, leave it out." However, there are several cases where the conventions are clear enough that there should be no doubt.

B. Commas are usually used in the following instances:

1. To set off a word, phrase, or clause before the subject of the sentence. (Some writers omit the comma if the introductory phrase is short.) For example:

   Wanting to impress all their friends, Jane and Jack Jones bought a Rolls-Royce.
   Because they wanted to impress their friends, Jane and Jack Jones bought a Rolls-Royce.
   In the spring of last year, Jane and Jack Jones bought a Rolls-Royce.
   Actually, they prefer to ride bicycles.

   but:

   Yesterday Jane and Jack bought a Rolls-Royce.

2. To separate items in a list:

   For the picnic, they packed *cheese, ham, egg salad, and roast beef.*
   They had no *electricity, gas, plumbing, or central heating.* (Baker, p. 295)

3. To set off words, phrases, and clauses that are inserted as additional information at any position in the sentence. The reader does not need this information to understand the meaning of the independent clause. For example:

   Sally's boss, *a powerful individual,* refused to give her the day off.
   Sally's boss, *however,* refused to give her the day off.
   Sally's boss, *who had headed the company for fifteen years,* refused to give her the day off.

Sally's boss refused to give her any time off, *not even the day Sally had requested to attend her sister's wedding.*

You can think of these commas as a set of handles: they let you lift the enclosed words out of the sentence. After you do that, the reader will still be able to understand the sense of the independent clause: for example, "Sally's boss refused to give her the day off."

4. To set off a quotation:

F. Scott Fitzgerald said to his daughter, "Don't worry about anyone getting ahead of you."
"Don't worry about anyone getting ahead of you," F. Scott Fitzgerald said to his daughter.

5. To separate complete sentences joined by one of the seven connecting words *(and, but, or, nor, so, for, yet).* In your reading, you might sometimes see the comma omitted. However, if you follow this convention and include the comma, it will not be considered wrong.

I came from a home in which my father never did any housework, and I had never been obliged to do any either. (Beer, p. 284)

Note: A comma is *not* used before a clause introduced by the subordinating word *that:*

It was astonishing that they had any energy left. (Baker, p. 295)
He said that she should not worry.

C. Examine all the uses of commas in paragraphs 6 to 9 in the selection "From *Poor Russell's Almanac*" by Russell Baker on pp. 241–242. Try to fit each comma use into one of the five categories in Item B.

Example:
Nowadays, most fathers sit in glass buildings . . . . (The comma sets off a word before the subject of the sentence.)

(See Answer Key, p. 309.)

Editing Advice

To make sure that every comma in your essay is necessary, examine each comma use and ask these questions:

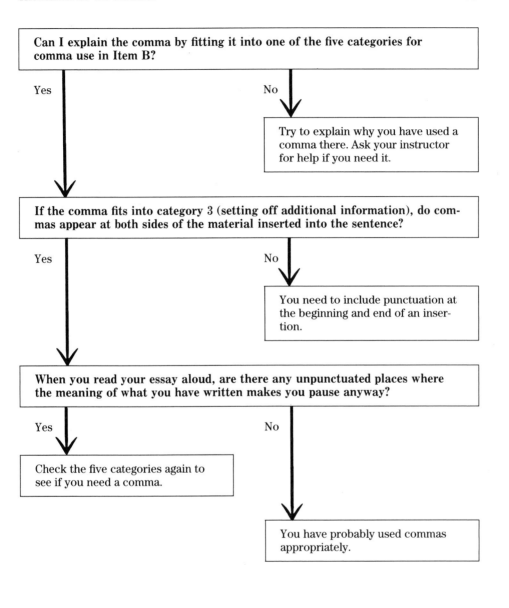

Can I explain the comma by fitting it into one of the five categories for comma use in Item B?

Yes   No

Try to explain why you have used a comma there. Ask your instructor for help if you need it.

If the comma fits into category 3 (setting off additional information), do commas appear at both sides of the material inserted into the sentence?

Yes   No

You need to include punctuation at the beginning and end of an insertion.

When you read your essay aloud, are there any unpunctuated places where the meaning of what you have written makes you pause anyway?

Yes   No

Check the five categories again to see if you need a comma.

You have probably used commas appropriately.

PART III ✳

MATERIALS ✳
Pictures
and Readings

Part III contains sets of pictures and readings grouped around five themes: Places, Possessions, Work, Family, and Men and Women. These materials will provide ideas to stimulate your thinking. You can refer to the materials when you do your own writing. They will also provide helpful vocabulary and structures that you can use when you write.

Chapter 2 of Part I asks you to choose a set of materials in Part III and to think about and write answers to the Preview Questions. You should then look at the pictures, read the passages, and answer some of the "Explorations" questions.

Each reading passage is glossed. The gloss defines the word in the context of the passage. The definitions are intended to help you understand the word in the sentence, so that you can continue reading quickly and enjoy the passage. The definitions are not intended to provide an understanding of all uses of the word.

1 ✳ Places

PREVIEW QUESTIONS

1. What places in your past evoke the strongest emotions for you—emotions such as pleasure, fear, hatred, or boredom? What places in your present life evoke strong emotions?

2. What places do you know that are undergoing change? What kind of change?

3. If you could choose any place in the world to live, where would you choose?

4. What places do you know that contrast greatly with each other?

1

Study and library in the house of Bronson Alcott, father of author Louisa May Alcott, Concord, Massachusetts, 1981, by Glynne Robinson Betts.

EXPLORATIONS

- What kind of person do you think this room belongs to?
- How would you change the room if you moved in?
- What similarities can you see between furnishing a room and doing a piece of writing?

2

Gas, 1940, by Edward Hopper.

EXPLORATIONS

- What kind of atmosphere does the picture create? For example, is it peaceful, exciting, sinister, frightening?
- What has Edward Hopper included in the painting that contributes to this atmosphere?
- Would the effect be different if there were more than one person in the picture?

3

The Empire of Lights, 1954, by Rene Magritte.

EXPLORATIONS

- How do you think the painter wants you to react to this painting?
- What general impression does the painting create, and which details help to form that impression?
- In this picture and the previous one, how do the artists use light, and for what effect?

4

Beach at Frederiksted, St. Croix, Virgin Islands, © by Phil Brodatz.

EXPLORATIONS

- Would you choose to spend a vacation here? Why or why not?
- Do you know any similar places in your own country? In which ways are they similar?
- What is the mood or atmosphere that the photographer wants to convey?

5

Jim Kalett/Photo Researchers.

EXPLORATIONS

- Which beach do you prefer: this one or the one in the previous picture? What kind of person would prefer the other beach?
- Which descriptive words (e.g., peaceful, exhausting) convey a general impression of what each beach is like? Which specific details in the photographs create this general impression?
- What sounds are evoked by this picture and the previous one?

6

Silver Peak, Nevada, 1940, by Arthur Rothstein.

EXPLORATIONS

- What kind of life do you think people lived in this town in 1940?
- How might the town have changed since 1940?
- Why do you think the photographer chose to photograph this place?
- Would you like to live there? Why or why not?

7

New York City, by Victor Laredo

EXPLORATIONS

- What are some advantages and disadvantages of living here, compared to where you live or compared to the town in the previous picture?
- This is obviously a big city. How has the photographer conveyed that impression so immediately?

8 *From* The Diary of a Young Girl

ANNE FRANK

Thursday, 9 July, 1942

Dear Kitty,*

So we walked in the pouring rain, Daddy, Mummy, and I, each with a school satchel° and shopping bag filled to the brim° with all kinds of things thrown together anyhow.°

We got sympathetic looks from people on their way to work. You could see by their faces how sorry they were they couldn't offer us a lift; the gaudy yellow star° spoke for itself.

Only when we were on the road did Mummy and Daddy begin to tell me bits and pieces about the plan. For months as many of our goods and chattels° and necessities of life as possible had been sent away and they were sufficiently ready for us to have gone into hiding of our own accord on July 16. The plan had had to be speeded up ten days because of the call-up,° so our quarters° would not be so well organized, but we had to make the best of it. The hiding place itself would be in the building where Daddy has his office. It will be hard for outsiders to understand, but I shall explain that later on. Daddy didn't have many people working for him: Mr. Kraler, Koophuis, Miep, and Elli Vossen, a twenty-three-year-old typist who all knew of our arrival. Mr. Vossen, Elli's father, and two boys worked in the warehouse;° they had not been told.

I will describe the building: there is a large warehouse on the ground floor which is used as a store. The front door to the house is next to the warehouse door, and inside the front door is a second doorway which leads to a staircase (A). There is another door at the top of the stairs, with a frosted glass window in it, which has "Office" written in black letters across it. That is the large main office, very big, very light, and very full. Elli, Miep, and Mr. Koophuis work there in the daytime. A small dark room containing the safe, a wardrobe, and a large cupboard leads to a small somewhat dark second office. Mr. Kraler and Mr. Van Daan used to sit here, now it is only Mr. Kraler. One can reach Kraler's office

°**satchel:** schoolbag
°**to the brim:** to the top
°**anyhow:** untidily

°**gaudy yellow star:** identification Jews were forced to wear by the Nazis
°**goods and chattels:** possessions

°**call-up:** summons to report to the S.S. (Special Guards) to be deported
°**quarters:** living space

°**warehouse:** storage area

*Anne Frank, a teenaged girl, gave the name *Kitty* to her diary to make it seem like a friend. She kept the diary for two years, while she and her family were hiding in Amsterdam during the Nazi occupation of the Netherlands. Anne Frank died in the concentration camp at Bergen-Belsen shortly before the end of World War II.

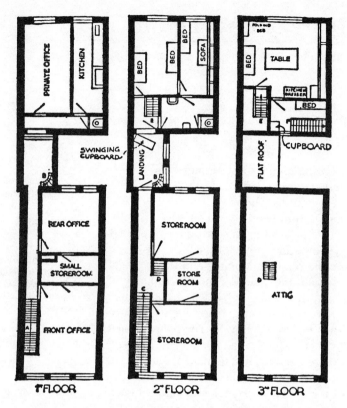

from the passage, but only via a glass door which can be opened from the inside, but not easily from the outside.

From Kraler's office a long passage goes past the coal store, up four steps and leads to the showroom of the whole building: the private office. Dark, dignified° furniture, linoleum and carpets on the floor, radio, smart lamp, everything first-class. Next door there is a roomy kitchen with a hot-water faucet and a gas stove. Next door the W.C.° That is the first floor.°

A wooden staircase leads from the downstairs passage to the next floor (B). There is a small landing at the top. There is a door at each end of the landing, the left one leading to a storeroom at the front of the house and to the attics. One of those really steep Dutch staircases runs from the side to the other door opening on to the street (C).

The right-hand door leads to our "Secret Annexe."° No one would ever guess that there would be so many rooms hidden behind that plain gray door. There's a little step in front of the door and then you are inside.

There is a steep staircase immediately opposite the entrance [E]. On the left a tiny passage brings you into a room which was

°**dignified:** formal-looking

°**W.C. (British):** water closet, toilet
°**first floor:** second floor (in American usage)

°**annexe:** additional part

to become the Frank family's bed-sitting-room, next door a smaller room, study and bedroom for the two young ladies of the family. On the right a little room without windows containing the washbasin and a small W.C. compartment, with another door leading to Margot's and my room. If you go up the next flight of stairs and open the door, you are simply amazed that there could be such a big light room in such an old house by the canal. There is a gas stove in this room (thanks to the fact that it was used as a laboratory) and a sink. This is now the kitchen for the Van Daan couple, besides being general living room, dining room, and scullery.°

°**scullery:** small room for washing dishes

   A tiny little corridor room will become Peter Van Daan's apartment. Then, just as on the lower landing, there is a large attic. So there you are, I've introduced you to the whole of our beautiful "Secret Annexe."

Yours, *Anne*

EXPLORATIONS

- If you did not have the map, could you visualize Anne Frank's Secret Annexe clearly?
- When you look at the map along with Anne Frank's description, how did she choose to organize the description? What plan did she use to organize her written description?

9 A Day in Shin-Ying

SIAO TAO KUO

It was six in the morning, but everybody in our family, including even our turkey and rooster, was awake. I didn't want to open my eyes because it seemed so bright outside. But I had to check and see if the mango° I had been watching for days had fallen into my mother's lily pond. This particularly good-looking mango had been hanging over the pond, from the highest limb of the tree. It was beyond the reach of a bamboo stick, even if you stood on a high stool. We just had to wait and hope it wouldn't fall into the muddy water. If that happened, it would be gone forever.

°**mango:** type of fruit

We lived in a Japanese style house in Shin-Ying, which is in the southern part of Taiwan. The front door of the house faced the front gate of the elementary school which every one of us children attended. My mother taught at the school. The school playground was our private playground during holidays. It was there that I learned how to ride a bicycle and to rollerskate.

Cleaning up the fallen leaves was my job every morning. We had all sorts of fruit trees in the front yard. Besides mango, there were banana, lichi, guava, and papaya trees. The grape vine was right by the pond and produced wonderful shade in the summer. My mother collected different colors of water lilies in this pond. We even tried to keep fish in there, because we had once bought too many for one meal. But most of them died a few days later. I think the sound of the fruit falling into the water upset the fish as much as it upset us.

I tried not to clean the yard too well, because I believed rotten leaves were good for the soil. Besides, I would have to clean up the next morning, anyway. When I saw the smoke from the chimney, I went in to wash myself, put on my school uniform, and have breakfast. I often ate ten pieces of toast, which amazed my friends.

Our high school was about an eight-minute bicycle ride from our house. School was fun. Normally, mornings went by faster than afternoons. At ten minutes to noon, my schoolmates and I would gather in front of the school and wait for lunch to arrive. My mother would usually rush home between classes to make my lunch and put it in a tin box, wrapped in a piece of cloth with a piece of fruit on the top of the box. A person who usually worked at the school would collect the lunch boxes from door to door and put them in two huge baskets that hung from the handlebars of his bicycle. He would bring them special delivery to the school.

190

When we caught sight of him, we crowded over and grabbed our lunch before he could park his bicycle.

A day wouldn't be complete if I didn't drop by Old Wang's stand to have a piece of corn. Old Wang made the best Bar-B-Q corn in the whole town. So, when I rode my bicycle home with a piece of corn in my hand, I was the happiest girl in the world.

After dinner, my family sat around under the grape vine, with the bright moon above us reflected in the water, drinking tea and talking about what had happened during the day. Sitting in the summer breeze, with the fragrance of flowers all around me, I felt more and more sleepy. After saying goodnight to everyone, on my way back to the house I heard, "Ker-plop-squish." My mango! I told myself there would be other mangoes, probably in my dreams that night.

EXPLORATIONS

- Which image forms a kind of frame for this essay, appearing in the opening and the concluding paragraphs?
- What does this image add to the piece of writing?

10 From "Returning to a Beloved Island"

RUTH GORDON

There are many places to which I return with pleasure again and again, but none more dripping with remembrance° and nostalgia° than the island of Martha's Vineyard: seven miles from the mainland of Cape Cod, a million miles from the world in which I do my work. For the island is now my home. Someone once said, "Home is where you keep your scrapbooks."° Mine are on Cottage Street in Edgartown.

°**dripping with remembrance:** full of memories
°**nostalgia:** sentimental thinking about the past
°**scrapbooks:** books for storing souvenirs

A little while ago, I stood across the road from the Teller House on Summer Street, looking into the distant, hazy° past.

°**hazy:** not clear

My father—once a rollicking° sea captain, later a melancholy° foreman at the Mellin's Food Company, 41 Central Wharf, Boston—always took his holidays somewhere by the sea. In the summer of 1898, when I was 2 years old, we came to Martha's Vineyard—I for the first time. Steam cars from Quincy to Boston, by sea to New Bedford, train to Woods Hole, ferry to Vineyard Haven, horsedrawn omnibus to Edgartown. A long day's journey. Now the trip takes 25 minutes by air.

°**rollicking:** high-spirited
°**melancholy:** sad

In Edgartown, we had stayed at the Teller House, and there it was, this Sunday afternoon, virtually unchanged° except that it is no longer a boardinghouse, but a private residence. At the town meeting last spring, the present owner approached me and invited me to come and visit—any time. Perhaps I shall. I would like to see the room where I spoke my first complete sentence. It was at breakfast. I was served a boardinghouse sliver° of cantaloupe. I am told that I looked up at the waitress, frowned and said, "When I'm home, I have *much!*" I do not remember the line, but I have a vague, indelible° memory of the place. I was to return to it intermittently° across the years, always meaning to stay longer and to come back more often—but life got in the way.

°**virtually unchanged:** almost unchanged

°**sliver:** very thin slice

°**indelible:** fixed
°**intermittently:** occasionally

EXPLORATIONS

- Are there any places to which you "return with pleasure again and again"? What are they?
- The author defines *home* as "where you keep your scrapbooks." How would you define *home*?
- What do you think the author means by "life got in the way"?

11 Mr. Doherty Builds His Dream Life

JIM DOHERTY

"To be a farmer and writer suggests a fickleness° of character. . ."—E. B. White

°**fickleness:** inconstancy, lack of stability

On a chilly morning not long ago, I went outside to feed the chickens and split some kindling° but ended up loafing° along the riverbank instead. Under a blanket of soggy° snow, the river was thawing. In the bare treetops, hundreds of red-winged blackbirds were fussing° and trilling.° Overhead, a skein° of Canada geese went gabbling by—then another and another. It was plain to see that the long Wisconsin winter was losing its grip. Back in the house after doing my chores, I wrote a hopeful little essay about spring and sent it off to a magazine. A few weeks later, a check arrived in the mail. It came, appropriately enough, on the first warm day of the year.

°**kindling:** sticks for a fire
°**loafing:** wasting time
°**soggy:** wet and heavy
°**fussing:** very active
°**trilling:** warbling (sound birds make)
°**skein:** flock (of geese)

There are two things I have always wanted to do—write and live on a farm. Today I'm doing both. I'm not in E. B. White's class as a writer or in my neighbors' league as a farmer, but I'm getting by. And after years of frustration with city and suburban living, my wife Sandy and I have finally found contentment here in the country.

It's a self-reliant sort of life. We grow nearly all of our fruits and vegetables. Our hens keep us in eggs, with several dozen left over to sell each week. Our bees provide us with honey, and we cut enough wood to just about make it through the heating season.

It's a satisfying life too. In the summer we canoe on the river, go picnicking in the woods and take long bicycle rides. In the winter we ski and skate. We get excited about sunsets. We love the smell of the earth warming and the sound of cattle lowing.° We watch for hawks in the sky and deer in the cornfields.

°**lowing:** mooing (sound cows make)

But the good life can get pretty tough. Three months ago when it was 30 below, we spent two miserable days hauling° firewood up the river on a toboggan. Three months from now, it will be 95 above and we will be cultivating corn, weeding strawberries and killing chickens. Recently, Sandy and I had to reshingle° the back roof. Soon Jim, 16, and Emily, 13, the youngest of our four children, will help me make some long-overdue improvements on the privy° that supplements our indoor plumbing when we are working outside. Later this month, we'll spray the orchard, paint the

°**hauling:** dragging

°**reshingle:** put on new roof shingles

°**privy:** outdoor toilet

barn, plant the garden and clean the hen house before the new chicks arrive.

In between such chores, I manage to spend 50 to 60 hours a week at the typewriter or doing reporting for the freelance° articles I sell to magazines and newspapers. Sandy, meanwhile, pursues her own hectic° rounds.° Besides the usual household routine, she oversees the garden and beehives, bakes bread, cans and freezes, chauffeurs° the kids to their music lessons, practices with them, takes organ lessons on her own, does research and typing for me, writes an article herself now and then, tends the flower beds, stacks a little wood and delivers the eggs. There is, as the old saying goes, no rest for the wicked on a place like this—and not much for the virtuous° either . . . .

°freelance: produced independently

°hectic: very busy
°rounds: activities

°chauffeurs: drives

°virtuous: good, pure

None of us will ever forget [our] first winter. We were buried under five feet of snow from December through March. While one storm after another blasted huge drifts up against the house and barn, we kept warm inside burning our own wood, eating our own apples and loving every minute of it.

When spring came, it brought two floods. First the river overflowed, covering much of our land for weeks. Then the growing season began, swamping us under wave after wave of produce. Our freezer filled up with cherries, raspberries, strawberries, asparagus, peas, beans and corn. Then our canned-goods shelves and cupboards began to grow with preserves, tomato juice, grape juice, plums, jams and jellies. Eventually, the basement floor disappeared under piles of potatoes, squash and pumpkins, and the barn became a repository° for bushels of apples and pears. It was amazing.

°repository: storage place

The next year we grew even more food and managed to get through the winter on six cords° of firewood—most of it our own—and only 100 gallons of heating oil. At that point I began thinking seriously about quitting my job and starting to freelance. The timing was terrible. By then, Shawn and Amy, our oldest girls, were attending expensive Ivy League schools° and we had only a few thousand dollars in the bank. Yet we kept coming back to the same question: Will there ever be a *better* time? The answer, decidedly, was no, and so—with my employer's blessings and half a year's pay in accumulated benefits in my pocket—off I went.

°cord: quantity of wood

°Ivy League schools: the top private colleges

There have been a few anxious moments since then, but on balance things have gone much better than we had any right to expect. For various stories of mine, I've crawled into black-bear dens for *Sports Illustrated,* hitched up dogsled racing teams for *Smithsonian* magazine, checked out the Lake Champlain "monster" for *Science Digest,* and canoed through the Boundary Waters wilderness area of Minnesota for *Destinations.*

I'm not making anywhere near as much money as I did when I was employed full time, but now we don't need as much either. I generate enough income to handle our $600-a-month mortgage payments plus the usual expenses for a family like ours. That includes everything from music lessons and orthodontist° bills to car repairs and college costs. When it comes to insurance, we have a poor man's major-medical policy with a $500 deductible for each member of the family. It picks up 80% of the costs beyond that. Although we are stuck with paying minor expenses, our premium is low—only $560 a year—and we are covered against catastrophe.° Aside from that and the policy on our two cars (a 1976 VW bus and a 1978 Ford Maverick) at $400 a year, we have no other insurance. But we are setting aside $2,000 a year in an IRA.°

We've been able to make up the difference in income by cutting back without appreciably lowering our standard of living. We continue to dine out once or twice a month, but now we patronize local restaurants instead of more expensive places in the city. We still attend the opera and ballet in Milwaukee but only a few times a year. We eat less meat, drink cheaper wine and see fewer movies. Extravagant Christmases are a memory, and we combine vacations with story assignments.

That kind of belt tightening° doesn't bother us as much as some other aspects of our new life do. Like killing chickens, for example. In any box of mixed chicks bought at a hatchery, about half the population will grow up into roosters that have to be butchered. If they're not, they gobble up a lot of feed without producing anything in return except a lot of trouble in the hen house. But when it came time to butcher our first batch of roosters, I was stumped.° First, I knew, you cut the head off—but *then* what?

Luckily, Sandy's folks, who live nearby, are a couple of chicken pluckers from way back° and they offered to teach us. We sharpened the hatchet and set up a regular production line on the lawn: chopping block, hot water, a cutting board, feather bags, newspapers for singeing, cold water, sharp knives and a pair of pruning shears. Then we went to work. Heads rolled, feathers flew and we got a terrific short course in poultry butchering from the old masters. We still don't like the job, but we can handle it.

We don't like bee stings either. We discovered early on that keeping bees means being stung—not just once or twice but about a dozen times a season. The how-to books play it down, and veteran beekeepers shrug it off.° Yet when three or four angry bees get trapped in a sleeve or a glove, it becomes a matter of real consequence to me. Still, there is no better way to develop a feeling of harmony with nature's rhythms than beekeeping, and getting stung is a small price to pay for honey fresh from the hive.

°**orthodontist:** dentist who corrects the position of teeth

°**catastrophe:** disaster

°**IRA:** Individual Retirement Account

°**belt tightening:** trying not to spend money

°**I was stumped:** I didn't know what to do
°**from way back:** from a long time ago

°**shrug it off:** think it is not important

To us, the satisfactions of the good life far outweigh the inconveniences, and yet we do experience real frustration from time to time. In fact, we're convinced that Murphy's Law° is more applicable in the country than just about anywhere else. Sooner or later, the well pump breaks down, the water softener goes haywire,° the septic-tank system backs up and the barn doors blow off in a storm.

°**Murphy's Law:** "If anything can go wrong, it will."

°**goes haywire:** breaks down

As a handyman, I've always subscribed to the maxim° that if something is worth doing well, it probably should be done by someone else. Now I have to muddle through, and surprisingly often I do. Recently, for example, I demonstrated that I am capable of wiring up a 220-volt mercury-vapor yard-light switch. In the process, though, I also demonstrated that I am capable of giving myself a horrendous shock. I have acquired a shaky proficiency at troweling° cement, hanging doors and repairing the sump pump. Yet I have fouled up° the furnace and the washing machine so badly that even professional repairmen were hard pressed to bail me out.°

°**maxim:** saying

°**troweling:** putting on with a trowel (a tool)
°**fouled up** *(slang):* ruined
°**bail me out:** help me out of a difficult situation

We've discovered a simple pleasure about living on a farm that tends to offset such predicaments:° people are usually glad to help. When our outhouse had to be moved a while ago, we invited some friends over for a "privy party," and the job got done in no time flat. In exchange for a couple of dozen eggs or apples, relatives are willing to push a paintbrush or weed a flower bed for a while. And we know we can always count on our neighbors for a tractor tow° or a load of manure.

°**predicaments:** embarrassing situations

°**tow:** pull

I suspect not everyone who loves the country would be happy living the way we do. It takes a couple of special qualities. One is a tolerance for solitude. Because we are so busy and on such a tight budget, we don't entertain much. During the growing season there is no time for socializing anyway. Jim and Emily are involved in school activities, but they too spend most of their time at home.

The other requirement is energy—a lot of it. The way to make self-sufficiency work on a small scale is to resist the temptation to buy a tractor and other expensive laborsaving devices. Instead, you do the work yourself. The only machinery we own (not counting the lawn mower) is a little three-horsepower rotary cultivator and a 16-inch chain saw.

How much longer we'll have enough energy to stay on here is anybody's guess—perhaps for quite a while, perhaps not. When the time comes, we'll leave with a feeling of sorrow but also with a sense of pride at what we've been able to accomplish. We should make a fair profit on the sale of the place too. We've invested about $35,000 of our own money in it, and we could just about double that if we sold today. But this is not a good time to sell.

Once economic conditions improve, however, demand for farms like ours should be strong again.

We didn't move here primarily to earn money though. We came because we wanted to improve the quality of our lives. When I watch Emily collecting eggs in the evening, fishing with Jim on the river or enjoying an old-fashioned picnic in the orchard with the entire family, I know we've found just what we were looking for.

EXPLORATIONS

- Would you ever want to do what Jim Doherty did?
- In what ways does the author think that the "quality of their lives" has been improved?
- This article was first published in *Money* magazine. Which parts of the article are aimed at the specialized audience of that magazine?

12 *From* Growing Up

RUSSELL BAKER

Morrisonville was a poor place to prepare for a struggle with the twentieth century, but a delightful place to spend a childhood. It was summer days drenched° with sunlight, fields yellow with buttercups,° and barn lofts° sweet with hay. Clusters of purple grapes dangled° from backyard arbors,° lavender wisteria° blossoms perfumed the air from the great vine enclosing the end of my grandmother's porch, and wild roses covered the fences.

On a broiling afternoon when the men were away at work and all the women napped,° I moved through majestic depths of silences, silences so immense I could hear the corn growing. Under these silences there was an orchestra of natural music playing notes no city child would ever hear. A certain cackle from the henhouse meant we had gained an egg. The creak of a porch swing told of a momentary breeze blowing across my grandmother's yard. Moving past Liz Virts's barn as quietly as an Indian, I could hear the swish of a horse's tail and knew the horseflies were out in strength. As I tiptoed° along a mossy bank to surprise a frog, a faint splash told me the quarry° had spotted me and slipped into the stream. Wandering among the sleeping houses, I learned that tin roofs crackle under the power of the sun, and when I tired and came back to my grandmother's house, I padded° into her dark cool living room, lay flat on the floor, and listened to the hypnotic° beat of her pendulum clock° on the wall ticking the meaningless hours away.

°**drenched:** soaked, completely covered
°**buttercups:** little yellow flowers
°**barn lofts:** top floors of farm buildings
°**dangled:** hung
°**arbors:** shady spots in a garden
°**wisteria:** climbing plant
°**napped:** slept briefly

°**tiptoed:** walked quietly on tips of toes
°**quarry:** something being followed or hunted
°**padded:** walked softly
°**hypnotic:** causing sleepiness
°**pendulum clock:** clock with swinging metal piece

EXPLORATIONS

- Do you know any places like Morrisonville? Describe them.
- Baker tells us about the "orchestra of natural music" that he hears. How does he explain to us what he means by that?
- How many specific sounds does Baker describe for us?

13 From "Homey Ski Spa in the Italian Alps"

BARBARA LAZEAR ASCHER

Light comes to the mountains while the valley sleeps. The only person who might witness the Alps' icy, gnarled° fingers probing° the dawn sky is the baker who drops a laundry basket of hot, crusty rolls on the hotel doorstep. It will be another two hours before life begins to fill Via Roma, the narrow, cobblestone° main street of Bormio, a village of 4,000 cradled in the Valtellina valley of northern Italy.

°**gnarled:** crooked
°**probing:** exploring

°**cobblestone:** rounded stone

The *barbiere*° is the first to arrive. The loud clang of his shop's metal gate sends out a wakeup call to those who slumber° in 14th- and 15th-century buildings lining the street. His lights go on, the broom comes out, and he prepares for a day of shaves, haircuts and gossip.

°**barbiere** *(Italian):* barber
°**slumber:** sleep

His first customer will be Renzo Pelosi, a white-haired, patrician° gentleman from the Posta, the neighboring 19th-century hotel bought by his mother when she arrived on horseback from Tirano in 1922. "She was a very cute woman," says her grandson, Giorgio Pelosi, who now runs the hotel.

°**patrician:** upper-class

The street is still dark, the sky and mountaintops sharing a yellow glow, when mother, father and two sons in their 20's arrive at 8:30 to open Rino Sport, two doors down from the *barbiere*. Skiers rely on this family's expertise to test the safety of bindings, choose the perfect boots and provide gloves and socks as insulation against frostbite on Bormio 3000 (Cima Bianca), the highest peak for winter skiing . . . .

[After a day of skiing,] you may sally forth° to join the evening parade on Via Roma. Shops and eyes closed for the 1 to 5 P.M. siesta° reopen. There is only room for six abreast;° the street is as narrow as it was four centuries ago. Skiers home from the mountain weave their equipment through the assembled as deftly° as needles through cloth. No cars intrude. Arms are linked, babies hoisted° and friends greeted. Kisses fly like dust. The pace is slow, the feet never quite lifted in a businesslike fashion. This is a time for glancing in windows, gathering in groups, stopping in at the Bormio Bar for cappuccino,° grappa° and pastries. Women visiting from the south gather here in Fendi furs opening to sequined° sweat shirts. Local children sit propped in chairs between parents and grandparents. Some are so small that only their eyes show.

°**sally forth:** go out

°**siesta:** afternoon rest time
°**six abreast:** six across in a line
°**deftly:** skillfully
°**hoisted:** picked up

°**cappuccino:** coffee with hot milk
°**grappa:** a type of liquor
°**sequined:** covered with sequins (small shiny discs)

199

The Via Roma, Bormio's main street, by Nicola Majocchi

Trails of chocolate lead from plate to open mouths below the
table's edge. Lovers leave powdered sugar on each other's lips;
postcard writers inadvertently° mix marzipan° and ink; teen-age
boys giggle into their *limonata*° . . . .

°**inadvertently:**
  accidentally
°**marzipan:** pastry
  made with almonds
°**limonata**
  (Italian): lemonade

EXPLORATIONS

- What do you like best about Bormio from this description?
- Which scenes described here resemble scenes from a film?
- Why do you think the writer presented them in this way?
- The author paints a lot of little scenes with words in the last paragraph. Why do
  you think she does that?

2 * Possessions

PREVIEW QUESTIONS

1. If there were a fire in your house, which three possessions would you try to save? Why?

2. What would you like to own that you don't own now? Do you think you will ever own those things?

3. How are people who strive for more possessions different from those who care only about their basic needs? Do you know people of both types?

4. How would you classify yourself and others in your family? Are you people who cling to possessions or who throw things away?

1

© Susan Shacter, 1984.

EXPLORATIONS

- Have you ever had "the blues"? Could gold ever cure that feeling?
- What do you imagine about the life of this woman as she is portrayed in the advertisement: her home, her family, her other possessions, her job?
- How has the photographer drawn attention to the theme of the advertisement: gold? Does the advertisement do a good job of selling gold?

2

Mahatma Gandhi's Worldly Possessions, Information Service of India, New York.

EXPLORATIONS

- This photo shows the belongings of Mahatma Gandhi. What do these possessions tell us about him?
- If you could have only the same number of possessions as Gandhi had, what would the picture of your possessions look like?
- Why do most people feel the need for more possessions than these?

3

© *Bill Owens*

EXPLORATIONS

- Everything the couple in the photo owns is in one room. Would you furnish a room in the same way as the couple?
- What does the way they have chosen to furnish and decorate their home tell you about their lives and their interests?
- What do you think the photographer feels about his subjects? Does he admire them, pity them, or what?

4

Bedroom Dresser, Shrimp Fisherman's House, Biloxi, Mississippi, 1945, by Walker Evans. Estate of Walker Evans.

EXPLORATIONS

- What kind of person is the shrimp fisherman? What can you tell about his life, interests, and values from this photograph of the objects on his dresser and in the room?
- Why do you think Walker Evans chose to photograph this subject?
- Does the photograph tell you anything about the photographer's attitude to his subject? For example, is he scornful, critical, sympathetic, admiring, pitying? What makes you draw your conclusions?

5

Why every kid should h:

Today, there are more Apples in schools than any other computer.

Unfortunately, there are still more kids in schools than Apples.

So innocent youngsters (like your own) may have to fend off packs of bully nerds to get some time on a computer.

Which is why it makes good sense to buy them an Apple® IIc Personal Computer of their very own.

The IIc is just like the leading computer in education, the Apple IIe. Only smaller. About the size of a three-ring notebook, to be exact.

Even the price of the IIc is small — under $1300*

Of course, since the IIc is the legitimate offspring of the IIe, it can access the world's largest library of educational software. Everything from Stickybear Shapes™

With a IIc your kid can do something constructive after school. Like learn to write stories. Or learn to fly. Or even learn something slightly more advanced. Like multivariable calculus.

for preschoolers to SAT test preparation programs for college hopefuls.

In fact, the IIc can run over 10,000

programs in all. More than a few of which you might be interested in yourself.

For example, 3-in-1 integrated business software. Home accounting and tax

programs. Diet and fitness programs.

Not to mention fun programs for the whole family. Like "Genetic Mapping" and

EXPLORATIONS

- How does this desktop compare to your own desktop?
- What do you think a typical day is like in the life of the person who owns this desk?

Courtesy of Apple Computer, Inc.

e an Apple after school.

zyme Kinetics."

And the Apple IIc comes complete h everything you need to start computing one box.

Including a free 4-diskette course to ch you how — when your kids get tired your questions.

An RF modulator that can turn almost y TV into a monitor.

As well as a long list of built-in tures that would add about $800 to the st of a smaller-minded computer.

128K of internal memory — twice

the power of the average office computer.

A built-in disk drive that would drive up the price of a less-senior machine.

And built-in electronics for adding accessories like a printer, a modem, an AppleMouse or an extra disk drive when the time comes.

In its optional carrying case, the IIc can even run away from home

So while your children's shoe sizes and appetites continue to grow at an alarming rate, there's one thing you know can keep up with them. Their Apple IIc.

To learn more about it, visit any authorized Apple dealer. Or talk to your own computer experts.

As soon as they get home from school.

- Why do you think the advertisement includes so many things other than an Apple computer when the purpose is to advertise the computer?

6

Esther Bubley, 1981.

EXPLORATIONS

- Why do children like stuffed animals so much?
- What were your favorite toys when you were the age of the boy in the picture?
- What stories can you remember about yourself and your childhood toys?
- What does the photograph lose or gain from showing only half of the child's face?

7 The Chrysler and the Comb

EVAN S. CONNELL

Mrs. Bridge, emptying wastebaskets, discovered a dirty comb in Ruth's basket.

"What's this doing here?" Ruth inquired late that afternoon when she got home and found the comb on her dresser.

"I found it in the wastebasket. What was it doing *there?*"

Ruth said she had thrown it away.

"Do you think we're made of money?" Mrs. Bridge demanded. "When a comb gets dirty you don't throw it away, you wash it, young lady."

"It cost a nickel,"° Ruth said angrily. She flung her books onto the bed and stripped off her sweater. °**nickel:** five cents

"Nickels don't grow on trees," replied Mrs. Bridge, irritated by her manner.

"Nickels don't grow on trees," Ruth echoed. She was standing by the window with her hand on her hips; now, exasperated,° she pointed to her father's new Chrysler,° which was just then turning into the driveway. °**exasperated:** annoyed, angry °**Chrysler:** type of American car

"Put the comb in a basin of warm water with a little ammonia and let it soak," Mrs. Bridge went on. "In a few minutes you can rinse the—"

"I know, I know, I know!" Ruth unzipped her skirt, stepped out of it, and threw it at the closet. She sat down on her bed and began to file her nails.

"So is a nickel going to break us up?" she asked, scowling.° °**scowling:** frowning angrily

"I wash my comb and I expect you to do the same. It won't hurt either of us," replied Mrs. Bridge. "Taking out without putting in will soon reach bottom," she added and left the room, shutting the door behind her.

For a few minutes Ruth sat on the bed quietly filing her nails and chewing her lower lip; then she snatched° the comb and broke it in half. °**snatched:** grabbed quickly

EXPLORATIONS

- If you had to take sides in the argument, would you agree with Mrs. Bridge or her daughter Ruth? Why?
- What does this short passage tell us in general about the attitudes of people to possessions?

8 An Interview with Ernest Hemingway

GEORGE PLIMPTON

Ernest Hemingway writes in the bedroom of his house in the Havana suburb of San Francisco de Paula. He has a special workroom prepared for him in a square tower at the south-west corner of the house, but prefers to work in his bedroom, climbing to the tower room only when "characters" drive him up there.

The bedroom is on the ground floor and connects with the main room of the house. The door between the two is kept ajar° by a heavy volume listing and describing *The World's Aircraft Engines*. The bedroom is large, sunny, the windows facing east and south letting in the day's light on white walls and a yellow-tinged° tile floor.

°**ajar:** slightly open

°**yellow-tinged:** slightly yellow

The room is divided into two alcoves° by a pair of chest-high bookcases that stand out into the room at right angles from opposite walls. A large and low double bed dominates one section, oversized slippers and loafers° neatly arranged at the foot, the two bedside tables at the head piled seven-high with books. In the other alcove stands a massive flat-top desk with a chair at either side, its surface an ordered clutter of papers and mementoes.° Beyond it, at the far end of the room, is an armoire° with a leopard skin draped across the top. The other walls are lined with white-painted bookcases from which books overflow to the floor, and are piled on top among old newspapers, bullfight journals, and stacks of letters bound together by rubber bands.

°**alcoves:** enclosed sections

°**loafers:** shoes

°**mementoes:** souvenirs
°**armoire:** clothes cabinet

It is on the top of one of these cluttered bookcases—the one against the wall by the east window and three feet or so from his bed—that Hemingway has his "work desk"—a square foot of cramped° area hemmed in° by books on one side and on the other by a newspaper-covered heap of papers, manuscripts and pamphlets. There is just enough space left on top of the bookcase for a typewriter, surmounted by° a wooden reading board, five or six pencils and a chunk of copper ore° to weight down papers when the wind blows in from the east window. . . .

°**cramped:** crowded
°**hemmed in:** surrounded

°**surmounted by:** topped by
°**copper ore:** reddish metal (Cu)

A man of habit, Hemingway does not use the perfectly suitable desk in the other alcove. Though it allows more space for writing, it too has its miscellany°: stacks of letters, a stuffed toy lion of the type sold in Broadway nighteries, a small burlap bag full of carnivore° teeth, shotgun shells, a shoehorn, wood carvings of lion, rhino, two zebras, and a wart-hog—these last set in a neat row across the surface of the desk—and, of course, books: piled on

°**miscellany:** collection of various objects

°**carnivore:** meat-eating animal

the desk, beside tables, jamming the shelves in indiscriminate° order—novels, histories, collections of poetry, drama, essays. A look at their titles shows their variety. On the shelf opposite Hemingway's knee as he stands up to his "work desk" are Virginia Woolf's *The Common Reader*, Ben Ames Williams's *House Divided*, *The Partisan Reader*, Charles A. Beard's *The Republic*, Tarle's *Napoleon's Invasion of Russia*, *How Young You Look* by Peggy Wood, Alden Brooks's *Will Shakespeare and the Dyer's Hand*, Baldwin's *African Hunting*, T. S. Eliot's *Collected Poems*, and two books on General Custer's fall at the battle of the Little Big Horn.

°**indiscriminate:** unorganized

The room, however, for all the disorder sensed at first sight, indicates on inspection an owner who is basically neat but cannot bear to throw anything away—especially if sentimental value is attached. One bookcase top has an odd assortment of mementoes: a giraffe made of wood beads, a little cast-iron turtle, tiny models of a locomotive, two jeeps° and a Venetian gondola, a toy bear with a key in its back, a monkey carrying a pair of cymbals, a miniature guitar, and a little tin model of a U.S. Navy biplane (one wheel missing) resting awry° on a circular straw place mat—the quality of the collection that of the odds-and-ends which turn up in a shoe-box at the back of a small boy's closet. It is evident, though, that these tokens have their value, just as three buffalo horns Hemingway keeps in his bedroom have a value dependent not on size but because during the acquiring of them things went badly in the bush which ultimately turned out well. "It cheers me up to look at them," he says. . . .

°**jeeps:** military vehicles

°**awry:** crooked

EXPLORATIONS

- This passage forms part of the introduction to an interview with Hemingway. Why do you think the interviewer thought it important to include all this information before the interview?
- What things do you keep for sentimental value?
- Why do you think people keep things that have no monetary value but only sentimental value, as Hemingway did?

9 Treasures

JOAN COSTELLO

Treasured objects have special significance° for people who invest them with personal meaning. Often cherished objects serve as visible links to loved ones, events, or traditions of the past. For example, I treasure an ancient ebony° necklace I found among my grandmother's possessions after she died. I never saw her wear it. It was, in fact, a gift from her closest friend's daughter after her friend's death, and thus a link to someone close to my grandmother. A girl who lived with me once borrowed it without my permission and lost it. She found it later, but I felt bereft while it was missing and somehow whole again after it was recovered. As is the case with most treasures, there is much mystery in my attachment to this necklace; I do not know what it really means, but it means a lot.

Early Treasures.   Children form attachments to objects at an early age. Most children select a blanket or toy animal to cherish.° Usually it is one that they have nearby as they fall asleep. Typically the object evokes° a sense of comfort and its soothing qualities may substitute somewhat for the attention of loved ones. As children grow, their early attachments to blankets or teddy bears fade and they invest other objects with special meanings. It is often unclear why they choose certain objects over others; nor is it clear even to them precisely what these things mean. It is likewise° uncertain exactly when their interests in some of their early treasures disappear; sometimes they have been put on the back burner° waiting to be rekindled at some later date. Few parents escape at least one desperate outburst° when a child learns that a favorite old object he is searching for has been thrown out or given away long ago. Mysteriously, old treasures sometimes take on additional meaning as new ones are found.

Collections.   As children approach their middle years they tend to expand their treasures into collections. Sometimes these are motivated by fads—baseball cards, bottle caps, stickers, and the like—and they provide children with a certain peer-group identity. Such collections also allow children to practice negotiation° skills in acquiring and exchanging property. They are, however, different from collections of personal treasures. Smooth stones, surf-polished glass, rings from cans, or bits of found metal can actually mean more to a child than expensive collections of dolls, stuffed animals, scale models, or video games. There is a

°**significance:** meaning

°**ebony:** very dark, almost black wood

°**cherish:** treasure, love

°**evokes:** produces

°**likewise:** similarly

°**put on . . . burner:** not paid attention to for a while
°**outburst:** display of anger

°**negotiation:** discussion

212

special pleasure in touching, thinking about, and rearranging one's treasures. The meanings given to them—even if not fully explainable—their power, beauty, size, and shape reflect on and reinforce° good feelings about the self: one must be a fine person to have such fine treasures.

°**reinforce:** make stronger

Expressions of the Self.   Children also derive° satisfaction from displaying such collections. Even though parents may at times look on them as clutter,° it is important to keep in mind that these objects may in effect serve as public statements of what a child may think is important and unique about himself. A child may therefore fiercely defend a collection or materials adults may classify as junk. However, by protecting these prized objects, adults offer children some assurance that they are respected as individuals with their own tastes, idiosyncrasies,° and personal lives. Children flourish° when adults permit them the space and respect to invest personal meaning in possessions of their own.

°**derive:** get

°**clutter:** mess

°**idiosyncrasies:** individual peculiarities
°**flourish:** grow and develop well

Besides, adults have their treasures too—things they especially like to look at, hear, touch, and wear, and things they keep in special, even secret places to check on now and then. Whatever their monetary° or artistic value, our treasures help us to feel good and special, and even give us a little something to fall back on to help us carry on. Seldom are we able to explain fully our attachment to them or their particular meaning to others but there is really no need to do so. They are there for our safekeeping, to give away when we want to share something important to us, and to abandon° when they no longer hold personal significance.

°**monetary:** financial

°**abandon:** leave

EXPLORATIONS

- Do you treasure anything that used to belong to a relative?
- What did you collect when you were a child?
- Who is the author writing for? That is, who does she envisage as her readers? What tells you the answer? Where is that audience specifically addressed in this piece of writing?

10 Lure* of Possessions: Do You Cling to Objects or Throw Away Your Past?

BARBARA LANG STERN

I've got to get rid of some of this stuff; I'm surrounded by things!" We say it, mean it, give ourselves incentives° for disposal: "I'll feel better; my clothes won't be mashed, my bookcase won't collapse, my passport will turn up; I even can take a tax deduction. . . ." But more often than not, a different set of rationalizations° wins out: "It might come in handy, come back in style, make a good costume, grow valuable in time, give the kids something to play with . . . I better hang on to it: I'll *want* it some day!"

So we rearrange things, temporarily creating more space and wondering why it's so difficult to divest° ourselves. Are we materialistic?° Sentimental? Insecure? Do we harbor a hidden pack-rat gene? And what about people who do the opposite, and get rid of everything that's not of immediate use?

"There is a basic human need to find psychological comfort through relationships to things external to ourselves," says Paul C. Horton, M.D., practicing psychiatrist, consultant to the Meriden Child Guidance Clinic for Central Connecticut, and author of *Solace: The Missing Dimension In Psychiatry* (University of Chicago Press). "We've all seen infants during the early weeks of life selecting their first soothers°—a blanket, diaper, or soft toy. These 'transitional objects,' as the English analyst Donald W. Winnicott termed them, help the child to separate from the mothering person by providing a symbolic connection that stands for, 'I'm not alone,' and 'I'm not completely separated from. . . .' "

As we mature, Dr. Horton suggests, we turn to more sophisticated° and culturally acceptable items. So the adolescent who feels uncomfortable hugging a stuffed animal in the presence of her peers may become a guitar player. She, like many adults, also might keep her stuffed animal and find comfort in knowing it still exists. "Women tend to be better than men at insisting on having some solacing° elements in their lives," says Dr. Horton. "These solaces may be intangible°—music, poetry, religion, philosophy; or tangible—art, plants, photographs, clothing, antique furniture, automobiles, workshop equipment; . . . they help us to continue to grow and especially to find some consoling° meaning in life, or even in sickness and death."

°**incentives:** motivation

°**rationalizations:** explanations

°**divest:** dispossess
°**materialistic:** mainly interested in possessions

°**soothers:** comforters

°**sophisticated:** experienced

°**solacing:** comforting
°**intangible:** nonmaterial

°**consoling:** comforting

*lure: attraction

But what's happening when we feel overwhelmed, rather than consoled, by too many objects that we nonetheless don't want to part with and continue collecting? "To generalize, people like this usually have had difficulty crossing a developmental hurdle,° especially in the area of intimacy or closeness with other people," says Dr. Horton. "So, as adults, instead of finding a special individual with whom to feel at one, from whom to find the most important kind of comfort, they seek solace in patchwork fashion—a little here, a little there—which can become addictive° because it never satisfies. The solacing objects, which for most people promote development, now become regressive,° causing the person to turn away from what she needs to do in order to grow still further."

°**hurdle:** obstacle, block

°**addictive:** causing a habit or addiction

°**regressive:** going backwards

Stuart S. Asch, M.D., professor of clinical psychiatry in the Cornell University Medical College and attending psychiatrist, The New York Hospital, observes, "What we do with our possessions reflects our philosophical/psychological view of the world: how much do I value a remembrance of things past? How much do I plan ahead for the future?

"A small minority of individuals cares only about what's going on *now*. 'What do I need now? What will I be needing *soon*?' Everything else quickly gets thrown out—including sometimes the property of others. Actually, such people are closely related to those who save everything, except that the 'throwers' struggle *against* their strong wish to hold on, denying the wish: 'It's not *me* that wants to be a child; *I* don't need anything from my past, from my parents or their parents; I'll order new things and trash all of that.' Their intolerance° of people who save is a tip-off, saying, in effect, 'Everyone should be as independent as I am, because if others are dependent upon the past, it will be too seductive° to me, struggling as I am against my own wishes to hold on."

°**intolerance:** lack of tolerance, dislike

°**seductive:** attractive

Just as many of us are aware of saving special things to preserve memories or enhance relationships, we've also felt that by getting rid of gifts, photos, letters, we're marking the *end* of a period or relationship. But why do we have conflicting feelings about saving more mundane,° less emotionally charged objects?

°**mundane:** ordinary

Dr. Asch suggests that most of us keep as much "stuff" as we need at any time in order to feel sufficiently full and to avoid fears of depletion.° He adds that in two illnesses, depression and senility,° exaggerated collecting and holding on to things are specific symptoms.°

°**depletion:** using up, emptying
°**senility:** mental problems in old age
°**symptoms:** visible signs of illness

"All our possessions are in a sense part of our identity or the identity of somebody who might have been important to us," says Dr. Asch. "Deciding whether to save something usually becomes difficult because it's *not* a simple, logical question of, 'Will this one day be useful or valuable?" Rather, the real, unconscious problem involves our own sense of personal limits, integrity,° and the need to preserve something that has become a part of us.   °**integrity:** honesty

"When you find yourself accumulating° more than you want to, being aware that you're acting not out of logic but for personal psychological reasons sometimes can help you to be more realistic and to recognize that you don't really need all of this."   °**accumulating:** collecting

EXPLORATIONS

- Have you ever thrown away a possession and then regretted it? If so, what was it? Why did you throw it away?
- What examples can you think of in which you "clung to objects" or "threw away your past"?
- Who does the author quote from, and why do you think she includes these quotations?

11 Object Lessons

MIHALY CSIKSZENTMIHALYI
EUGENE ROCHBERG-HALTON

A lawyer who had accumulated° many valuable things in his home over a lifetime spoke of most of them with indifference.° When asked what his most private possession was, however, he paused, and then invited the interviewer into the basement family room. There, from an old chest, he carefully unpacked a trombone. It turned out that he had played the instrument in college; for a middle-aged lawyer, it epitomized° a life of freedom and spontaneity° that he looked back on with nostalgia.° Even now, when depressed or overwhelmed by responsibilities, he retires to the basement and blows on the old trombone.

°**accumulated:** collected
°**indifference:** lack of interest

°**epitomized:** was an example of
°**spontaneity:** unplanned behavior
°**nostalgia:** longing for the past

To understand what people are and what they might become, it helps to understand what things they cherish° and why. Yet it is surprising how little is known about what things mean to people. By and large, social scientists have neglected to investigate the relationship between people and objects. In 1974 we decided to make such a study. The goal was to see how and why people in contemporary urbanized° America relate to things, by examining the role of objects in people's definition of who they are, who they have been, and who they wish to become.

°**cherish:** love, treasure

°**urbanized:** changed from country to city

We interviewed members of 82 families in the Chicago metropolitan area in their own homes, asking: "What are the things in your home which are special for you?" We then asked *why* each object named was special, what it would mean to the respondent to be without it, where it was kept, and how and when it was acquired. Half the families belonged to the upper-middle class, and half were lower-middle class. In each family, we talked to at least one of the children, both parents, and at least one grandparent. There were 79 respondents in the youngest generation, 150 in the middle one, and 86 in the oldest generation, for a total of 315. Forty-four percent were male; 67 percent were Caucasian,° 30 percent Afro-American, and 3 percent Oriental.

°**Caucasian:** term for white people

In all, the people with whom we talked mentioned 1,694 things; this comes to slightly more than five objects apiece. We developed an empirical° typology or "grammar" by sorting the objects into 41 categories. We used a similar process of classification to organize the 7,875 reasons given that the objects were special and

°**empirical:** relying upon observation

217

constructed 37 meaning categories, such as "souvenir" or "enjoyment."

The category most often mentioned as special was furniture, cited° by 36 percent of the respondents. The other categories in the top 10 and the percentage of subjects who mentioned at least one special object in each category were: visual art (26), photographs (23), books (22), stereos (22), musical instruments (22), TVs (21), sculpture (19), plants (15), plates (15).

°**cited:** mentioned

Who Treasures What?

Children	Percentage mentioning	Parents	Percentage mentioning	Grandparents	Percentage mentioning
Stereos	45.6	Furniture	38.1	Photos	37.2
TVs	36.7	Visual art	36.7	Furniture	33.7
Furniture	32.9	Sculpture	26.7	Books	25.6
Musical instruments	31.6	Books	24.0	TVs	23.3
Beds	29.1	Musical instruments	22.7	Plates	22.1
Pets	24.1	Photos	22.0	Visual art	22.1
Miscellaneous	20.3	Plants	19.3	Sculpture	17.4
Collectibles	17.7	Stereos	18.0	Appliances	15.1
Sports equipment	17.7	Appliances	17.3	Miscellaneous	15.1
Books	15.2	Miscellaneous	16.7	Plants	12.8
Vehicles	12.7	Plates	14.7	Collectibles	11.6
Radios	11.4	Collectibles	12.0	Musical instruments	10.5
Refrigerators	11.4	Glass	11.3	Silverware	10.5
Stuffed animals	11.4	Jewelry	11.3	Weavings	10.5
Clothes	10.1	TVs	11.3	Whole room	10.5
Photos	10.1				

The most cherished things in the home, as viewed by the three generations in the authors'
study. The clear-cut differences in the rankings (as determined by the percentage who
mentioned each object) suggest that things play a different role at different stages of life.
In general, the younger generation cherishes objects that invite action; grandparents prefer
things that lend themselves to contemplation; and the middle generation finds meaning in
both objects of action and objects of contemplation.

The preeminent° place of furniture over other objects might be
that furniture can be displayed more easily, that it is supposed to
be useful, and that it usually constitutes° heavy investments of
money. But comments by our subjects suggest other, more complex reasons. For example, here is what a teenage boy said about
why he selected the kitchen table and chairs as being special to
him: " 'Cause I can set on 'em, eat on 'em, play on 'em, do lots of
things with the chairs and table." When asked what it would mean
to him not to have those things, he responded, "It would mean
that I couldn't play as good 'cause I love the feel of that table."

°**preeminent:** most
important

°**constitutes:** forms

His short answer illustrates several trends° in the answers of
the younger generation. The meaning of kitchen furniture for this
youngster revolved around the active experiences he could have
by interacting with it; the accent was on comfort and enjoyment,
and the meaning referred exclusively to him. The table did not
provide a link with other people or with some ideal to be achieved.

°**trends:** styles

Among women of the middle generation, the reasons for cherishing furniture were very different. One middle-aged woman
found two upholstered chairs special: "They are the first two

chairs me and my husband ever bought, and we sit in them and I just associate them with my home and having babies and sitting in the chairs with babies." Her quotation illustrates different meanings from the ones mentioned by younger respondents. Gone is the emphasis on comfort and enjoyment; one finds, instead, important memories, relationships, and past experiences.

Subjects gave a total of 638 meanings for why furniture was special. Only 5 percent of these were utilitarian, that is, focused on usefulness. Most often, furniture was said to be special because it brought to mind memories of relationships with parents, children, or spouses.°

°**spouses:** husbands or wives

The large proportion of people mentioning visual art (26 percent) reflects the fact that we did not count only original or recognized works of art in this category. Paintings made by family members were also included.

One would expect people to cherish paintings because of their beauty and originality, or because of the artist's skills; in short, for aesthetic reasons. Yet only 16 percent of the time were any of those characteristics mentioned. It appeared, rather, that people value their pictures because they help them relive memorable occasions and pleasing relationships.

Visual art was not very meaningful to the youngest generation. Fewer than 10 percent of the children mentioned one or more pictures as special, as opposed to 37 percent and 22 percent of their parents and grandparents, respectively.

The preference for photographs shows a similarly dramatic age difference: 10 percent of the children mentioned at least one photograph as special, compared with 22 percent of the parents and 37 percent of the grandparents. For the youngest generation, photographs are the 16th category in order of frequency; for grandparents, they are the first.

Photographs are the prime vehicle for preserving the memory of one's close relations. For that reason older respondents often describe them as "irreplaceable." When a picture represents a deceased° relative, it often bears a freight° of vivid emotions for people in the middle generation as well. An adult woman burst into tears while explaining why a picture of her brother was special: "It's the only formal picture that we have of him. And, too, because he's gone, passed away."

°**deceased:** dead
°**freight:** heavy load

Books were cited almost as often as photographs, and again, almost exclusively by adult respondents. For professionals, whose identity as productive adults is intimately related to written knowledge, books signify a central dimension of the self. Although professional books are usually kept in the office rather than in the home, lawyers, doctors, teachers, and other people whose livelihood depends on book knowledge keep some of these volumes at home. Many voiced the fear of what it would mean to be deprived of the props° of a professional identity: "It would be terrible. I would be very upset. It has to do with my sense of being OK."

°**props:** supports

One-fifth of the respondents mentioned a stereo set or a tape player as special. Age made a tremendous difference in the preference for stereos or tape players in a way that was almost a mirror image of the preference for photographs. Here 46 percent of the youngest generation cited a stereo set versus 18 percent of the parents and only 6 percent of the grandparents. A stereo is the object most frequently mentioned by children. The younger person's attraction to stereos cannot be explained only in terms of familiarity with technology; it is probably bound up with the extraordinary importance music has in the lives of teenagers. One typical adolescent said: "Because when I'm not real happy and gay, I turn it on and it makes me happy again." Not to have it would mean that all my good days would turn into bad days . . . 'cause it helps me recover good, recover from the bad days." The same theme pervaded the answer of a policeman: "Well, I like music and I would be kind of lost without it. It's just a way of soothing me if I've had a rough night, made a lot of arrests, have to write up a review, prepare to go to court; it's just soothing."

Thus music seems to act as a modulator° of emotions, a way of compensating for negative feelings. The importance of this function is great in adolescence, when mood swings are significantly greater than in later life. . . .

°**modulator:** regulator

Terminal Materialism   A recurrent° theme in the answers was that of kinship.° On the whole, 82 percent of the people cherished at least one object because it reminded them of a close relative. But numbers do not begin to express the importance of kinship ties among our respondents. It was the cumulative effect of hearing them talk about their parents, spouses, and children, and the depth of their emotions in doing so, that we found so impressive.

°**recurrent:** occurring again and again
°**kinship:** family relationship

Many people, despite their attachment to things, were not materialistic in the usual sense of the term. They cherished things not because of the material comfort they provided but for the information they conveyed about the owner and his or her ties to others.

In general, attachment to things seemed to go hand in hand with attachment to people. Some respondents were upset by our questions about special objects. They said that they were not materialists, and that things meant nothing to them. "You should ask me how I feel about people, not things," they would say. They refused to single out any object as special, or perhaps mentioned only one or two photographs of persons to whom they felt close. This rejection of the symbolic meaning of things in favor of direct human ties seemed attractive at first, until we began to notice that people who denied meanings to objects also lacked close networks of human relationships. Those who were most vocal° about prizing friendship over material concerns seemed to be the most lonely and isolated. That does not mean, of course, that things are indispensable to objectify relationships with loved ones. It does seem, however, that those who have ties to people tend to represent them in concrete objects.

°vocal: outspoken

Few of the people we interviewed prized objects that symbolized an identification with any particular cultural or religious tradition. Homes in the past may have been centered around household gods, crucifixes, icons, historical pictures, flags—symbols of attachment to widely shared cultural ideals. But in our study such objects were conspicuous only by their absence.

Only 7 percent of the sample mentioned religous meanings, and 9 percent, ethnic ones. Political allegiance was not represented visibly, except for pictures of a few heroes like John F. Kennedy or Martin Luther King, Jr. The ideals mentioned were often very fragmentary and idiosyncratic°; the closest to a widely shared cultural ideal was perhaps the ecological consciousness symbolized by plants.

°idiosyncratic: individualistic, different

The transpersonal goals in which people invest attention tend to be rather primitive in the sense that they include close kin, ancestors, and descendants in preference to some larger, more universal body. The strongest ties established are to relatives, not to abstract principles, institutions, or groups.

Beyond their value as status symbols—indeed, quite unrelated to any such function—objects were cherished by many in our study as instruments for discovering and articulating° personal values. These people reflected what we call "instrumental materialism" as opposed to "terminal," or merely acquisitive, materialism.

°articulating: expressing

One of the men we talked to proved to be a striking example of how people can relate constructively to objects. Asked what it would mean not to have the objects he had mentioned, he answered:

"I honestly think it would mean almost nothing. One way that you could say that is that we have so many things that we like that a few more or less wouldn't be particularly noticed. Beyond that, there's something very close between the freedom to love and the freedom to go without. The place that loss would be felt most severely would be in family objects, and for that reason they are irreplaceable. Another rosewood desk [one of his special objects] would not be the one that came down through the family. We have a four-poster bed that we like very much, and another would be very beautiful, but it wouldn't be the one that my wife's grandfather was born in."

EXPLORATIONS

- Do you value any objects that remind you of close relatives? What are they?
- Which things in the chart on p. 219 do you treasure?
- Which objects do your family members cherish? Do you notice any generational differences in the objects they treasure?

12 *From* Minor Characters

JOYCE JOHNSON

I'm thinking, painfully, of a room. It has a red couch with a green slipcover, a gold-upholstered chair covered in maroon, a needlepoint piano bench also covered in green—hunter green, it was called. The Oriental rug, bought just before the Depression, is red and blue and gets vacuumed every day.* The table with curved bow legs—used only for important family occasions—is in the style known as French provincial. A lamp stands on it, Chinese, on little teak° feet, its silk shade covered with cellophane.°

°**teak:** type of wood
°**cellophane:** transparent wrapping

The piano dominates everything—a baby grand, bought while my mother was still working, before I was born. It's a Steck, an obscure° make that's supposedly every bit as good as a Steinway. For years she'd saved up for it out of her small, secretary's salary. Her picture as a young woman, placed on the polished lid that's never opened except when the piano tuner comes, is in a heavy silver frame of ornate° primitive design brought by my uncle from Peru. She's slender and so pretty, graciously smiling in the long organza dress she'd made herself, white camellias° pinned to the flounce° on her shoulder. She could very well be what she never became, a concert singer, but she's engaged to my father, who stands beside her in a dark suit. He's a small man, round-faced like I am, with a sweet, serious look. Above the piano is an oil representation° of me done by an artistic neighbor when I was eight—the golden era of my career as a daughter. I had to hold my head in one position for hours and hours, dreaming of the chocolate eclair° I'd always get at the end of the session. And after all the sitting still, I never liked the portrait of the stolid° child in the flowered pinafore dress with two fat blonde pigtails.

°**obscure:** not well known

°**ornate:** decorated

°**camellias:** type of flower
°**flounce:** frill

°**oil representation:** oil painting
°**eclair:** type of cream-filled pastry
°**stolid:** not emotional
°**poignancy:** emotional feeling
°**gratifications:** satisfaction
°**deferred:** delayed
°**tensions of gentility** strains caused by caring about respectability
°**aspiration:** ambition, desire to succeed
°**frayed:** worn, threadbare

There's the terrible poignancy° in this room of gratifications° deferred,° the tensions of gentility.° It's as if all these objects—the piano, the rug, the portrait—are held in uneasy captivity, hostages to aspiration.° If the slipcovers ever come off, if the heavy drapes are drawn aside letting in the daylight, everything that has been so carefully preserved will be seen to have become frayed° and faded anyway.

You could just as well have gone to hell with yourself and enjoyed all that naked upholstery from the start.

---

*The Depression was a decline in the American economy in the 1930s when the value of money dropped and unemployment rose.

EXPLORATIONS

- Why does the author say that the time when she was eight was "the golden era" of her "career" as a daughter?
- Does the author like the room she is describing and the things in it? How do you form your opinion?
- What is the connection between the use of "cover" and "covered" (four times) in paragraph 1 and the use of "naked" in the last paragraph?

3 * Work

PREVIEW QUESTIONS

1. What kind of work would you most like to do? Why?

2. What are the three most important things you would look for in your ideal job?

3. In your country which jobs are the most respected and earn one the most money?

4. If you suddenly came into a lot of money, would you choose to work or not? Why?

1

Welders, 1943, by Ben Shahn.

EXPLORATIONS

- In your country, what kind of pay would workers like these earn compared to teachers?
- Do you think that "blue-collar workers" like these welders should earn more than "white-collar workers" because of the dangers of the job? Why or why not?
- Why do you think the artist chose to emphasize the worker's hand by making it come out of the frame?

2

Spring Hoeing, by Li Feng-Lan.

- Who usually does farmwork in your country? Men or women or both? Why?
- Which kind of work do you think is more satisfying: manual labor in the fields or manual labor on a construction site? Why?
- How is this style of painting different from the style of Edward Hopper on p. 232?

3

Jim Kalett/Photo Researchers.

EXPLORATIONS

- Is the job of the people behind the counter appealing to you? Why or why not?
- How much do you think they should earn for their job compared to the workers in the first picture of this section?
- What do you think the photographer was most interested in here? What did he choose to emphasize? What point is he making with this picture?

4

Young Housewife, Bethnal Green, by Bill Brandt.

EXPLORATIONS

- Do you think the woman in the photo is working for pay? What makes you think that?
- Here she is scrubbing the floor. What do you think she does the rest of the day?
- Who does the housecleaning in your home?

5

Office at Night, 1940, by Edward Hopper.

EXPLORATIONS

- Edward Hopper painted this picture in 1940. In what ways would a modern office differ from this one?
- Why do you think these two people are in the office at night?
- How would the effect of the painting be different if the woman were at the desk and the man at the file cabinet?
- Does this office look like a happy place to work? Why or why not? What kind of atmosphere does the artist convey, and how does he convey it?

6

Jim Kalett/Photo Researchers.

EXPLORATIONS

- When you were younger, were your teachers mostly men or women?
- In your country, is a teacher a respected member of society?
- Who were the good teachers you have had? What made them good?
- Is the photographer drawing our attention to the classroom setting, to the students, or to the teacher? What details make you choose your answer?

7 *From* Working: *Nancy Rogers*

STUDS TERKEL

At twenty-eight, she has been a bank teller for six years. She earns five-hundred dollars a month.

What I do is say hello to people when they come up to my window. "Can I help?" And transact their business, which amounts to taking money from them and putting it in their account. Or giving them money out of their account. You make sure it's the right amount, put the deposits on through the machine so it shows on the books, so they know. You don't really do much. It's just a service job.

We have a time clock. It's really terrible. You have a card that you put in the machine and it punches the time that you've arrived. If you get there after eight-forty-five, they yell and they scream a lot and say, "Late!" Which I don't quite understand, because I've never felt you should be tied to something like a clock. It's not that important. If you're there to start doing business with the people when the bank opens, fine.

I go to my vault,° open that, take out my cash, set up my cage, get my stamps set out, and ink my stamp pad. From there on until nine o'clock when the bank opens, I sit around and talk to the other girls.

°**vault:** place to keep valuables

My supervisor yells at me. He's about fifty, in a position that he doesn't really enjoy. He's been there for a long time and hasn't really advanced that much. He's supposed to have authority over a lot of things but he hasn't really kept informed of changes. The girls who work under him don't really have the proper respect that you think a person in his position would get. In some ways, it's nice. It's easier to talk to him. You can ask him a question without getting, "I'm too busy." Yet you ask a question a lot of times and you don't get the answer you need. Like he doesn't listen.

We work right now with the IBM.° It's connected with the main computer bank which has all the information about all the savings accounts. To get any information, we just punch the proper but-

°**IBM:** computer made by the IBM company

Note: This passage is an excerpt from Studs Terkel's book *Working,* which consists of transcriptions of interviews with people in different jobs. So what you read here is closer to speech than to a polished piece of writing; there are sentence fragments, colloquial expressions, and even some instances of nonstandard English.

tons. There are two tellers to a cage and the machine is in between our windows. I don't like the way the bank is set up. It separates people. People are already separated enough. There are apartment houses where you don't know anybody else in the building. They object to your going into somebody else's cage, which is understandable. If the person doesn't balance, they'll say, "She was in my cage." Cages? I've wondered about that. It's not quite like being in prison, but I still feel very locked in. . . .

A lot of people who work there I don't know. Never talk to, have no idea who they are. You're never introduced. I don't even know who the president of the bank is. I don't know what he looks like. It's really funny, because you have to go have okays on certain things. Like we're only allowed to cash up to a certain amount without having an officer okay it. They'd say, "Go see Mr. Frank." And I'd say, "Who's that? Which one? Point him out." The girl who's the supervisor for checking kept saying, "You don't know who he is? You don't know who he is? He's the one over there. Remember him? You waited on him." "Yeah, but I didn't know what his name was. Nobody ever told me."

I enjoy talking to people. Once you start getting regular customers, you take your time to talk—which makes the job more enjoyable. It also makes me wonder about people. Some people are out working like every penny counts. Other people, it's a status thing with them. They really like to talk about it. I had a man the other day who was buying stock. "Oh well, I'm buying fifty-thousand dollars worth of AT&T,° and I'm also investing in . . ." He wouldn't stop talking. He was trying to impress me: I have money, therefore I'm somebody.

°**AT&T:** very large international company

Money doesn't mean that much to me. To me, it's not money, it's just little pieces of paper. It's not money to me unless *I'm* the one who's taking the money out or cashing the check. That's money because it's mine. Otherwise it doesn't really mean anything. Somebody asked me "Doesn't it bother you, handling all that money all day long?" I said, "It's not money. I'm a magician. I'll show you how it works." So I counted out the paper. I said, "Over there, at this window, it's nothing. Over there, at that window, it's money." If you were gonna° think about it every minute: "Oh lookit,° here's five thousand dollars, wow! Where could I go on five-thousand dollars? Off to Bermuda—" You'd get hung-up° and so dissatisfied of° having to deal with money that's not yours, you couldn't work.

°**gonna** *(colloquial):* going to
°**lookit** *(colloquial):* look at this
°**hung-up** *(slang):* very involved
°**dissatisfied of** *(nonstandard):* dissatisfied with

People are always coming in and joking about—"Why don't you and I get together? I'll come and take the money and you ring the alarm after I've left and say, 'Oh, I was frightened, I couldn't do anything.' " I say, "It's not enough." The amount in my cash drawer isn't enough. If you're going to steal, steal at least into the hundreds of thousands. To steal five or ten thousand isn't worth it. . . .

EXPLORATIONS

- What would be the good and the bad things about working in a bank?
- In a job, how important is it to have a good boss?
- What can a boss do to make one's life better or worse?

8 *From* Blooming: A Small-Town Girlhood

SUSAN ALLEN TOTH

In Ames everyone worked. Fathers had jobs and mothers were homemakers, a word religiously observed in a town whose college was famed for its Division of Home Economics. Some mothers had outside jobs, not for pleasure but because they needed the money. Everyone knew that Mrs. McCallum clerked° at the Hy Valu because her husband drank, Mrs. Olson managed the Dairy Dreme because her husband had deserted their family, my mother taught because she was a widow and had to support two daughters. A few other women, mainly faculty wives, worked even though they were securely married; but they were idiosyncratic° individuals who somehow made their own rules and were not judged by ours.

°**clerked:** worked as a clerk

°**idiosyncratic:** different from others

As soon as I can remember, my friends and I wanted to get jobs. We looked forward to being sixteen, the magic age when most employers would be able to put us legally on their payrolls. Until then, we had to scrabble° furiously for what summer and after-school jobs we could dig' up in a small town whose work force did not usually expand at the times we were available. All girls babysat. Boys mowed lawns, raked leaves, shoveled walks and delivered papers. In junior high school, we all detasseled° corn in the summer. But by high school, we began to look more seriously for jobs that might "lead to something," jobs that seemed more important, jobs that offered what our high-school vocational counselor portentously° called "preparation for life." As a sixteen-year-old reporter on the Ames *Daily Tribune*, I did a photo feature on teenagers' summer jobs, ostentatiously° lugging my large black box camera around town to interview my friends. Kristy ran the elevator between the basement, first, and second floors of Younkers; Jack washed dishes at the Iowa State Union cafeteria; Emily was a carhop° at the A&W Root Beer Stand; Patsy clerked at her aunt's fabric store; Charlie was cutting and hauling sod° on an outlying farm. Kristy told me, confidentially, that her job was numbingly° dull; Jack was planning to quit in a few weeks, when he'd saved enough for golf clubs; Emily hated the rude jibes° she had to endure with her tips; Patsy didn't get along with her old-maid aunt; and Charlie said his job was about as much fun as football practice, and a lot dirtier. But we were all proud of ourselves, and the Ames *Daily Tribune* was proud too: my pictures

°**scrabble:** struggle

°**detasseled:** removed the flowering part from

°**portentously:** significantly, solemnly
°**ostentatiously:** showily

°**carhop:** waitress at a drive-in restaurant
°**sod:** turf, grass

°**numbingly:** extremely
°**jibes:** insulting remarks

ran on the front page, a visible testament° to the way the younger   °testament: proof
generation was absorbing the values of its elders. . . .

What did I actually learn from all my summer and after-school
jobs? Each one may have given me some small skills, but the
cumulative° effect was to deepen my belief that work was the   °cumulative: total
essential aspect of grown-up life. Even now, I am sometimes filled
with anxieties at the prospect of stretches of free time. When I do
not immediately rush to fill that time with work, I have to fight off
guilt, struggling mentally against a picture of a Real Grown-up
shaking a finger at me, someone with the droning voice of our
high-school career counselor, but with firm overtones of former
employers, teachers, even my mother. "This," the voice beats re-
lentlessly° into my ear, "is your preparation for life."   °relentlessly: steadily

EXPLORATIONS

- Have you ever had a job? What was it?
- Do teenagers in your country take summer jobs to earn money and gain experi-
  ence?
- When Susan Allen Toth mentions Mrs. McCallum, Mrs. Olson, and her own
  mother, what point is she making with these details?
- How many examples does the author give us of teenagers' summer jobs?

9 Dulling of the Sword

DAVID H. AHL

. . . . Until quite recently—15 to 20 years ago—nearly all Japanese marriages were arranged. With such a system, neither the man nor woman looked to the marriage for much personal fulfillment. The social life of a man was with his business associates, and it was rare for a wife to meet her husband's friends or vice versa.

However, largely as a result of American movies and television, the concept of romantic love has blossomed in Japan. Thus, today, more than one-quarter of Japanese marriages are "love marriages" rather than arranged ones. As a result, marriage partners are beginning to look to each other for fulfillment. Moreover, beyond the man/woman relationship, the wider effect is an erosion° of values and changing of expectations.

°**erosion:** wearing away

The widely held perception is that Japanese workers love their jobs so much that they willingly work long hours, skip vacations, and sacrifice their personal lives to their employers and their country. Not any more, says a recent report issued by the Aspen Institute for Humanistic Studies. The study examined how well jobs and worker values were matched.

Of the six countries included in the study—Britain, Israel, Japan, Sweden, the U.S., and West Germany—Japan ranked lowest. Only 32 percent of the Japanese questioned felt their jobs and values were well-matched; Britain was second lowest with 36 percent. In contrast, 49 percent of American workers and 55 percent of Israeli workers felt their values and jobs were well-matched. As for Japan, the report concludes, "The changing value standards of the younger Japanese job-holders may well cause significant changes in tomorrow's Japanese—and world—economy."

Many Japanese researchers and managers agree. Tamotsu Sengoku, director of the Japan Youth Research Institute, observes that younger Japanese workers are more like Americans than the older generations. They work very hard on the job, but when the workday is over, they move quickly to their own pursuits, to family and friends. Traditionally, before and after the formal workday, Japanese workers spent time with their peers and supervisors in quality control circles or having a drink discussing how to improve their company's products. Says Atsuko Toyama, author of *A Theory on the Modern Freshman* (the name for a new college

graduate), "The younger workers do what they are told and not
one iota° more."   °iota: bit

According to a study by the Japan Recruitment Center, more
recent college graduates describe themselves as oriented to the
home (72 percent in 1983 compared to 66 percent in 1976). On the
other hand, the divorce rate has also increased sharply in the past
five years. Still far less than the U.S., about two percent of all
Japanese households consist of a mother raising children under
20 years old. Furthermore, the number of women raising children
born out of wedlock° has increased by 250 percent over the past   °born out of
ten years.   wedlock: born to
                                                                      unmarried parents
Unlike the U.S., divorced women in Japan generally do not
receive alimony° or child support from the father. Instead, it is   °alimony: regular
common for men to pay their wives a lump sum upon separation.   payment by divorced
While this trend has not had a noticeable impact on the economy   spouse
to date, it is likely that in the future an increasing number of
women will have to work during the years they are traditionally
expected to spend at home with their children. This is likely to
further erode the traditional work ethic and values of the youngsters in these households.

In an article about the Japanese work ethic in *Fortune* (May 14,
1984), Lee Smith opines,° "In a sense, the rejection of work as a   °opines: expresses an
total way of life is not only understandable but healthy. Economic   opinion
prosperity isn't supposed to be an end in itself. It's supposed to
deliver people from exhausting drudgery° so they can find plea-   °drudgery: unpleasant
sure in life beyond day-to-day survival."   work

Smith concludes, "The Japanese work ethic will almost certainly not collapse, although it may sag enough to slow the country down."

EXPLORATIONS

- Why do you think David Ahl begins by talking about marriage and goes on to
  discuss work? What is the connection?
- What reasons are given in the article for the conclusion drawn in the last paragraph—that the Japanese work ethic is not so strong and may slow the country
  down?
- Would you ever sacrifice your personal life to your employer and your country?

10 *From* Poor Russell's Almanac

RUSSELL BAKER

It is not surprising that modern children tend to look blank and dispirited° when informed that they will someday have to "go to work and make a living." The problem is that they cannot visualize what work is in corporate America.°

°**dispirited:** unhappy

°**corporate America:** the big-business part of America

Not so long ago, when a parent said he was off to work, the child knew very well what was about to happen. His parent was going to make something or fix something. The parent could take his offspring° to his place of business and let him watch while he repaired a buggy° or built a table.

°**offspring:** child
°**buggy:** horse-drawn carriage

When a child asked, "What kind of work do you do, Daddy?" his father could answer in terms that a child could come to grips with. "I fix steam engines." "I make horse collars."

Well, a few fathers still fix steam engines and build tables, but most do not. Nowadays, most fathers sit in glass buildings doing things that are absolutely incomprehensible° to children. The answers they give when asked, "What kind of work do you do, Daddy?" are likely to be utterly mystifying° to a child.

°**incomprehensible:** not understandable
°**mystifying:** puzzling

"I sell space." "I do market research." "I am a data processor." "I am in public relations." "I am a systems analyst." Such explanations must seem nonsense to a child. How can he possibly envision° anyone analyzing a system or researching a market?

°**envision:** imagine

Even grown men who do market research have trouble visualizing° what a public relations man does with his day, and it is a safe bet that the average systems analyst is as baffled° about what a space salesman does at the shop as the average space salesman is about the tools needed to analyze a system.

°**visualizing:** imagining
°**baffled:** confused

In the common everyday job, nothing is made any more. Things are now made by machines. Very little is repaired. The machines that make things make them in such a fashion that they will quickly fall apart in such a way that repairs will be prohibitively expensive.° Thus the buyer is encouraged to throw the thing away and buy a new one. In effect, the machines are making junk.

°**prohibitively expensive:** too expensive to afford

The handful° of people remotely° associated with these machines can, of course, tell their inquisitive children "Daddy makes junk." Most of the work force, however, is too remote from junk production to sense any contribution to the industry. What do these people do?

°**handful:** very few
°**remotely:** slightly

Consider the typical twelve-story glass building in the typical American city. Nothing is being made in this building and nothing is being repaired, including the building itself. Constructed as a piece of junk, the building will be discarded° when it wears out, and another piece of junk will be set in its place.

°**discarded:** thrown away

Still, the building is filled with people who think of themselves as working. At any given moment during the day perhaps one-third of them will be talking into telephones. Most of these conversations will be about paper, for paper is what occupies nearly everyone in this building.

Some jobs in the building require men to fill paper with words. There are persons who type neatly on paper and persons who read paper and jot notes in the margins. Some persons make copies of paper and other persons deliver paper. There are persons who file paper and persons who unfile paper.

Some persons mail paper. Some persons telephone other persons and ask that paper be sent to them. Others telephone to ascertain° the whereabouts of paper. Some persons confer about paper. In the grandest offices, men approve of some paper and disapprove of other paper.

°**ascertain:** find out

The elevators are filled throughout the day with young men carrying paper from floor to floor and with vital° men carrying paper to be discussed with other vital men.

°**vital:** important

What is a child to make of all this? His father may be so eminent° that he lunches with other men about paper. Suppose he brings his son to work to give the boy some idea of what work is all about. What does the boy see happening?

°**eminent:** important

His father calls for paper. He reads paper. Perhaps he scowls° at paper. Perhaps he makes an angry red mark on paper. He telephones another man and says they had better lunch over paper.

°**scowls:** looks angry

At lunch they talk about paper. Back at the office, the father orders the paper retyped and reproduced in quintuplicate,° and then sent to another man for comparison with paper that was reproduced in triplicate last year.

°**quintuplicate:** five copies

Imagine his poor son afterwards mulling over the mysteries of work with a friend, who asks him, "What's your father do?" What can the boy reply? "It beats me,"° perhaps, if he is not very observant. Or if he is, "Something that has to do with making junk, I think. Same as everybody else."

°**beats me** *(slang):* I have no idea

EXPLORATIONS

- Do you think this essay is totally serious? What parts of the essay help you form your opinion?
- Do you ever find it difficult to imagine what people actually do all day on their jobs? Which jobs in particular?
- How does Russell Baker illustrate his point that paper occupies nearly everyone in a twelve-story office building?

11 Getting Ready for the Jobs of the Future

MARVIN J. CETRON

One thing is certain about tomorrow's job markets: dramatic shifts will occur in employment patterns. These changes are going to affect how we work and how we are educated and trained for jobs.

Major shifts in the job market won't necessarily mean major changes in the numbers of people employed. What the changes do mean is that many of the old jobs will disappear—and not just because of robots and computers. Manufacturing will provide only 11% of the jobs in the year 2000, down from 28% in 1980. Jobs related to agriculture will drop from 4% to 3%. The turn of the century will find the remaining 86% of the work force in the service sector, up from 68% in 1980. Of the service-sector jobs, half will relate to information collection, management, and dissemination.°

Unemployment will be an ongoing problem. If the current recession° were to end tomorrow, probably 1.2 million of the more than 11 million unemployed in the United States today would never be able to return to their old jobs in the automobile, steel, textile, rubber, or railroad industries. This loss of jobs is called structural unemployment.

Foreign competition in low-wage countries will eliminate about one-sixth of the 1.2 million jobs; another one-sixth will disappear because of the nationalization° of many major industries in other countries that results in "dumping" of products on the U.S. market and undercutting American prices. "Computamation" (robotics, numerically-controlled equipment, CAD/CAM [computer-aided design and computer-aided manufacturing], and flexible manufacturing) will assist in the demise° of the remaining two-thirds of the jobs eliminated.

As this technological transition takes place, productivity will increase. For example, the use of a robot or a CAD/CAM system in the automotive industry can replace up to six workers if operated around the clock. Quality control increases fourfold, and scrap° is reduced from 15% to less than 1%.

Japan already uses some of these new jobs and technology. It had no choice. Currently, it imports 96% of its energy. By the year 2000, that will rise to 98%. Eighty-seven percent of all of Japan's resources come from the outside. These statistics contributed to the decision to go robotic. But the essence of Japan's problem is

°**dissemination:** spreading of information

°**recession:** decline in the economy

°**nationalization:** government control of business

°**demise:** death

°**scrap:** left-over material

243

that, between 1985 and 1990, 20% of the entire work force will
retire at 80% of their base pay for the rest of their lives. Japan was
forced to go robotic to remain competitive. The United States, too,
will be filling many of today's blue-collar jobs with robots. The
displaced workers will have to learn the new skills necessary to
build and maintain the robots.

White-collar workers in the office of the future will also see
some dramatic changes in their jobs. Currently, about 6,000 word
lexicons—machines that type directly from speech—are in use.
After a person dictates into the machine, a word lexicon types up
to 97% of what was said. In addition, it can translate the material
into nine languages, including Hebrew, which it types backwards,
and Japanese kanji symbols, which it types sideways and the user
reads down the columns. Machines such as this will eliminate 50%
of all clerical and stenographic° jobs. But instead of going to an   °stenographic: typing
unemployment line, many of these workers may find jobs control-
ling the robots in factories using word-processing equipment.

As the types of jobs change, so will the definition of full employment. Currently [in 1983], a 4.5% unemployment rate is considered full employment. But by 1990, 8.5% unemployment will be
considered full employment. This figure is not as disturbing as it
first appears, for at any given time 3.5% of the work force will be
in training and education programs preparing for new jobs.

Workers will be able to take time out for retraining, in part,
because of the shift in job patterns. In 1980, 45% of American
households had two people working. In 1990, this proportion will
increase to 65%, and in 2000, 75% of family units will have two
incomes. This shift will allow easier transitions from the work
force to training programs and back to the work force. Forecasts
estimate that every four or five years one of the spouses or partners will leave the ranks of the employed to receive the additional
knowledge and skills demanded by changes in technology and the
workplace.

With these changes already taking place, workers must learn to
do new jobs now and in the future. Vocational educators and
trainers must gear up° to provide this vital education and training   °gear up: prepare
to the work force of the next two decades—jobs related to robots,   themselves
lasers, computers, energy and battery technology, geriatric° social   °geriatric: related to
work, hazardous-waste management, and biomedical electron-   the aged
ics. . . .

EXPLORATIONS

- How does Marvin Cetron capture the reader's attention at the beginning? Does
  he make you want to read on?
- Does the article make you look forward to the future or not? Why?

12 Work in the 1980s and 1990s

JULIA KAGAN

Feeling satisfied and working hard—[our] exploration of the American workplace, based on the survey done by the Public Agenda Foundation, [has] explored these two issues. We've found that most American jobholders are satisfied with their work, that a majority—especially women—believe in the work ethic° and that, although most say they put a lot of extra effort into work, they admit that they are not working as hard as they could be. We've also discovered a large difference between what many say they have in their jobs and what they wish they had. Is this gap responsible for the declining growth rate of the nation's productivity?

°ethic: principle of what is right

One of the major findings of the Public Agenda survey is that the link between rewards and performance on the job has been severed.° Less than a quarter of the work force see a close connection between how hard they work and how much they are paid. Yet more than 60 percent want a job where pay is tied to performance; they want to be able to work hard without feeling like fools for doing so.

°severed: cut

Would giving workers what they want make them work harder? A growing body of research indicates that this would not necessarily be the result. For many years, researchers have made distinctions between rewards that make workers more satisfied (satisfiers) and rewards that motivate them to work harder (motivators). Yet this message has been slow to reach management.

In a major 1975 study of job satisfaction and productivity, Daniel Yankelovich, president of the Public Agenda Foundation, and Raymond A. Katzell, PhD, professor of psychology at New York University, found that many policymakers assume that these two goals are causally° linked, that increasing job satisfaction automatically increases productivity. This turns out to be an expensive mistake. Efforts based on this assumption, they found, "are more likely than not to leave productivity unchanged, or at best to improve it marginally,° and may even cause it to decline." The jobholders in the Public Agenda survey confirm the motivators/satisfiers distinction.

°causally: by cause and effect

°marginally: slightly

A note about the charts: Items marked with an asterisk also appeared on the list of workers' top-ten job wishes that ran in last month's column, indicating that they probably are particularly im-

245

The Top Ten Motivators

Managers and Professionals		Blue-collar workers		Clerical workers
Men	Women	Men	Women	Women
A good chance for advancement (48%/29%)*	A good chance for advancement (47%/22%)*	Good pay (50%/22%)*	Good pay (44%/28%)*	A good chance for advancement (56%/19%)*
A great deal of responsibility (45/28)	A job that enables me to develop my abilities (44/18)*	A good chance for advancement (47/23)*	A good chance for advancement (42/17)*	A job that enables me to develop my abilities (52/24)
Recognition for good work (44/32)*	Recognition for good work (43/30)*	Pay tied to performance (47/28)*	Pay tied to performance (41/30)*	A challenging job (47/23)
A job where I can think for myself (44/29)	A great deal of responsibility (40/22)	Recognition for good work (42/37)*	A challenging job (37/23)	A job where I can think for myself (45/21)
A job that enables me to develop my abilities (42/28)*	A job where I can think for myself (38/33)	Interesting work (38/34)*	A job where I can think for myself (35/29)	A job that allows me to be creative (45/25)
A challenging job (42/29)	Good pay (37/30)*	See end results of my efforts (38/32)	Interesting work (35/28)*	See the end results of my efforts (45/30)
A job that allows me to be creative (41/29)	Pay tied to performance (37/33)	A job that enables me to develop my abilities (36/29)	A job that enables me to develop my abilities (34/27)	Good pay (42/35)*
A job with pay tied to performance (40/39)*	A challenging job (35/25)	A challenging job (34/38)	See end results of my efforts (34/31)	A great deal of responsibility (42/37)
A say in important decisions (39/33)	A say in important decisions (32/33)	A job that allows me to be creative (34/34)	A job that allows me to be creative (33/33)	Recognition for good work (39/32)*
A place that does quality work (39/29)	A place that does quality work (32/32)	A job where I can think for myself (33/39)*	Recognition for good work (32/39)*	Interesting work (37/41)*

The first figure in parentheses is the percentage in the group that rated this factor a motivator; the second shows those who called it a satisfier.
*Items marked with an asterisk were on the list of the top-ten job features this group of workers most wanted more of (*Working Woman*, June 1983)

portant to jobholders. The numbers in parentheses indicate how strong a motivator or satisfier the factor in question is—in some cases, workers are almost evenly divided on the issue. These numbers will give managers an indication of how strongly they can rely on these factors in designing job-reward systems. Male clerical workers were not included because there are so few of them.

Intrinsic Rewards The most obvious difference between the lists of motivators and satisfiers is that motivators concern the job itself almost exclusively. Working conditions and fringe benefits—both considered important to workers—do not appear to promote productivity, although these factors are prominent° satisfiers.   °**prominent:** important

Ambition, in the form of a desire for money and advancement, tops the lists of motivators. In some groups, though, good pay is surprisingly low on the list—for male managers and professionals, it ranked number 11 and doesn't even appear here. What is most interesting about the lists is the importance of the content of the job itself. Managers also would do well to notice that the nature of work, the degree to which it allows an employee to grow and develop her abilities, is also important to blue-collar and clerical workers.

There is a difference, though, in what one could call the power need of managers and professionals and that of lower-level workers: Managers are more hungry for a great deal of responsibility and a say in important decisions. There is little difference, however, between what motivates male and female managers.

In addition, the survey sounds a warning to companies involved in office automation. These firms would do well to study the motivators of women with clerical jobs. In the May issue of *Working Woman*, Karen Nussbaum (executive director of 9 to 5, a national advocacy group for office workers) pointed out the negative effects on the mental and physical health of office workers when companies transformed relatively varied clerical jobs into minutely divided, repetitive tasks, designed around VDTs.° This survey shows that, to motivate clerical workers, jobs must enable them to advance and develop their abilities, must be challenging and permit the worker to think for herself, be creative and see the end results of her work. Automated office systems that ignore these factors are likely to have the opposite effect on her motivation—and, ultimately, her productivity.

°VDTs: video display terminals (computer screens)

More backing for the importance of intrinsic° rewards in job motivation comes from *In Search of Excellence*, the thoughtful new book on America's best-run companies by Thomas J. Peters and Robert H. Waterman, Jr. (Harper & Row, 1982). Concerning recognition for good work, Peters and Waterman note that the best companies design reward systems that make most employees feel like winners. (For example, IBM's sales quotas are set so that 70 to 80 percent of the sales force can meet them.) The authors also stress the importance of immediate and positive reinforcement.

°intrinsic: internal

The Peaceable Kingdom   The lists of satisfiers provide a dramatic contrast to the motivators. What everyone wants most of all, it seems, is peace and quiet—a job without too much rush and stress. Judging by their reaction, male managers and professionals feel particularly hard-pressed.° Another stereotype that bites the dust° is that women are more concerned with human relations. Both sexes value working with people they like and getting along with their supervisors.

°hard-pressed: pressured
°bites the dust *(idiom):* dies

Why don't fringe benefits, lack of stress and good working con-

The Top Ten Satisfiers

Managers and professionals		Blue-collar workers		Clerical workers
Men	Women	Men	Women	Women
Job without too much rush and stress (71%/6%)	Job without too much rush and stress (57%/15%)	Job without too much rush and stress (57%/20%)	Job without too much rush and stress (55%/20%)	Convenient location (69%/13%)
Good working conditions (67/9)	People really care about me as a person (57/12)	Good working conditions (57/13)	Being informed about what goes on (55/10)	Working with people I like (69/8)
Convenient location (65/9)	Working with people I like (56/14)	Convenient location (53/10)	Getting along well with supervisor (51/17)	Job without too much rush and stress (66/12)
Being able to control work pace (61/9)	Convenient location (55/12)	Working with people I like (52/22)	Working with people I like (48/16)	Being able to control work pace (62/8)
Flexible working hours (61/15)	Getting along well with supervisor (54/17)	Getting along well with supervisor (52/20)	Flexible working hours (48/11)	Good working conditions (60/14)
Working with people I like (56/15)	Good fringe benefits (52/21)*	Being informed about what goes on (50/19)	Being able to control work pace (45/19)	Informal work environment (59/16)
Good fringe benefits (53/25)*	Job security, little chance of being laid off (52/27)	People who listen to your ideas (50/28)	People treat me with respect (45/17)*	All the tools I need to do my job (59/21)
Never asked to do anything improper or immoral (53/11)	Good working conditions (51/11)	Informal work environment (49/7)	Convenient location (44/14)	Efficient, effective managers (58/20)
Place I'm so proud of I want everyone to know I work there (53/20)	Never asked to do anything improper or immoral (50/15)	Being able to control work pace (47/29)	Good working conditions (44/14)	Fair treatment (54/15)*
Employer with good reputation (52/21)	Flexible working hours (48/19)	Fair treatment (46/26)	People who listen to your ideas (44/17)	Getting along well with supervisor (54/27)*

The first figure in parentheses is the percentage of the group that rated this factor a satisfier; the second is the percentage that rated it a motivator.
*Items marked with an asterisk were on the list of the top-ten job features this group of workers most wanted more of (*Working Woman*, June 1983).

ditions produce motivation to hard work? In the 1950s, industrial psychologist Frederick Herzberg found that factors extrinsic° to a job (he called them hygiene factors because they included working conditions as well as supervision, company policies, interpersonal relations, benefits and job security) had the power to make people feel dissatisfied and perform poorly if they fell below a certain level but did not increase job performance if they rose to an optimum level. In their 1975 study, Yankelovich and Katzell pointed out that many people are satisfied with their jobs precisely because their work is undemanding and requires minimal effort.

°extrinsic: external

The reader should not leave this article with the impression that it would be wise—to say nothing of moral—to mount a full-scale attack on fringe benefits and other satisfiers in the company compensation plan in order to replace them with motivator-based benefits. As Herzberg found, when "hygiene" factors become unacceptably low, they make employees so unhappy that negative effects on productivity result. What is important is that companies pay attention to designing jobs to create maximum levels of intrinsic interest and to provide financial and nonfinancial rewards for those who put in maximum effort.

EXPLORATIONS
- What point is Julia Kagan making? Does she present a convincing case?
- Which of the motivators and satisfiers listed would be important to you? Why?

4 ✳ Family

PREVIEW QUESTIONS

1. In what setting and in what pose would your family choose to be photographed?

2. What occasions does your family regularly celebrate?

3. Is your own family life centered around a nuclear family (parents and a few children) or an extended family (grandparents, parents, and lots of other relatives)?

4. Which member of your family do you try to please the most?

5. Do you think family life is changing? If so, in what ways?

251

1

Family Portrait, Courtesy of the Raimes family.

EXPLORATIONS

- In what decade do you think this photograph was taken? What makes you think that?
- Who do you think was the most influential person in this family? Why do you think that?
- What can you speculate about the daily life of the various family members?
- Which member of this family looks the most interesting to you, and why?

2

Nina Leen

EXPLORATIONS

- Why do you think the family members chose to arrange themselves in this way for their family portrait?
- Who do you think is the most powerful and important member of this family?
- How do you imagine the daily routine of the various members of this family?

3

Chester Higgins, Jr. Photo Researchers Inc.

EXPLORATIONS

- How would you identify the family relationships of the people in the picture? Which woman, for example, is the man's wife?
- Why do you think the family is in the boat? What are they doing? Where are they going? What do you think they will do next?
- What kinds of activities do the members of your family like to do together?

4

Sailor Home on Leave, by Eve Arnold.

EXPLORATIONS

• Does this family seem harmonious to you? Why or why not?
• What does this photograph suggest about the relationship of the children with their parents?
• What can you gather about this family's values from this one scene?

5

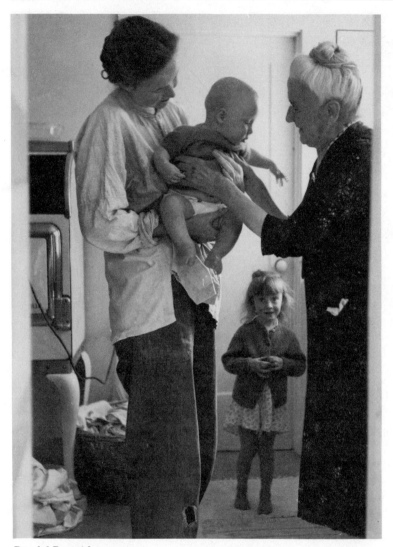

Rondal Partridge

EXPLORATIONS

- Which adjectives would you use to describe the people in this photo?
- Do different generations live together in your family? If so, is this usual in your country?
- Do you think it is advantageous to have several generations living together? If so, what are the advantages? If not, what are the disadvantages?

6

Greek family at Easter dinner, James L. Stanfield.

EXPLORATIONS

- What does this picture tell you about this family?
- What festivals or holidays do you celebrate with a family meal in your country?
- Which members of the family organize the celebration and the meal, and what foods are traditionally prepared?

7 *The Old Man and His Grandson*

JACOB AND WILHELM GRIMM

There was once a very old man, whose eyes had become dim, his ears dull of hearing, his knees trembled, and when he sat at table he could hardly hold the spoon, and spilt the broth° upon the table-cloth or let it run out of his mouth. His son and his son's wife were disgusted at this, so the old grandfather at last had to sit in the corner behind the stove, and they gave him his food in an earthenware bowl, and not even enough of it. And he used to look towards the table with his eyes full of tears. Once, too, his trembling hands could not hold the bowl, and it fell to the ground and broke. The young wife scolded him, but he said nothing and only sighed. Then they bought him a wooden bowl for a few half-pence,° out of which he had to eat.

°**broth:** soup

°**half-pence:** small amount of money

They were once sitting thus when the little grandson of four years old began to gather together some bits of wood upon the ground. "What are you doing there?" asked the father. "I am making a little trough,"° answered the child, "for father and mother to eat out of when I am big."

°**trough:** bowl

The man and his wife looked at each other for a while, and presently began to cry. Then they took the old grandfather to the table, and henceforth always let him eat with them, and likewise said nothing if he did spill a little of anything.

EXPLORATIONS

- How many sections does this fairy tale fall into, and what marks the sections?
- What is the point (the moral) of the story?
- Do you think this is an effective story? Why or why not?

8 F. Scott Fitzgerald's 21 Pieces of Advice to His Daughter on Living

F. SCOTT FITZGERALD

1. Worry about courage.
2. Worry about cleanliness.
3. Worry about efficiency.
4. Worry about horsemanship.
5. Don't worry about popular opinion.
6. Don't worry about dolls.
7. Don't worry about the past.
8. Don't worry about the future.
9. Don't worry about growing up.
10. Don't worry about anyone getting ahead of you.
11. Don't worry about triumph.
12. Don't worry about failure unless it comes through your own fault.
13. Don't worry about mosquitoes.
14. Don't worry about flies.
15. Don't worry about insects in general.
16. Don't worry about parents.
17. Don't worry about boys.
18. Don't worry about disappointments.
19. Don't worry about pleasures.
20. Don't worry about satisfactions.
21. Think about: What am I really aiming at?

EXPLORATIONS

- Do all these pieces of advice seem to you to be equally serious? Why or why not?
- What kind of advice would you give to a daughter?
- Are there any special pieces of advice a daughter or son could give to parents?

9 *Table Manners*

EVAN S. CONNELL

Mrs. Bridge said that she judged people by their shoes and by their manners at the table. If someone wore shoes with run-over heels, or shoes that had not been shined for a long time, or shoes with broken laces, you could be pretty sure this person would be slovenly° in other things as well. And there was no better way to judge a person's background than by watching him or her at the table.

°slovenly: sloppy

The children learned it was impolite to talk while eating, or to chew with the mouth open, and as they grew older they learned the more subtle° manners—not to butter an entire slice of bread, not to take more than one biscuit at a time, unless, of course, the hostess should insist. They were taught to keep their elbows close to their sides while cutting meat, and to hold the utensils in the tips of their fingers. They resisted the temptation to sop up° the gravy with a piece of bread, and they made sure to leave a little of everything—not enough to be called wasteful, but just a little to indicate the meal had been sufficient. And, naturally, they learned that a lady or a gentleman does not fold up a napkin after having eaten in a public place.

°subtle: not obvious

°sop up: soak up

The girls absorbed these matters with greater facility° than Douglas, who tended to ask the reason for everything, sometimes observing that he thought it was all pretty silly. He seemed particularly unable to eat with his left hand lying in his lap; he wanted to leave it on the table, to prop himself up, as it were, and claimed he got a backache with one arm in his lap. Mrs. Bridge told him this was absurd,° and when he wanted to know why he could not put his elbow on the table she replied, "Do you want to be different from everyone else?"

°facility: ease

°absurd: ridiculous

Douglas was doubtful, but after a long silence, and under the weight of his mother's tranquil° gaze, he at last concluded he didn't.

°tranquil: calm

The American habit of switching implements, however, continued to give him trouble and to make him rebellious.° With elaborate° care he would put down the knife, reach high across his plate and descend on the left side to pick up the fork, raising it high over the plate again as he returned to the starting position.

°rebellious: resistant
°elaborate: complicated

"Now stop acting ridiculous," she told him one day at lunch.

"Well, I sure bet the Egyptians don't have to eat this way," he
muttered, giving "Egyptians" a vengeful° emphasis.   °**vengeful:** wanting
                                                                        revenge
"I doubt if they do," she replied calmly, expertly cutting a tri-
angle of pineapple from her salad, "but you're not an Egyptian. So
you eat the way Americans eat, and that's final."

EXPLORATIONS

* Do similar disagreements to the one at the Bridges' meal table happen in your
  family? If so, why do these kinds of arguments take place?
* What other issues do families tend to argue about at mealtimes?
* How do table manners and eating habits in your country differ from the ones
  described here?

10 *From* Ivy Days

SUSAN ALLEN TOTH

More and more I worried that I might let everyone down. If I didn't graduate Summa,° how could I face my professors? . . .

Most of all, though, I worried about facing my mother. Even as I write that sentence, I feel it sounds unfair. My mother probably didn't ever wonder if I was going to graduate with a Latin word tacked after my name. I do not think she ever asked about my grades or even urged me to do well. She didn't need to. All my life I had wanted to make her happy, to make up to her somehow for her pain and trouble, to reassure her that no matter what, I was doing OK. More, I wanted to show her I was doing wonderfully. I was pleased when I could bring an honor home, whether it was a "100" on my spelling paper, a prize for an essay on the United Nations, or a report card full of A's. From some deep inner place that had no connection with how often she told me she was proud of me, I felt that nothing I could do was ever enough. A Summa might be, though, I thought. To march with the other Summas past my mother, who would have driven all the way from Ames, Iowa, to let her see the culmination° of her years of care and effort, to be crowned with the highest academic honor Smith° could offer: surely that would be enough.

°**Summa** *(Latin):* *summa cum laude;* with the highest praise

°**culmination:** highest point
°**Smith:** a private women's college

EXPLORATIONS

- In what ways have you tried to please a member of your family?
- Have you ever been worried about facing a member of your family? What was the occasion?
- Do parents sometimes expect too much from their children? What evidence do you have for your answer?

11 *The Analysts Who Came to Dinner*

As any homemaker who has tried to maintain order at the dinner table knows, there is far more to a family meal than meets the palate°. . . . Sociologist Michael Lewis has been observing 50 families to find out just how much more. . . . The basic conclusion is . . . clear: with all that is said and done at the dinner table, food may be the least significant ingredient of the evening meal.

°there . . . the palate: there is more than food

Lewis and his colleagues at the Educational Testing Service in Princeton, N.J., conducted their research by videotaping the families while they ate ordinary meals in their own homes. They found that parents presiding over° small families tend to converse actively with each other and their children. But as the brood° gets larger, conversation gives way to the parents' efforts to control the inevitable° uproar.° That can have important implications° for the kids. "In general, the more question-asking the parents do, the higher the children's IQ's,"° Lewis says. "And the more children there are, the less question-asking there is."

°presiding over: in control of
°brood: number of children in one family
°inevitable: unavoidable
°uproar: loud noise
°implications: results
°IQ's: Intelligence Quotients, measured by tests

'Invisible': The study also offers a clue to why middle children often seem to have a harder time in life than their siblings.° Lewis found that in families with three or four children, dinner conversation tends to center on the oldest child, who has the most to talk about, and the youngest, who needs the most attention. "Middle children are invisible," says Lewis. "When you see someone get up from the table and walk around during dinner, chances are it's the middle child." There is, however, one great equalizer that stops all conversation and deprives everyone of attention: "When the TV is on," Lewis says, "dinner is a non-event."

°siblings: brothers and sisters

Despite the feminist movement, Lewis's study indicates that preparing dinner continues to be regarded as woman's work— even when both spouses° have jobs. Some men do help out, but for most husbands dinnertime remains a relaxing hour. While the female cooks and serves, Lewis says, "the male sits back and eats."

°spouses: husbands or wives

EXPLORATIONS

- What observations can you make from your own experience about middle children?
- What are the most common topics of conversation during mealtimes with your family?
- Do you think mealtimes are important family events?

12 *Photos Speak Volumes About Relationships*

JANE E. BRODY

Among the many pictures in the family album was a prescient° family portrait: Mother was off to one side holding the dog, father was hugging their son and daughter, and all were grinning happily. Shortly after this picture of seeming familial contentment° was taken, the couple divorced, the father took custody of the children and the mother kept the dog.

Another woman was struck by an unmistakable pattern in the pictures of her family when she was a child. In every photo of the four of them, she and her brother were touching their mother and their father stood apart, with both physical distance and hands-in-pockets stance° precluding° any contact with his children. Her eyes filled with tears as she began to understand why she had never felt close to her father. And when she looked at the pictures of her own family, a similar pattern was obvious: She and her daughter were always close together and her husband was off to one side. No wonder she felt so distant from him, she thought; he was just like her father.

Somewhere in nearly every American household lie powerful documents of the family's emotional as well as social history, photographs that can help people understand relationships and recall long-forgotten or repressed events that have continuing significance.

"Everyone takes pictures and everyone has pictures, but no one looks at them to see what they tell us about ourselves, our families, our relationships," remarked Dr. Alan D. Entin, a family therapist° in Richmond, Va.

A sophisticated reading of photographs can give anyone a better sense of a family situation. But this is proving especially so in psychotherapy as a growing number of therapists use family pictures and other forms of "phototherapy" to facilitate° treatment and to deepen people's insights about themselves and their families. An international society of phototherapists has recently been formed and a biennial° journal is being published. Various dimensions of the technique are described in a recently published professional text, *Phototherapy in Mental Health,* edited by Dr. David A. Krauss and Dr. Jerry L. Fryrear, and published by Charles C Thomas.

°**prescient:** telling the future

°**familial contentment:** family happiness

°**stance:** way of standing
°**precluding:** preventing

°**therapist:** person who treats psychological disorders

°**facilitate:** help

°**biennial:** once every two years

264

Although the first recorded use of photographs in treatment dates to 1856 when Dr. Hugh Diamond photographed patients at the Surrey County Lunatic Asylum in England, modern interest in the technique is but 10 years old. According to Dr. Robert U. Akeret, who revived the interest with the publication in 1973 of a popular book, *Photoanalysis*, pictures can help to arouse awareness, diminish resistance to therapy, correct a distorted° self-image and distorted memories of events, document important changes in a family or individual, and help people to acknowledge otherwise "unacceptable" feelings and thoughts.

°**distorted:** misrepresented

Other therapists have since shown that photographs can help therapists reach those who are otherwise unreachable, such as children who are autistic° or deaf, juvenile delinquents, people from other cultures and people whose feelings are so buried that they seem to have no feelings at all.

°**autistic:** very withdrawn

But Dr. Entin and other leaders in the field say that the insights to be gained from perusing° family and other pictures are accessible° to anyone who chooses to look beyond the obvious. In many cases, the pictures themselves tell a significant story; in others, they trigger° memories that help to put present events and feelings into a more realistic perspective;° in still others, they provoke an awareness of emotions and concerns that might otherwise go unrecognized.

°**perusing:** examining
°**accessible:** easily reached
°**trigger:** set off
°**perspective:** view

For one distressed young man who was deeply ashamed of his immigrant family's ghetto° background, an examination of old pictures brought about a wholly new view. Looking at photos of his grandparents, he began to talk about how his father's father was renowned° for his fine ironwork and how his mother's parents had tended the exquisite formal garden of an aristocratic° estate. As he recounted the stories, a sense of pride and admiration for his family heritage emerged.

°**ghetto:** poor section of a city
°**renowned:** famous
°**aristocratic:** upper-class

Dr. Akeret, a New York psychoanalyst, said he had found photos "a quick way to get at things, a powerful means of creating an intense experience that can lead to change."

Dr. Entin believes that pictures often say more than words because "people do not guard their body language with the same vigor° as their words." He suggests that when people look at family pictures they consider such questions as who stands where, who is touching whom, who is not in the picture, whether one person is always in the center or off to the side, how the children are positioned, what expressions are on people's faces and whether there are significant gaps in the family's photographic chronicle.°

°**vigor:** enthusiasm

°**chronicle:** historical record

Typically, in times of family stress or illness, or when children reach their teens and become camera-shy, few if any pictures get taken, Dr. Entin remarked. He noted that in his own family, he can no longer take pictures of his teen-age son and daughter together. "They don't get along with each other in real life, so they refuse to be photographed together."

One person may be missing from most of the family pictures because he or she is the one who takes them. "But this too could be saying something about the person," Dr. Entin noted. "Is he or she the one who's trying to control everything?"

Dr. Entin cautions against overinterpreting a single picture. "It's the pattern that counts, the repetition of the same position or posture or expression in picture after picture," he said in an interview.

Pictures taken over a period of many years can reveal generational patterns (have the men in the family always stood rigid and apart?), values (are objects or pets more important than people?) and traditions (are all the family weddings well-documented?), Dr. Entin explained. . . .

On another level, Dr. Akeret suggests that analysis of the photographs of famous people can be both enlightening and entertaining. In a portrait of the Kennedy family, for example, he noted that all the boys were centrally located close to their parents but the girls were positioned peripherally.°

°**peripherally:** on the edges

"We all know how the Kennedy men were pushed by their parents and what they became," Dr. Akeret observed. "Here we can actually see the emphasis that the Kennedys placed on the male children and the way the children acted out parental expectations."

EXPLORATIONS

- What patterns could someone see in your own family photographs that tell something about the family relationships?
- What connection is there between what the organization of a family photograph tells us and what the arrangement of a piece of writing tells us?

13 *The American Family in the Year 2000*

ANDREW CHERLIN · FRANK F. FURSTENBERG, JR.

• At current rates, half of all American marriages begun in the early 1980s will end in divorce.

• The number of unmarried couples living together has more than tripled since 1970.

• One out of four children is not living with both parents.

The list could go on and on. Teenage pregnancies: up. Adolescent suicides: up. The birthrate: down. Over the past decade, popular and scholarly commentators have cited° a seemingly endless wave of grim statistics about the shape of the American family. The trends have caused a number of concerned Americans to wonder if the family, as we know it, will survive the twentieth century.

°**cited:** quoted

And yet, other observers ask us to consider more positive developments:

• Seventy-eight percent of all adults in a recent national survey said they get "a great deal" of satisfaction from their family lives; only 3% said "a little" or "none."

• Two-thirds of the married adults in the same survey said they were "very happy" with their marriages; only 3% said "not too happy."

• In another recent survey of parents of children in their middle years, 88% said that if they had to do it over, they would choose to have children again.

• The vast majority of the children (71%) characterized their family life as "close and intimate."

Family ties are still important and strong, the optimists argue, and the predictions of the demise° of the family are greatly exaggerated.

°**demise:** death

Neither the dire° pessimists° who believe that the family is falling apart nor the unbridled° optimists° who claim that the family has never been in better shape provide an accurate picture of family life in the near future. But these trends indicate that what we have come to view as the "traditional" family will no longer predominate.°

°**dire:** threatening
°**pessimists:** people who expect bad things
°**unbridled:** uncontrolled
°**optimists:** people who expect good things
°**predominate:** be the most important

Diverse Family Forms   In the future, we should expect to see a growing amount of diversity in family forms, with fewer Americans spending most of their life in a simple "nuclear" family consisting of husband, wife, and children. By the year 2000, three kinds of families will dominate the personal lives of most Americans: families of first marriages, single-parent families, and families of remarriages.

In first-marriage families, both spouses will be in a first marriage, frequently begun after living alone for a time or following a period of cohabitation.° Most of these couples will have one, two, or, less frequently, three children.

°**cohabitation:** living together

A sizable° minority, however, will remain childless. Demographer° Charles F. Westoff predicts that about one-fourth of all women currently in their childbearing years will never bear children, a greater number of childless women than at any time in U.S. history.

°**sizable:** fairly large
°**demographer:** person who studies human populations

One other important shift: in a large majority of these families, both the husband and the wife will be employed outside the home. In 1940, only about one out of seven married women worked outside the home; today the proportion is one out of two. We expect this proportion to continue to rise, although not as fast as it did in the past decade or two.

Single-Parent Families The second major type of family can be formed in two ways. Most are formed by a marital separation, and the rest by births to unmarried women. About half of all marriages will end in divorce at current rates, and we doubt that the rates will fall substantially in the near future.

When the couple is childless, the formerly married partners are likely to set up independent households and resume life as singles. The high rate of divorce is one of the reasons why more men and women are living in single-person households than ever before.

But three-fifths of all divorces involve couples with children living at home. In at least nine out of ten cases, the wife retains° custody° of the children after a separation.

°**retains:** keeps
°**custody:** care, guardianship

Although joint custody has received a lot of attention in the press and in legal circles, national data show that it is still uncommon. Moreover, it is likely to remain the exception rather than the rule because most ex-spouses can't get along well enough to manage raising their children together. In fact, a national survey of children aged 11 to 16 conducted by one of the authors demonstrated that fathers have little contact with their children after a divorce. About half of the children whose parents had divorced hadn't seen their father in the last year; only one out of six had managed to see their father an average of once a week. If the current rate of divorce persists, about half of all children will spend some time in a single-parent family before they reach 18.

Much has been written about the psychological effects on children of living with one parent, but the literature has not yet proven that any lasting negative effects occur. One effect, however, does occur with regularity: women who head single-parent families typically experience a sharp decline in their income relative to before their divorce. Husbands usually do not experience a decline. Many divorced women have difficulty reentering the job market after a long absence; others find that their low-paying clerical or service-worker jobs aren't adequate to support a family.

Of course, absent fathers are supposed to make child-support payments, but only a minority do. In a 1979 U.S. Bureau of the Census survey, 43% of all divorced and separated women with children present reported receiving child-support payments during the previous year, and the average annual payment was about $1,900. Thus, the most detrimental° effect for children living in a single-parent family is not the lack° of a male presence but the lack of a male income.

°**detrimental:** harmful
°**lack:** absence

Families of Remarriages   The experience of living as a single parent is temporary for many divorced women, especially in the middle class. Three out of four divorced people remarry, and about half of these marriages occur within three years of the divorce.

Remarriage does much to solve the economic problems that many single-parent families face because it typically adds a male income. Remarriage also relieves a single parent of the multiple burdens° of running and supporting a household by herself.

°**burdens:** problems

But remarriage also frequently involves blending together two families into one, a difficult process that is complicated by the absence of clear-cut ground rules for how to accomplish the merger.° Families formed by remarriages can become quite complex, with children from either spouse's previous marriage or from the new marriage and with numerous sets of grandparents, step-grandparents, and other kin° and quasi-kin.°

°**merger:** union

°**kin:** relatives
°**quasi-kin:** resembling relatives

The divorce rate for remarriages is modestly higher than for first marriages, but many couples and their children adjust successfully to their remarriage and, when asked, consider their new marriage to be a big improvement over their previous one.

The Life Course: A Scenario for the Next Two Decades
Because of the recent sharp changes in marriage and family life, the life course of children and young adults today is likely to be far different from what a person growing up earlier in this century experienced. It will not be uncommon, for instance, for children born in the 1980s to follow this sequence of living arrangements: live with both parents for several years, live with their mothers after their parents divorce, live with their mothers and stepfathers, live alone for a time when in their early twenties, live with some-

one of the opposite sex without marrying, get married, get divorced, live alone again, get remarried, and end up living alone
once more following the death of their spouses.

Not everyone will have a family history this complex, but it is
likely that a substantial° minority of the population will. And many
more will have family histories only slightly less complex.

°substantial: rather
large

Overall, we estimate that about half of the young children alive
today will spend some time in a single-parent family before they
reach 18; about nine out of ten will eventually marry; about one
out of two will marry and then divorce; and about one out of three
will marry, divorce, and then remarry. In contrast, only about one
out of six women born in the period 1910 to 1914 married and
divorced and only about one in eight married, divorced, and remarried.

Without doubt, Americans today are living in a much larger
number of family settings during their lives than was the case a
few generations ago.

The life-course changes have been even greater for women
than for men because of the far greater likelihood of employment
during the childbearing years for middle-class women today compared with their mothers and grandmothers. Moreover, the increase in life expectancy has increased the difference between
men's and women's family lives. Women now tend to outlive men
by a wide margin, a development that is new in this century.
Consequently, many more women face a long period of living
without a spouse at the end of their lives, either as a widow or as
a divorced person who never remarried.

Long-lived men, in contrast, often find that their position in the
marriage market is excellent, and they are much more likely to
remain married (or remarried) until they die. . . .

EXPLORATIONS

• What kind of family life is dominant in your country now?
• What kind of family life do you expect will predominate in your country in the
  year 2000? Will it be similar to the one predicted for North America?

5 * Men and Women

PREVIEW QUESTIONS

1. How would you define the roles of men and women in your country?

2. Is there such a thing as a "typical man" or a "typical woman" in your country? If so, what is that typical person like?

3. Who are the "role models" for men and women? (That is, who are the people that other men and women want to be like?)

4. How are the roles of men and women changing in your country?

A lot of men have made a lot of money dressed like this.

1

Outside a Bistro, France, 1968–69, by Henri Cartier-Bresson.

EXPLORATIONS

- How do you react when you see this picture?
- When you look closely at the composition of the photograph, how does your eye travel? Look at the man's arm, the dog's head, the angle of the woman's body. Do you think that Henri Cartier-Bresson noticed what you noticed before or after he took the picture?
- Does this picture show a typical scene of "young love"?

2

Drowning Girl, 1963, by Roy Lichtenstein.

EXPLORATIONS

- How do you imagine the relationship between the woman in the picture and Brad?
- What could Brad have done to make the drowning woman say that she would rather sink than call for help?
- Could anyone you know ever say anything similar? Under what circumstances?
- This is a large painting (67⅝ by 66¾ inches) made to look like one frame of a cartoon strip. Why do you think the artist, Roy Lichtenstein, chose this style of presentation?

3

John Wayne 1971, The Bettmann Archive

EXPLORATIONS

- Does this picture of John Wayne fit your image of a typical cowboy?
- What details in the photograph help you answer that question?
- The cowboy incorporated all the virtues of "masculinity" in the days of the American "Wild West." Is there a modern-day equivalent of the cowboy?

4

AP/Wide World Photos, Inc.

EXPLORATIONS

- Marilyn Monroe was a famous American movie star. What kind of ideal of beauty did she represent? How is it similar to or different from your ideal of female beauty?
- What kind of life would you expect someone like Monroe to lead?
- How do you imagine that someone like Marilyn Monroe would spend a day at home? How would it be different from the way you would spend a day at home?

5

Women's Activities in Arsenals: Acetylene Welding on Cylinder Water Jacket, 1918.

EXPLORATIONS

- What do you imagine this woman's life to be like? How do you think she feels about her job?
- What jobs do women do now that men used to do almost exclusively?
- Has the work role of women changed recently in your country?

6

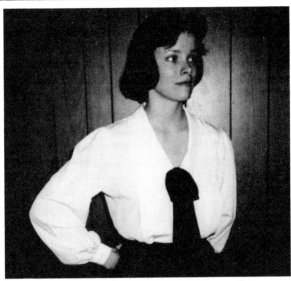

A lot of men have made a lot of money dressed like this.

EXPLORATIONS

- Do you think men and women should wear similar clothes? Why or why not?
- What image of women is this advertisement presenting?
- Has the advertiser designed an effective advertisement for a blouse? Why or why not?

7

More Choosing the Single Life

Three-fourths of the U.S. population (age 25–64) is married, acccording to a newly released study. However, more of us, as a percentage of the population, are choosing the single life than in 1970.

Percent who are single

Men	1970	1983*
25–34	15.5%	29.4%
35–44	7.8%	8.5%
45–64	6.4%	5.1%
Total	39.7%	43.1%
Women		
25–34	10.0%	19.2%
35–44	5.7%	6.3%
45–64	6.1%	4.4%
Total	21.8%	29.9%

*Latest data available
Source: Metropolitan Life Insurance Co. By Bob Laird, USA TODAY

EXPLORATIONS

• The statistics in the above table show that in 1985, a greater percentage of the United States population chose the single life than did so in 1970. Do you think a similar trend toward the single life is occurring in your own country? Why do you hold that opinion?
• What are the implications of more men and women choosing to remain single?
• What other ways are there to present the same information? Is the table an effective and clear method?

8 Are Women Bosses Better?

MARY SCHNACK

In sharp contrast to polls° taken only a few years ago, a new survey shows that two-thirds of all Americans would not mind working for a woman. °**polls:** opinion surveys

This growing acceptance of women in positions of authority doesn't surprise Natasha Josefowitz, a professor of business administration at the University of California in San Diego.

In fact, based on her interviews with hundreds of executives for her book *Paths to Power: A Woman's Guide From First Job to Top Executive* (Addison-Wesley, 1980), Ms. Josefowitz says that women are *better* managers than men. They are more sensitive to office politics and the feelings of subordinates.° °**subordinates:** people working in lower positions

"Women are skilled at noticing small details and subtle° changes in events. Because a woman detects a potential problem early, she often can defuse° it before it turns into a real conflict," Josefowitz says. °**subtle:** not obvious °**defuse:** make less tense

She disregards the theory that, because they did not participate in team sports in their earlier years, women cannot deal with conflict or manage groups as well as men can. "While boys were developing good team behavior, girls were talking to one another and developing social and verbal skills. As you rise up the corporate ladder, you go from needing good technical skills to good social skills."

Other experts say that because most women in positions of authority had to work their way up through the same jobs that their subordinates hold, they are more empathetic° and are apt° to create a good working environment by giving frequent praise and constructive criticism. They also spend more time with their employees than men do. When Ms. Josefowitz surveyed male and female managers in various areas of business, she found that women were more likely than their male counterparts to encourage interruptions by employees and to take calls at home from them. °**empathetic:** understanding °**apt:** likely

Some people have criticized women for this open-door policy. Others say that it works to their advantage by earning them employee respect and cooperation. Says Sandy Inbody-Brick, a savings and loan vice-president from California, "We realize that we need the people below us to make us good managers. In turn, we feel an obligation to help them advance."

Right now, women still hold only 6 percent of middle-management positions and one percent of jobs in upper management. But this will change, says one female executive, as more companies— and women who have been diffident° about aspiring to° these jobs—realize that you don't have to be a "barracuda"° to be a good boss.

°**diffident:** timid, not aggressive
°**aspiring to:** aiming at
°**barracuda:** vicious type of fish

EXPLORATIONS

• The author, Mary Schnack, asks a question in the title. What answer does she provide in her article?
• What evidence does she provide to support her point of view?
• Would you rather work for a man or a woman? Why?

9 *What Do Women Really Want?*

WILLIAM NOVAK

Women have always valued success in men, but today it seems that they are looking for a whole other set of qualities as well. Mr. Right must be strong, but he must also be supportive of a woman's strengths. He must be vulnerable° and tender without being weak. He must be encouraging to women without being condescending.° He must be tough but also loving and gentle. It's a tall order—and some men believe it's unrealistic.

°**vulnerable:** open to attack
°**condescending:** acting superior

In the course of investigating the apparent shortage of eligible° men for today's women, I interviewed many single men, most of whom were middle-class professionals and businessmen in their 30s and 40s, either divorced or never married. A common complaint among them was that women—especially those in their late 20s and in their 30s who have delayed marriage to launch careers—want to have things both ways.

°**eligible:** suitable for marriage

"They want us to be two different people at the same time," said Tom, a divorced stockbroker in his late 30s. "At work we're supposed to be tough, aggressive, successful. Women still want us to be earning a good income, especially if they hope to have children at some point. They like to see that we're moving forward in our careers. It doesn't seem to make much difference that they themselves are increasingly successful. If anything, that confirms for them that we should be even *more* ambitious, because women want men to be ahead of them in their careers.

"If I weren't successful," Tom said flatly, "most of the women I know would lose interest in me, but success is difficult, and you pay a high price for it. If I am successful, it's because I'm dedicated, competitive and driven. But it's not fair to value the result if you disparage° the process. It's hypocritical.° Women who admire my success are always saying that men like me are driven. Driven? Of *course* we're driven. How on earth do they expect me to be successful *without* being driven? Just by being a nice guy?

°**disparage:** criticize
°**hypocritical:** false, insincere

"Some women understand that I have to be driven at work, but then they want me to be a totally different person with them. They're looking for somebody who's John D. Rockefeller° at the office and Dr. Benjamin Spock° at the dinner table. But that's impossible because one set of qualities cancels out the other. I'm sorry, but I'm only one person, not two."

°**John D. Rockefeller:** millionaire businessman
°**Dr. Benjamin Spock:** famous children's doctor

Many of the men I interviewed spoke angrily about this di-
lemma.° "Society just doesn't allow you to be emotionally inte-   °**dilemma:** problem
grated," a Chicago lawyer explained. "Something has to give. Ei-
ther you end up being too soft at work, or else you're too tight
and controlled at home.

"I know some men who have made important and admirable
changes in their lives," he continued, "but these are the same guys
who aren't doing well at work. There's very little place in the
business world for emotional honesty or for caring. You have to
be realistic.

"But women are anything *but* realistic about this. They seem to
be searching for some kind of androgynous° man, a man who has   °**androgynous:** with
all the qualities and sensitivities of a woman. I think they want   male and female
some new kind of species that hasn't evolved yet."   characteristics

It is not clear whether the new sensitive man that this attorney
describes is, as he suspects, an imaginary hybrid° of women's   °**hybrid:** mixture
fantasies or whether he is just over the horizon, waiting to appear
on the scene. What is clear, however, is that few such men exist
today, although women still seem surprised and disappointed
when they can't find them. It's not only that very few men have
been able to incorporate both sides of the emotional spectrum;
there are also few models for men who want to be both strong
and tender, vulnerable without being weak, attentive and loving
as fathers, husbands or lovers while at the same time reasonably
successful in their working lives. Even if the Chicago lawyer is
wrong, and such paradoxical° combinations are eminently possi-   °**paradoxical:** contradictc
ble,° who is going to lead the way? Where are the pioneers?   °**eminently
                                                                             possible:** very
Aside from the lack of role models, many men are not entirely   possible
convinced that their relationships with women would benefit from
such a transformation: they suspect that women are somewhat
less than sincere about their new expectations.

Like many other men I talked to, Mark, a professor, is angry at
what he sees as the hypocrisy of women on the issue of emotional
expressiveness and vulnerability in men. "Women *say* they want
men who are vulnerable and tender, but what they really want are
old-fashioned men who show occasional flashes of tenderness and
self-awareness. When faced with a choice between the new sensitive man and the old-fashioned macho man, they choose the old-
fashioned one. They may *talk* about a long-term relationship with
a kind and nurturing guy, but they continue to be attracted to men
of power and achievement. They're saying one thing and doing
another.

"If a man paid attention to what women *said* they wanted and
acted accordingly, he'd soon discover that they don't really mean

it after all. Their ideology° is out of whack° with their basic emotional responses. Let's face it: These 'new' women are as old-
fashioned as the men they keep choosing, which leaves other men
bitter, angry and confused." . . .

°**ideology:** set of
   beliefs
°**out of whack**
   (slang): not in line
   with

EXPLORATIONS

- What point is William Novak making? What evidence does he provide for his
  point of view? Is his argument convincing?
- What points might you make in an article called "What Do Men Really Want"?

10 *From* Househusbands

WILLIAM R. BEER

[My wife and I] share most housework fairly equally, although we do not do the same tasks all the time. There are only a few jobs that only one of us does, and the rest are thought of as common obligations.° This situation evolved° naturally rather than being the result of some conscious design.° The sharing of housework is the direct counterpart° of our both having careers and contributing to the income of the household. If either of us, for some reason, stopped working outside the home, the division of responsibility would certainly change.

°**obligations:** duties
°**evolved:** developed
°**design:** plan
°**counterpart:** opposite side

Since I began doing housework on an equal basis, what has struck me is how easy it is. I do not mean that all of housework itself is easy; I mean that to take over tasks conventionally° regarded as "women's work" was not as difficult a personal experience as I had expected. Much of the activity, literature, and rhetoric° of the feminist movement over the past decade° has focused on the difficulties women encounter—both inside themselves and in the world around them—in assuming roles ordinarily performed by men. "Consciousness-raising" is aimed at least as much at overcoming women's own resistance to being "liberated" as at coping with° the hostile° reactions of husbands, other men, and other women. I expected, then, that I would not only encounter curious, if not derisive,° attention from other people, but that I would have difficulty personally adjusting to doing housework. This expectation was all the greater because I came from a home in which my father never did any housework, and I had never been obliged to do any either. With all the emphasis on "role models" and the supposedly dire° impact of the schooling of the sexes in sex-segregated° jobs, I should have undergone some sort of trauma° in starting activities for which I had not been trained at all.

°**conventionally:** usually regularly

°**rhetoric:** persuasive language
°**decade:** ten years

°**coping with:** dealing with
°**hostile:** unfriendly
°**derisive:** mocking

°**dire:** dreadful
°**segregated:** separated
°**trauma:** emotional shock

I was quite surprised, then, when not only did I not receive so much as a lifted eyebrow when wheeling a baby carriage down the middle of my street, but I found myself enjoying these new tasks far more than I had expected. Not that I enjoy every aspect of child care, cooking, and cleaning. A few things about child care are unpleasant, such as having to wake up at five in the morning when a little girl wants to play or taking care of a baby who can only cry because she can't tell you that her head hurts or she has a fever. But the whole experience made me curious about the experiences of other men who were taking over housework as I had done. I wondered how they felt about it, whether they found it as much of an adventure as I did, if they learned about themselves as much as I had.

EXPLORATIONS

- Do married couples in your country ever share housework? If so, what kinds of housework do they do?
- William Beer calls taking over housework "an adventure." What do you think about his choice of words?
- What kind of role model do fathers in your country provide for their children?

11 *The Working Mother as Role Model*

ANITA SHREVE

A 3-year-old boy, whose mother is a businesswoman, is asked to identify 20 items on the Stanford-Binet Vocabulary Test, one of which is a picture of a sport coat. "That's Mommy's dress," he says with total confidence.

When asked what jobs mothers can do, 9-year-old Andrew responds that mothers can be lawyers, cops° and presidents—and, as an afterthought, that fathers can be lawyers, cops and presidents, too.

°cops: police officers

A 3-year-old girl, whose mother is a businesswoman—described by colleagues and friends as so well-organized that she is something of a "superwoman"—announces one morning that she wants to be a father when she grows up. "Why?" asks an adult friend. The girl has no trouble answering: "Because mommies work too hard."

Women whose own mothers probably did not work have entered the work force in droves° as a result of the social changes of the late 1960's and early 1970's. More than two-thirds of the mothers in this country are working women. Middle- and upper-middle-class women dress in business attire in the morning, share cornflakes with their children, kiss them goodbye and go off to jobs as doctors, lawyers and corporate executives. The children know where their mothers are going and in most cases even understand the nature of their mothers' careers. As a result of this change in American life, children's perceptions of women and mothers are different from those held a generation ago.

°in droves: in large numbers

It has always been true that mothers have been role models for their daughters. It has also been true that large numbers of women have always had to work out of economic necessity. Yet today's working mother differs as much from the working middle-class women of the past as she differs from her own mother who did not work. She dreams, not of escaping from the job, but of being promoted to vice president or made a partner. For career mothers, even those who feel that they *must* work to make ends meet, combining work and family can be an attractive proposition—an attitude that is inevitably° conveyed to their children.

°inevitably: unavoidably

These developments intrigue child psychologists. Studies suggest that independent and achieving mothers engender° similar qualities in their daughters, and that these daughters have higher

°engender: produce

career aspirations and greater self-esteem than daughters of non-working mothers.

Child specialists also believe that as more children grow up in the families of working mothers, both boys and girls will find it easier to balance their masculine and feminine characteristics than their parents did. Says Dr. E. Kirsten Dahl, an assistant professor of anthropology at Yale University's Child Study Center: "No one, even in more traditional families, is totally masculine or feminine. We all have within us these two forces. The recognition of certain masculine traits° troubled women of my generation. But the children of this generation may not see feminine and masculine traits as being so irreconcilable."°

°**traits:** characteristics

°**irreconcilable:** impossible to unite

But the pervasiveness° of working mothers also raises questions of a political, economic and social nature. Will their children grow to be better persons and parents, or will they experience conflict as a result of being presented with too many options? Will they be overwhelmed by having to live up to the standards of two achieving parents? Will pressures of the working world force mothers to abandon their time-honored role of nurturer?° Will sexual stereotypes° be erased or reinforced?

°**pervasiveness:** spreading in many places

°**nurturer:** person who provides care and nourishment
°**stereotypes:** conventional types

"The next generation of young women will start from a different place—a more confident place about what it means to be a woman," says the feminist author Betty Friedan. "To be sure, they may face a new set of problems, but there won't be that automatic shrinking away, that sense of being something less. I believe women will enjoy better mental health and more political power and will relish° both their careers and their motherhood. Their sense of possibilities will be lovely."

°**relish:** enjoy

On Bradford Avenue in Westfield, N.J., a street that seems to have come from the era of "Father Knows Best,"° with its small brick and clapboard° houses and trim° lawns,° the Swingle-Nowicki family rises early each morning. Dr. David E. Nowicki, a 32-year-old periodontist,° is up at 5:30, making coffee for himself and waiting for his two daughters, Kate, 3½, and 13-month-old Christine, to wake up at 6. Then he steers them both in the direction of the sunny kitchen, where he feeds his children breakfast under a conspicuous° sign that reads, "This is an equal opportunity kitchen."

°**"Father Knows Best":** 1950s TV show
°**clapboard:** wooden boards
°**trim:** neat, tidy
°**lawns:** patches of grass
°**periodontist:** dentist specializing in gum disease
°**conspicuous:** obvious

At 7:15, the children's mother, Dr. Elaine M. Swingle, 34, makes her appearance in the kitchen, ready for work in a tailored yellow dress. When she gets to her office, she will don° a white coat and start her day as a busy and successful general dentist. Because Dr. Swingle is not a "morning person," her husband tends to take on the morning child-care duties, while she has responsibility in the evening.

°**don:** put on

Dr. Elaine Swingle and her daughter Kate

Dr. Swingle holds Christine on her lap and talks with Kate about what she will be doing that day. The housekeeper, Maribel Canales, comes in the back door and says hello all around. Miss Canales, 30, will take care of the children while the parents work.

Soon it is time for Dr. Swingle to go to the office. Kate gets her kisses and asks for more. The baby looks momentarily bereft,° but Dr. Swingle kisses her affectionately and then slips out quickly. °**bereft:** sad

When asked where her mother had gone, Kate replies that she is at work. "If I were a mommy," Kate says, "I'd be a doctor—the doctor that fixes teeth." And if she were a daddy? "I'd do all the things that mommies do," she says.

"Kate accepts it as a given that women work," says Dr. Swingle, who feels her responsibility as a role model very keenly. "I have to have an impact when I am with her, because I am away during the day. I encourage her to be feminine and to have strong love of the family, but I want her to believe that she can do many things.

Although I like her to wear dresses about half the time, I'm the one who brought her a dump truck, a football and a set of carpenter's tools. I encourage her to be independent, and I tell her from time to time that she doesn't need me, or anybody else, along. If she puts her clothes on backward, I send her to school that way. If she attempts to make her own bed, I don't run in to fix it. It's more important for her to do things for herself than to have someone else doing them for her."

Dr. Swingle was one of seven children, and her mother's days were engulfed° by child-rearing and housekeeping. Her parents' roles were distinct and separate. Her mother took care of the children; her father earned the money.

°engulfed: taken over completely

In the Swingle-Nowicki family, however, there is no chore or task that is the exclusive responsibility of one or the other parent. "We both do everything," says Dr. Swingle. "On a very basic level, Kate and Christine are growing up aware that both their parents work and both their parents take care of them. Kate rejoices when I come in the door at night, in the same way I used to rejoice when Dad came home at night when I was little."

"Studies that were done in the 1940's and 1950's showed that children unconsciously regarded mothers as less intelligent and less competent than fathers," says Dr. Jerome Kagan, a professor of developmental psychology at Harvard University. "I'd like to see the same types of studies done today. Is it still true? Do children today think mothers are as competent as fathers?"

"Mommy is very smart, and Daddy is very smart," says Kate Nowicki. "And I'm very smart, too." . . .

EXPLORATIONS

- In what ways were children's perceptions of women and mothers different a generation ago?
- Do you know any families like the one described in the article?
- The article begins by telling three short stories about different children. Why do you think the author, Anita Shreve, begins her piece like this? What do the stories have in common, and what point do they lead up to?

12 *John Wayne: A Love Song*

JOAN DIDION

In the summer of 1943 I was eight, and my father and mother and small brother and I were at Peterson Field in Colorado Springs. A hot wind blew through that summer, blew until it seemed that before August broke, all the dust in Kansas would be in Colorado, would have drifted over the tar-paper barracks° and the temporary strip° and stopped only when it hit Pikes Peak. There was not much to do, a summer like that: there was the day they brought in the first B-29,° an event to remember but scarcely a vacation program. There was an Officers' Club, but no swimming pool; all the Officers' Club had of interest was artificial blue rain behind the bar. The rain interested me a good deal, but I could not spend the summer watching it, and so we went, my brother and I, to the movies.

°**barracks:** housing for soldiers
°**strip:** airstrip, runway

°**B-29:** type of airplane

We went three and four afternoons a week, sat on folding chairs in the darkened Quonset hut° which served as a theater, and it was there, that summer of 1943 while the hot wind blew outside, that I first saw John Wayne.* Saw the walk, heard the voice. Heard him tell the girl in a picture called *War of the Wildcats* that he would build her a house, "at the bend in the river where the cottonwoods° grow." As it happened I did not grow up to be the kind of woman who is the heroine in a Western, and although the men I have known have had many virtues° and have taken me to live in many places I have come to love, they have never been John Wayne, and they have never taken me to that bend in the river where the cottonwoods grow. Deep in that part of my heart where the artificial rain forever falls, that is still the line I wait to hear.

°**Quonset hut:** metal building with semicircular roof

°**cottonwoods:** type of tree

°**virtues:** good characteristics

I tell you this neither in a spirit of self-revelation° nor as an exercise in total recall, but simply to demonstrate that when John Wayne rode through my childhood, and perhaps through yours, he determined forever the shape of certain of our dreams. It did not seem possible that such a man could fall ill, could carry within him that most inexplicable and ungovernable° of diseases. The rumor struck some obscure° anxiety, threw our very childhoods into question. In John Wayne's world, John Wayne was supposed

°**self-revelation:** telling about oneself

°**ungovernable:** uncontrollable
°**obscure:** indistinct

*John Wayne was a famous American film star who played in many Westerns. He died of cancer in 1979.

290

to give the orders. "Let's ride," he said, and "Saddle up." "Forward
ho," and "A man's gotta do what he's got to do." "Hello, there," he
said when he first saw the girl, in a construction camp or on a
train or just standing around on the front porch waiting for somebody to ride up through the tall grass. When John Wayne spoke,
there was no mistaking his intentions; he had a sexual authority
so strong that even a child could perceive it. And in a world we
understood early to be characterized by venality° and doubt and   °**venality:** dishonesty
paralyzing ambiguities,° he suggested another world, one which   °**ambiguities:**
may or may not have existed ever but in any case existed no more: uncertainties
a place where a man could move free, could make his own code
and live by it; a world in which, if a man did what he had to do, he
could one day take the girl and go riding through the draw° and   °**draw:** valley
find himself home free, not in a hospital with something going
wrong inside, not in a high bed with the flowers and the drugs and
the forced smiles, but there at the bend in the bright river, the
cottonwoods shimmering in the early morning sun.

EXPLORATIONS

- Is there any public figure of the opposite sex whom you have admired? What
  were your reasons?
- Can you think of a line (from literature, real life, or the movies) that you have
  always wanted to hear? If so, what is it?
- Do you think that most women admire the type of person that John Wayne
  portrayed on the screen? Why or why not?
- John Wayne is not mentioned until paragraph 2. What do you think Joan Didion
  intended paragraph 1 to do?

13 *In Fighting Trim*

BRUCE MAYS

I'm not a man who picks fights at the ball park or waits in bars for a brawl.° But even so, this is the way it goes:

    °brawl: fight

I'm on the subway by myself (subways are perfect for this); or walking up a deserted street; or in my car, at a light, late at night. The details aren't important. What matters is that I'm alone, and there's a strange man near me in what might, by a small twist of my urbanized° imagination, become a threatening situation. It doesn't matter that this other man is probably thinking about nothing more than the dinner he's late for, or the girlfriend he's just left, or even, a little worriedly, about me. Because the first thing I do, whenever there's even a remote chance of a confrontation, is to start sizing things up.° And the conclusion I come to, the footing on which I rest my peace of mind, is a purely physical one: Can I take this guy, or not?

    °urbanized: influenced by the city

    °sizing things up: figuring out the situation

Of course I know—I mean really *know*—that if imaginary push ever came to real-life shove,° I wouldn't cover myself with glory. I've never hit anybody, at least not the way they do in Steve Canyon.° I can't box. I paid for a course in judo and never took the first lesson. On Chicago's West Side, where I grew up, I was always known as the one who read. But still: Can I take him? If the answer is yes, I feel better. If no, I start looking for a way out.

    °if . . . push . . . came to . . . shove *(idiom)*: if something actually happened
    °Steve Canyon: comic strip

I think that it's something every man feels, wherever he grew up and whatever he does for a living. Maybe it isn't always so physical. Questions like, "Am I smarter than this guy?" and "If we start talking about jobs, will mine sound more impressive?" are part of the same response. So is "Am I better looking (or thinner, or funnier)?" It's the competitive instinct reduced to its pettiest° essence, but there it is. Boys are taught to win. If winning involves beating some other boy who wants to win just as badly, then you've got to take him or suffer the consequences. Who teaches us this instinct? Where does the habit come from?

    °pettiest: least important

We're driving in our car, right? My dad's got me and one of my friends in the back seat of our old family blunderbuss,° and there's a car to our right. We're on a highway, driving north to Wisconsin. It's 20 years ago, in the days before speed limits of 55 miles per hour, and the road narrows from two lanes to one half a mile ahead. We're neck and neck.° The car next to us is also a few

    °blunderbuss: old-fashioned rifle; here, big car

    °neck and neck: together, in the same position

years past its prime,° and as these two old whales put on the speed, I can see that there are kids in the other car, too, and that they're giving their old man the same push we are. "Come on, Dad!" these two crazy carloads are saying at the same time. *"Take him!"*

Or another time. A friend of mine—my size, maybe a little bigger—was walking fast down Michigan Avenue, of all places, when these two construction workers cut behind him, gave one of his heels a little tweak° and sent him tripping. He looked back—there was no mistaking that the tweak was deliberate. There the two of them were, slowing down, watching my friend, just waiting for him to say something. What was he going to say? They were both young and tanned, arms like whipcords.° They could have taken him easily, and all three knew it. My friend walked away and didn't look back again.

That's the language that men speak, the level on which their bodies communicate. That's why even good friends, when they're sparring° in fun, don't hit each other hard enough to make it seem like a challenge. A man doesn't ever really have to fight: I mean, if I *look* like I can take someone, who's going to gamble that I can't? But as a man, I've got to know that the possibility exists; it means I've been given a copy of the rules.

I had another friend, a big Irish rugby player who had recently stopped playing and was cutting down his weight. He said the thing that bothered him most about losing the weight was that he had to back down from fights now instead of bluffing° his way through. Those are the rules, as rank° and as subtle° as the signs known by dogs in the pack: Can I take this guy, or not? That's the way the system works.

My wife is pregnant now, and talks about raising our son or daughter in a nonviolent, nonsexist way. And who could argue that this wouldn't be the best of all possible worlds? But until I see it, I'm holding out the possibility that the world is going to continue in its dog-pack, Wild West show, high-sticking ways.

I took my wife to the airport a while ago, and as we were walking through the terminal together we passed the man she used to live with. When I had first known her, this man had always seemed a threat. Now, though, it had been years since we'd seen him, so I was able to look at him pretty objectively. We all smiled at each other and said hello. And on the way home, I felt much better. I'd checked him out. I knew I could take him.

°**past its prime:** old

°**tweak:** small pull

°**whipcords:** thin, strong cords

°**sparring:** boxing

°**bluffing:** pretending
°**rank:** strong
°**subtle:** hardly noticeable

EXPLORATIONS

- Could a woman have written an article like this one? Why or why not?
- Do you think you would like to have Bruce Mays, the author of this article, as a friend? Why or why not?
- Have you ever had competitive feelings similar to the ones described here?
- The article ends with the author describing an incident. What is the purpose of telling that, and how does it tie in with the rest of the article?

14 *From* Growing Up

RUSSELL BAKER

I was enjoying the luxuries of a rustic° nineteenth-century boy-hood, but for the women Morrisonville life had few rewards. Both my mother and grandmother kept house very much as women did before the Civil War.* It was astonishing that they had any energy left, after a day's work, to nourish° their mutual disdain.° Their lives were hard, endless, dirty labor. They had no electricity, gas, plumbing, or central heating. No refrigerator, no radio, no tele-phone, no automatic laundry, no vacuum cleaner. Lacking indoor toilets, they had to empty, scour,° and fumigate° each morning the noisome° slop jars° which sat in bedrooms during the night.

°**rustic:** relating to the country

°**nourish:** feed
°**disdain:** dislike

°**scour:** clean by rubbing hard
°**fumigate:** disinfect, clean thoroughly
°**noisome:** filthy, disgusting
°**slop jars:** pots used for toilets

For baths, laundry, and dishwashing, they hauled° buckets of water from a spring at the foot of the hill. To heat it, they chopped kindling° to fire their wood stoves. They boiled laundry in tubs, scrubbed it on washboards until knuckles were raw, and wrung it out by hand. Ironing was a business of lifting heavy metal weights heated on the stove top.

°**hauled:** carried
°**kindling:** sticks of wood

They scrubbed floors on hands and knees, thrashed rugs with carpet beaters, killed and plucked their own chickens, baked bread and pastries, grew and canned their own vegetables, patched the family's clothing on treadle-operated° sewing ma-chines, deloused° the chicken coops, preserved fruits, picked po-tato bugs and tomato worms to protect their garden crop, darned° stockings, made jelly and relishes, rose before the men to start the stove for breakfast and pack lunch pails, polished the chimneys of kerosene lamps, and even found time to tend the geraniums, hollyhocks, nasturtiums, dahlias, and peonies that grew around every house. By the end of a summer day a Morrisonville woman had toiled like a serf.°

°**treadle-operated:** run by foot pedal
°**deloused:** got rid of lice (bugs)
°**darned:** sewed up holes

°**serf:** slave

At sundown the men drifted back from the fields exhausted and steaming. They scrubbed themselves in enamel basins and, when supper was eaten, climbed up onto Ida Rebecca's porch to watch the night arrive. Presently the women joined them, and the twilight music of Morrisonville began:

The swing creaking, rocking chairs whispering on the porch planks,° voices murmuring approval of the sagacity° of Uncle Irvey

°**planks:** wooden boards
°**sagacity:** wisdom

---

*The Civil War between the North and the South in the United States was fought from 1861 to 1865.

as he quietly observed for probably the ten-thousandth time in his life, "A man works from sun to sun, but woman's work is never done."

EXPLORATIONS

- Do you know people who work as hard as the men and women described here? If so, what do they do?
- Are the jobs of men and women clearly defined in your country? If so, what are these jobs?
- In this piece, which one sentence provides for you the main idea Russell Baker wants to convey? How does he illustrate that idea?

Answer Key

Note: There is often more than one correct answer to an exercise. If your answer is different from the answer here, do not assume your answer is wrong. You may have found an alternative solution. Check with your instructor.

PART I

Chapter 14: Improve Style

Classroom Activity 7: Pronouns and Noun Phrases to Which Pronouns Refer

his (ears): a very old man
his (knees): a very old man
he: a very old man
he: a very old man
it: the broth
his (mouth): a very old man
His (son): a very old man
his (son's wife): a very old man
this: spilt the broth *or* let it run out of his mouth
they: his son and his son's wife
him: a very old man
his (food): a very old man
it: food
he: a very old man
his (eyes): a very old man
his (hands): a very old man
it: the bowl
him: a very old man
he: a very old man
they: his son and his son's wife
him: a very old man
he: a very old man
they: his son and his son's wife
you: the little grandson
I: the little grandson
I: the little grandson
his (wife): the man
they: the man and his wife

him: the old grandfather
them: the man and his wife
he: the old grandfather

Chapter 16: Prepare Final Copy and Proofread

Individual Assignment 4: Proofreading Corrections

their families
the job they have loses its glamour . . .
Even when some women could make a good salary in a job . . .
will improve *or* will be improved
Her children's happiness comes . . .

PART II

Troublespot 1: Sentence Structure and Boundaries

A. Standard Sentences in Written English

Note: There are more possibilities than those given here. If you have other versions, check them with your instructor.

1. The sun came out.
2. OK
3. The beach looked lovely. [Punctuation needed at end.]
4. The waves were splashing on the sand. *or* The beach looked lovely, with the waves splashing on the sand.
5. We were playing games. *or* We played games.
6. We ate our picnic. *or* We played games and ate our picnic.
7. We ate ham sandwiches.
8. We ate chocolate cake, too. *or* We ate ham sandwiches and chocolate cake.
9. OK
10. We were having such a good time. *or* Because we were having such a good time, we stayed there for four hours, sunbathing and swimming.

B. Correcting Sentence Fragments

1. Fragment: A great big black one.
   The little girl saw a spider, a great big black one. *or* The little girl saw a great big black spider.
2. Fragment: To try to scare the spider.
   She screamed loudly to try to scare the spider.
3. Fragment: Because she was frightened.
   Because she was frightened, she ran into another room.
4. Fragment: Her legs still shaking.
   Her legs were still shaking. *or* She sat down next to her mother, her legs still shaking.

Troublespot 2: Combining Sentences: Coordinating

D. Linking Expressions

moreover: adds an idea
in fact: emphasizes by giving an example
however: points out a contrast
of course: emphasizes
thus: shows result
for instance: provides an example
overall: makes a general statement
in contrast: points out a contrast
moreover: adds an idea
consequently: shows result
in contrast: points out a contrast

E. Connecting Sentences

Only one of the possibilities for each pair is listed:
1. . . . ; for instance, he always wrote standing up.
2. . . . ; in addition, he was an active sportsman.
3. . . . . However, he shifted to his typewriter when the writing was easy for him. . . .
4. . . . . He was, nevertheless, a neat person at heart.
5. . . . ; in fact, he hardly ever threw anything away.
6. . . . ; for example, he wrote the ending to *A Farewell to Arms* thirty-nine times.
7. . . . . Then, after lunch, . . .
8. . . . . As a result, his landlady worried that he wasn't eating enough.

F. Using Connecting Words or Linking Expressions

His parents took him to the United States in 1946. The family spoke. . . .
Now my grandfather no longer speaks Polish or German at home; he speaks only English.
His children don't speak Polish at all. However, they understand it a little.

Troublespot 3: Combining Sentences: Subordinating

D. Combining Sentences

Here are a few of the possibilities:
Since Jack, our administrative assistant, wanted to make a good impression, he wore his
    brother's new suit, the pants of which kept falling down because the suit was big for
    him.
To make a good impression, Jack, our administrative assistant, wore his brother's new
    suit, but the pants kept falling down because the suit was big for him.
Although our administrative assistant, Jack, wore a new suit belonging to his brother in
    order to make a good impression, the suit was too big for him, so the pants kept
    falling down.

E. Combined Sentences

1. There are two independent clauses: *Jack wore his brother's new suit.* and *The suit was so big for him.*
2. Subject + verb = *Jack wore* and *the suit was*
3. The independent clauses are connected by *but.*
4. There is one subordinate clause: *that the pants kept falling down* (result).
5. Other attachments are condensed phrases: *wanting to make a good impression, our administrative assistant.*

F. Separating Sentences

Her picture is in a heavy silver frame.
The frame is of ornate primitive design.
The frame was brought by my uncle from Peru.
The picture shows her as a young woman.
The picture is placed on the polished lid [of the piano].
The lid is never opened.
The piano tuner comes and opens it.

G. Combining Sentences

Only one or two possibilities for each group of sentences is given below. There are others. Check with your instructor to find out if yours is accurate:
1. As I watched a little girl carrying a big shopping bag, I felt so sorry for her that I offered to help.
2. When my huge family met at my grandparents' house every holiday, there were never enough chairs, so I always had to sit on the floor.
3. Computers save so much time that many businesses are buying them, but the managers sometimes don't realize that they have to train people to operate the machines.
4. All their lives they have lived with their father, a powerful politician who has made lots of enemies.
5. Wanting to be successful, she worked day and night for a famous advertising agency until eventually she became a vice-president.
6. Although he really wants to go skiing, he has decided to go to a beach resort in California since his sister, who(m) he hasn't seen for 10 years, lives there. *or* Although he really wants to go skiing, he has decided to go to a beach resort in California to visit his sister, whom he hasn't seen for 10 years.

Troublespot 5: Negatives

F. Verb Forms with *Neither . . . Nor*

The verb agrees with the last item of the pair in the *neither . . . nor* subject:
the childen have (plural subject—plural verb form: no *-s*)
the mother has (singular subject—singular verb form: *-s*)

G. Alternative Forms of Negation

Workaholics have no time for their family. They think nothing is as important as their job
. . . . Workaholics can never really relax . . . . They won't go anywhere unless . . . .
Often, on a weekend away, workaholics won't talk to anybody . . . .

Troublespot 6: Nouns

F. Identify and Categorize Nouns

1. luxuries: common/countable/plural
   boyhood: common/countable/singular
   women: common/countable/plural
   life: common/uncountable
   rewards: common/countable/plural
2. mother: common/countable/singular
   grandmother: common/countable/singular
   house: common/uncountable (idiom = to keep house)
   women: common/countable/plural
   Civil War: proper
3. electricity: common/uncountable
   gas: common/uncountable
   plumbing: common/uncountable
   heating: common/uncountable
4. baths: common/countable/plural
   laundry: common/uncountable
   dishwashing: common/uncountable
   buckets: common/countable/plural
   water: common/uncountable
   spring: common/countable/singular
   foot: common/countable/singular
   hill: common/countable/singular
5. floors: common/countable/plural
   hands: common/countable/plural
   knees: common/countable/plural
   rugs: common/countable/plural
   carpet beaters: common/countable/plural
   chickens: common/countable/plural
   bread: common/uncountable
   pastries: common/countable/plural
   clothing: common/uncountable
   sewing machines: common/countable/plural
6. end: common/countable/singular
   day: common/countable/singular
   woman: common/countable/singular
   serf: common/countable/singular
7. [men]: common/countable/plural
   basins: common/countable/plural

supper: common/uncountable
porch: common/countable/singular
night: common/countable/singular
8. women: common/countable/plural
   twilight: common/uncountable (used here as adjective)
   music: common/uncountable
   Morrisonville: proper

G. Mistakes with Noun Capitals and Plurals

Corrections of errors:
suitcase: suitcases
all the store: all the stores
Town: town
three dress: three dresses
spain: Spain

Troublespot 7: Verb Tenses

C. Switch in Time Zone

The writer signaled the switch in time zone with the word *once*, telling us that she was going to describe an event in the past.

D. Identify Verb Phrase, Time Zone, Time Relationship, and Signal

love: Present/simple present
watch: Present/simple present
can get: Present/simple present
was: Past/simple past (signal: three months ago)
spent: Past/simple past
will be: Future/simple future (signal: three months from now)
will be cultivating . . . , weeding . . . killing: Future/in progress at a known time in the
       future
had to reshingle: Past/simple past (signal: recently)
will help: Future/simple future (signal: soon)
supplements: Present/simple present
are working: Present/in progress at a known time in the present
will spray . . . , paint . . . , plant . . . clean: Future/simple future (signal: later this month)
arrive: Future/simple present (in time clause)

Troublespot 8: Verb Forms

C. Underline Complete Verb Phrase

1. had divorced, hadn't seen, had managed (to see), persists, will spend, reach, has been
   written, has (not yet) proven, occur, does occur, head, experience, do (not) experience
2. is made, are made, is repaired, make, make, will fall apart, will be, is encouraged (to
   throw away and buy), are making

Troublespot 9: Agreement

B. Identify Verbs

- The verbs are: pursues, oversees, bakes, cans, freezes, chauffeurs, practices, takes, does, writes, tends, stacks, delivers
- With a plural subject ("Sandy and her sister") all these verbs will change to the "no -*s*" form: *pursue, oversee,* etc.
- Other changes:
  her: their
  she: they
  herself: themselves

E. Determine Whether "There Is" or "There Are" Is Correct

1. There are, 2. There is, 3. There is, 4. There is, 5. There are, 6. There is, 7. There are, 8. There are, 9. There is, 10. There are.

Troublespot 10: Active and Passive

E. Determine Active and Passive Verbs

1. consider: active
    is being made: passive
    is being repaired: passive
    will be discarded: passive
    wears out: active
    will be set: passive
2. will forget: active
    were buried: passive
3. is: active
    will occur: active
    are going to affect: active
    work: active
    are educated: passive
    (are) trained: passive
4. is: active
    will retire: active
    was forced: passive
    will be filling: active

Troublespot 11: Pronouns

C. Answers to Specific Questions (e.g., What does *this* refer to?)

1. beauty, originality, and skills
2. the one just described, with the run-over heels, etc.
3. the one before
4. the fact that women hold so few management positions

D. Personal Pronouns/Demonstratives and People/Objects They Refer To

it: a blanket or toy animal
they: most children
they: most children
its: the object's (referent is *object*)
their: children's (referent is *children*)
they: children
they: children
them: children
these: certain objects

Troublespot 12: Articles

E. Articles and Determiners with Nouns and Their Special Categories

a lawyer: countable/singular/nonspecific
many valuable things: countable/plural/quantity word (nonspecific)
his home: countable/singular/possessive adjective (specific)
a lifetime: countable/singular/nonspecific
indifference: uncountable/nonspecific
his most private possession: countable/singular/possessive adjective (specific)
the interviewer: countable/singular/specific
the basement family room: countable/singular/specific
an old chest: countable/singular/nonspecific
a trombone: countable/singular/nonspecific
the instrument: countable/singular/specific (refers back to *trombone*)
in college: idiomatic usage: nonspecific (generalization)
a middle-aged lawyer: countable/singular/nonspecific
a life: countable (here)/singular/nonspecific
freedom and spontaneity: uncountable/nonspecific
nostalgia: uncountable/nonspecific (compare *with indifference*)
responsibilities: countable/plural/nonspecific
the basement: countable/singular/specific
the old trombone: countable/singular/specific

Troublespot 13: Adjectives

F. Categories in Noun Phrases

1. that: determiner
   sophisticated: opinion
   young: age
   Italian: nationality
   model: head noun
2. his: determiner
   comfortable: opinion
   white: color
   velvet: material
   couch: head noun

3. two: determiner
   middle-aged: age
   Catholic: religion
   bishops: head noun
4. their: determiner
   charming: opinion
   little: size
   wood: material
   cabin: head noun

G. Categories in Noun Phrases

1. bookcase: noun
2. wood: material
3. a: determiner
   little: size
   cast-iron: material
4. a: determiner
   Venetian: nationality
5. a: determiner
   little: size
   tin: material
6. a: determiner
   circular: shape
   straw: material
   place: noun
7. three: determiner
   buffalo: noun
8. an: determiner
   ancient: age
   ebony: material

Troublespot 14: Adverbs

C. Adverbial Forms

happily, simply, carefully, successfully, fortunately, basically, angrily, possibly

G. Identify Adverbs

equally, naturally, conventionally, ordinarily, personally, supposedly

Troublespot 15: -ing and Participle Forms

D. Examples of Some of the Possibilities

• Past tense form:
  The loud radio *annoyed* Julie as she lay on the beach in the sun.

- *-ing* form:

Julie found the radio *annoying*.

The loud radio was *annoying* to Julie.

The loud radio was so *annoying* that Julie left the beach.
- Participle form:

Annoyed by the loud radio, Julie left the beach.

Julie was so *annoyed* by the loud radio that she left the beach.

E. *"-Ing"* Forms or the Participle Form

1. saving, getting rid, marking
2. collecting, fishing, enjoying, found, looking
3. constructed, discarded, set
4. forced, filling, displaced
5. surprised, disappointed

F. Combine Sentences with *"-ing"* or a Participle

1. Wanting to get the job, she arrived early for the interview.
2. The gray-haired man wearing a blue coat is my father.
3. We saw an exciting movie last week.
4. Confused by the examination questions, the student failed the exam.
5. The painting stolen from the museum yesterday was extremely valuable.
6. Asked to share his toys, the little boy screamed and cried. *or* When asked to . . . , . . .
7. She twisted her ankle (while) playing in the tennis tournament.

Troublespot 16: Relative Clauses

G. Combine Sentences with Relative Clause

Only one method of combining is given here. Others are possible. Check with your instructor.

1. The man who won the race was awarded a prize.
2. The girl who is sitting in the front row asks a lot of questions.
3. The people [that] I met at a party last night are from California.
4. The house [that] he is living in is gigantic.
5. Ms. McHam, who lives next door to me, is a lawyer. [This clause has commas around it.]
6. The journalist whose story you read yesterday has won a lot of prizes.
7. The radio [that] I bought was made in Taiwan.
8. She told her friends about the book [that] she had just read.
9. The man whose dog I am looking after is a radio announcer.

H. Combine Sentences with Relative Clause

1. At the lecture there were thirty-three people, most of whom lived in the neighborhood.
2. They waited half an hour for the committee members, some of whom just did not show up.
3. I sang three songs, one of which was "Singing in the Rain."

4. The statewide poetry competition was held last month, and she submitted four poems, none of which won a prize.
5. On every wall of his house he has hundreds of books, most of which are detective novels.

Troublespot 17: Conditions

D. Rewrite with Conditional Clause

1. If I had seen him, I would have paid him the money I owed him.
2. If she spent more time with her children, she would know their friends.
3. If he had locked the windows, a burglar would not have climbed in and taken his jewelry.
4. If the woman had been able to find an ambulance, her husband wouldn't have died on the street.
5. If he had someone to help him, he would finish the job on time.

Troublespot 18: Quoting and Citing Sources

A. Answers to Questions

1. a. When part of a sentence is quoted, the part does not begin with a capital letter: "and I've lost the address . . . ."
   b. When a whole sentence is quoted, it begins with a capital letter, begins and ends with quotation marks, and the quotation marks come after the punctuation that signals the end of the quotation: "What's this?" she asked. A quoted complete sentence that does not appear at the end of the written sentence ends in a comma, not a period: "Ah, here it is," the woman exclaimed.
   c. When more than one sentence is quoted, quotation marks do not appear at the beginning and end of every sentence, but only at the beginning and end of the passage quoted: Mrs. Stein said, "What does that mean? Does that mean we'll all get it?"

2. Quotation marks regularly come after the end-of-quotation punctuation: "Marilyn and I are going to that new Italian place," she said.

3. A comma: Mrs. Stein said, "What does that mean? . . ."

4. A capital letter is used when a complete sentence is quoted. If the quotation begins in the middle of a sentence, no capital letter is used: "Marilyn and I are going to that new Italian place," she said, "and I've lost the address . . . ."

5. A new paragraph marks a change of speaker.

Troublespot 19: Reporting and Paraphrasing

A. Determine the Differences in the Sentences

There are seven differences: no comma, no capital letter for *where*, no quotation marks, *are/were*, *my/her*, statement word order, no question mark.

B. Quote Directly

One version follows: Charlie Brown came along, sat down, and said, "I have deep feelings of depression." Then he asked, "What can I do about this?" Lucy replied, "Snap out of it! Five cents please."

C. Change to Reported Speech

One version follows, providing an example of a reported statement, question, and command: Charlie Brown came along, sat down, and said that he had deep feelings of depression. He asked Lucy what he could do about that. She advised him to snap out of it and politely asked him for five cents.

E. Change to Reported Speech

One version follows. Others are possible.

Mrs. Stein told the people in the room that she and Marilyn were going to a new Italian restaurant, an elegant place where they served everything burning on a sword. However, she had lost the address. At that point, Priscilla started coughing, and Lee wondered aloud if the cough was psychosomatic. Mrs. Stein didn't know what that word meant and wanted to know if they would all get the cough. Lee said they probably would. Suddenly, Mrs. Stein found the piece of paper with the address on it. As Priscilla put her hand in her mink-coat pocket, Mrs. Stein told her not to light another cigarette, but Priscilla pulled out a little box and told Lee it was for him. It was a Tiffany's box, and in it he found a pair of gold cuff links.

Troublespot 20: Apostrophes for Possession

A. Answers to Questions

All four sentences include an apostrophe.
Sentence 2b has the apostrophe after the final -*s*.
Sentence 2b has the apostrophe after the -*s* because the word *girls* already ends in -*s*. None of the other nouns (*girl, man, men*) end in -*s*.

B. Rewrite with Apostrophes

1. The baby's toys are all over the floor.
2. The babies' crying kept everyone awake.
3. My family's house is gigantic.
4. Ms. Johnson's son is a lawyer.
5. The women's plans are ambitious.
6. The politicians' plans are ambitious.

D. Rewrite with Apostrophes

1. their daughters' room
2. their son's room
3. the president's advice
4. the teachers' problems
5. Ms. Johnson's efforts
6. my brother's toothbrush
7. his mother-in-law's house
8. my family's decision

Troublespot 21: Commas

C. Fit Commas into Categories

. . . does with his day, and it is . . . . The comma separates complete sentences joined by *and.*

In the common everyday job, nothing is made any more. The comma sets off a phrase before the subject of the sentence.

In effect, the machines are making junk. The comma sets off a phrase that is inserted as additional information. This one could be moved: *The machines are, in effect, making junk.*

can, of course, tell their inquisitive children . . . . The commas set off a linking expression that is inserted as additional information.

Most of the work force, however, is too remote . . . . The commas set off a linking expression that is inserted as additional information.

nothing is being repaired, including the building itself. The comma sets off a phrase inserted as additional information.

Constructed as a piece of junk, the building . . . . The comma sets off a participial phrase before the subject of the sentence.

the building will be discarded when it wears out, and another piece of junk will be set in its place. The comma separates complete sentences joined by *and.*

Acknowledgments (continued from page iv)

p. 237: Excerpts from *Blooming: A Small-Town Girlhood*, pp. 122–125. Susan Allen Toth. Copyright © 1978, 1981 by Susan A. Toth. By permission of Little, Brown and Co. and The Aaron M. Priest Literary Agency, Inc.

p. 239: Excerpts from "Dulling of the Sword," p. 467. David H. Ahl. Reprinted from Creative Computing, August 1984. Copyright © 1984 AHL Computing, Inc.

p. 241: Excerpts from "The Paper Workingstuff," pp. 151–153. From *Poor Russell's Almanac* by Russell Baker (New York: Doubleday, 1972). Copyright © 1969 by The New York Times Company. Reprinted by permission.

p. 243: "Getting Ready for the Jobs of the Future," pp. 15–16. Martin J. Cetron. From *Jobs of The Future: The 500 Best Jobs; Where They Are and How To Get Them.* Marvin J. Cetron and Marcia Apple. Reprinted with permission of M. Cetron.

p. 245: Excerpts from "Survey: Work in the 1980s and 1990s, " pp. 16–18. Julia Kagan. Reprinted with permission from *Working Woman* magazine. Copyright © 1983 by HAL Publishers.

p. 259: "F. Scott Fitzgerald's 21 Pieces of Advice to His Daughter on Living," p. 288. From F. Scott Fitzgerald, *Letters to His Daughter*, ed. Andrew Turnbull (New York: Scribner, 1965). Reprinted with permission by Scribner and Laurence Pollinger Ltd.

p. 260: "Table Manners," pp. 14–16. From *Mrs. Bridge* © 1959 Evan S. Connell. Reprinted by permission of Harold Matson Co., Inc.

p. 262: Excerpt from *Ivy Days*, p. 156. Susan Allen Toth. Boston: Little, Brown, 1984.

p. 263: "The Analysts Who Came to Dinner," October 19, 1981, p. 92. Copyright © 1981 by *Newsweek* Inc. All rights reserved. Reprinted by permission.

p. 264: "Photos Speak Volumes About Relationships," July 17, 1984, III, 1:2. Jane E. Brody. Copyright © 1984 by The New York Times Co. Reprinted by permission.

p. 267: "The American Family in the Year 2000," pp. 7–10. Andrew Cherlin and Frank Furstenberg, Jr. Reprinted with permission from *The Futurist*, June 1983, published by The World Future Society.

p. 279: "Are Women Bosses Better?" p. 39, Mary Schnack. Reprinted by permission of The McCall Publishing Company, August 1981 issue.

p. 281: "What Do Women Really Want?" pp. 10–12, William Novak. Published in the February 1983 issue of *McCall's*. Reprinted with permission of The Axelrod Agency.

p. 284: "Househusbands: Men and Housework in American Families," pp. xix–xx. William Beer. Reprinted with permission from *Househusbands.* Copyright 1983 by Bergin & Garvey Publishers, Inc.

p. 286: "The Working Mother as Role Model." Anita Shreve. Published in the *New York Times Magazine*, September 9, 1984, pp. 39–41. Copyright © 1984 by Anita Shreve. All rights reserved. Reprinted by permission of the author. Photograph. Untitled. Courtesy of Francene Keery, photographer.

p. 290: Excerpt from "John Wayne: A Love Song," pp. 29–31. Joan Didion. Originally published in *Slouching Towards Bethlehem*, Farrar, Straus & Giroux. Reprinted by permission of Wallace & Shiel Agency, Inc.

p. 292: "In Fighting Trim." (About Men Feature) Bruce Mays, September 2, 1984, issue of *The New York Times Magazine*, p. 28. Reprinted with permission of the New York Times.

Picture credits

p. 166: *Peanuts* cartoon. Copyright © 1959. Courtesy of United Feature Syndicate, Inc.

pp. 179 and 181: *Gas*, Edward Hopper. (1940) Courtesy of The Museum of Modern Art, New York. Mrs. Simon Guggenheim Fund.

p. 182: *The Empire of Lights*, René Magritte. Courtesy of Patrimonie des Musées Royaux des Beaux-Arts de Belgique, Brussels.

p. 183: *Beach at Frederiksted, St. Croix.* From *Land, Sea, and Sky*, Dover Publications, Inc. New York © 1976. Courtesy of Phil Brodatz.

p. 184: Untitled. From *People and Crowds: A Photographic Album for Artists and Designers*, Dover Publications, Inc. New York © 1978. Courtesy of Jim Kalett/Photo Researchers.

pp. 179 and 185: *Silver Peak, Nevada, 1940.* Courtesy of the Library of Congress.

p. 186: *Looking South from 49th Street and Madison Avenue.* From *New York City: A Photographic Portrait.* Courtesy of Victor Laredo.

pp. 201 and 203: *Mahatma Gandhi's Wordly Possessions.* Courtesy of Harcourt Brace Jovanovich, Inc.

pp. 201 and 206–207: Advertisement for Apple. Photograph. Courtesy of Apple Computer, Inc.

p. 202: "Nothing Cures My End-of-Summer Blues Like Gold." International Gold Corporation. Photograph. © Susan Shacter, 1984.

pp. 204: *We've Been Married 2 Months and Everything We Own Is in this Room.* From *Suburbia.* Courtesy of Bill Owens, photographer.

p. 205: *Bedroom Dresser, Shrimp Fisherman's House, Biloxi, Mississippi.* (1945) Walker Evans, photographer. Courtesy of the Estate of Walker Evans.

p. 208: Untitled. *From World of Children in Photographs.* © 1981, Dover Publications, Inc. Courtesy of Esther Bubley.

p. 218: Untitled. Mark Kozlawski, photographer. Reprinted with permission of M. Kozlawski Photography Inc., appearing with article entitled "Object Lessons" by M. Czikszentmihalyi and E. Rochberg-Halton in *Psychology Today*, Dec. 1981.

pp. 227 and 228: *Welders*, Ben Shahn. (1943) Courtesy of Collection, The Museum of Modern Art, New York.

p. 229: *Spring Hoeing*, Li Feng-Lan. Courtesy of *Chinese Literature*, Beijing, China.

pp. 227 and 232: *Office at Night.* Edward Hopper. (1940) Courtesy of Collection Walker Art Center, Minneapolis; Gift of T. B. Walker Foundation, Gilbert M. Walker Fund, 1948.

p. 230: Untitled. From *People and Crowds: A Photographic Album for Artists and Designers*, Dover Publications, Inc. New York. Courtesy of Jim Kalett/Photo Researchers.

p. 231: *Young Housewife Bethnal Green.* Bill Brandt, photographer. Reprinted with permission of Estate of Bill Brandt. Courtesy of Mrs. Brandt.

p. 233: Untitled. From *People and Crowds: A Photographic Album for Artists and Designers*, Dover Publications, Inc. New York. Courtesy of Jim Kalett/ Photo Researchers.

pp. 251 and 257: *Greek Family at Easter Dinner.* By James L. Stanfield © 1983. National Geographic Society.

p. 253: *U.S.A.* (1948) Photograph. Nina Leen. Courtesy of *Life* Magazine, Time Inc.

p. 254: Untitled. Photograph by Ken Higgins. Appearing with article entitled "The American Family in the Year 2000," June 1983 issue of *The Futurist.*

p. 255: *Sailor Home on Leave.* From *In America*, 1983, by Eve Arnold. Courtesy of Magnum Photographers, Inc. New York.

p. 256: Untitled. From *The Family of Man.* Courtesy of Rondal Partridge, Photography, California.

p. 272: *Outside a Bistro, France.* Photograph. Henri Cartier-Bresson. Courtesy of Magnum Photographers, Inc. New York.

p. 273: *Drowning Girl.* (1963) Roy Lichtenstein. Courtesy of Collection, The Museum of Modern Art, New York. Philip Johnson Fund (by exchange) and gift of Mr. and Mrs. Bagley Wright.

pp. 271 and 274: *John Wayne on Horseback.* Photograph. The Bettmann Archive. New York.

p. 275: *Marilyn Monroe.* Photograph. World Wide Photos, Inc. New York.

p. 276: *Women's Activities in Arsenals, Etc. Acetylene Welding on Cylinder Water Jacket.* 1918. Signal Corps. No. 111-SC-35757 in National Archives.

p. 278: "More Choosing the Single Life." Graph. Bob Laird. Copyright, 1985. *USA Today.* Reprinted with permission.

Index

Note: Page numbers in italics refer to photographs and paintings.